Antoine de La Sale, Alexander Vance

The History and Pleasant Chronicle of Little Jehan de Saintre

And of the Lady of the Fair Cousins

Antoine de La Sale, Alexander Vance

The History and Pleasant Chronicle of Little Jehan de Saintre
And of the Lady of the Fair Cousins

ISBN/EAN: 9783337342968

Printed in Europe, USA, Canada, Australia, Japan

Cover: Foto ©ninafisch / pixelio.de

More available books at **www.hansebooks.com**

THE

HISTORY AND PLEASANT CHRONICLE

OF

LITTLE JEHAN DE SAINTRÉ

AND OF THE LADY OF THE FAIR COUSINS

Without being any otherwise named

NOW FIRST DONE INTO ENGLISH

BY

ALEXANDER VANCE

DUBLIN
MOFFAT AND CO., 6 D'OLIER STREET
LONDON: HAMILTON, ADAMS, & CO.
MDCCCLXVIII

INTRODUCTION.

AS few things would appear to me to be more discreditable; or, in the long run, more shortsighted, than for any man who has earned to himself some little reputation for taste and judgment, simply to attain some temporary end, deliberately to prostitute, or trifle with the same, I shall very candidly avow to the reader, had the translation of *Saintré* to be entered on afresh, it is not by any means a thing certain that I had been the effecter of the same. However if, when undertaken, surprised out of a more wonted wariness by the unexpected richness of a part, I may have been prevailed upon to look somewhat too good-naturedly on the work as a whole, it is still possible, envisaging it under all the apathy and reaction inevitable to the subsidence of a somewhat heightened enthusiasm, that I may now be allowing myself to think a little too hardly of it. It is, if not with the expectation, at least the hope, that the latter impression may prove to be the more grounded of the two, that it is now submitted to the public.

But few, it may be safely ventured to predict, will come to the last page of this romance with other feelings than those of regret and of surprise: regret, that a man who had shown himself equal to the dénouement, should have been at all the pains which he was to oblige us with the mystification of the same; (though, how well much more was to have been made of his subject, I must confess, I am at a loss to conceive): surprise, that such as it is, it should never till now have been rendered into the English tongue.

In truth, it is a very remarkable work. In some respects it is one of the most original productions that I ever remember to have met with. But with very little exaggeration it may be said to be the *Waverley*, and even *more* than the Waverley of a comparatively unlettered age. Or I am much deceived, let which will be the *second*, with it must ever remain the honour of being accounted the *first novel*, in the conventional and modern acceptation of the term, of which there is any record, originating either in France or in England; at any rate, the first *comic* one. This, of course, I do not undertake to assert; I merely state as much to be my impression. A dozen like it might easily be eluding the research of so erratic and capricious a reader as myself. Here we have a man, at a time when every forest was the haunt of fays; when every dungeon had its dragon, den its giant, court its dwarf; when hermits, palmers wept, recluses prayed; when every lady had her milk-white palfrey; unprotected female her champion; damsel her lover; virgin her ravisher or her deliverer; when every castle was enchanted, the very stones were bewitched:—in a word, when all kindred and contemporary literature was no better, or other, than one interminable and unintelligible rigmarole of, however picturesque, solemn, clumsy and unmanageable adventure, boldly discarding, at a swoop, all such auxiliaries; fearlessly retreating upon nature, pure, simple, unadulterate. Nor can the effect have been other than answerable to the design. I question if even *Don Quixote*, with all its strained, common-place, far-fetched hyperbole, extravagance, can have ever done so much with the ordinary sort, to open the eyes of the world to the weaker side of chivalry, as must the keen, fine irony, raillery of *Saintré*, among the more accomplished classes. Anything more creditable than the plot, all things considered; or characters more admirably sustained than those of the hero and the heroine, it would be difficult to find, and unreasonable to look for, at any such early day.

If I spoke, a moment ago, of *Saintré* being "the *Waverley*, and even more than the Waverley of a comparatively unlettered age," I must be understood to have been instituting a comparison simply between the originality, not the literary pretensions of the two works. That Scott was greatly struck with *Saintré*; more so, perhaps, than he was altogether aware of at the time, is evident. I think it will be very hard for any observant reader of our work, to resist the conclusion, that it was to it that he was indebted for the first hint of the general outline of the plan of the Waverley novel.

The romance of *Saintré* is generally supposed, though, to my mind, upon entirely inadequate grounds, to be of a semi-historical character. The impression may probably be traced to the editor of the Paris edition of 1724; a man in no way competent to have taken any such charge in hand. He has evidently, as he himself allows, been at no end of trouble to identify the "*Lady of the Fair Cousins*," with one or other of the nieces of the King; taking it for granted that she must have stood in such a relation to the crown. And this simply because the Queen calls her *Fair Cousin;* and that the Lady herself speaks of the royal dukes, as *Fair Uncles*. But as to the Queen's calling her *Fair Cousin*, that amounts to exactly nothing; as such condescension was then, in the interchange of familiarity and sprightliness, common enough. Besides, it would then be *niece*, not *cousin*. Whilst, that she should allude to the dukes, as *Fair Uncles*, weighs equally little with me. She only once, I think, either addresses them, or refers to them, as being her personal relatives. And this allusion may be either an oversight, or a misprint, or an interpolation; for anything more slovenly, disgraceful, barbarous, or, at times, unintelligible than the copy from which this translation is made, it would be literally impossible to conceive. *Fair Uncles*, which is the honorary with which a King would address his uncles, or the junior branches of a royal blood approach theirs, might clearly also be the one by which those dignitaries would be spoken of unceremoniously in a court, behind their backs. The lady can have been of no such rank, for abundant and very obvious reasons. *To be come of the kindred of the Fair Cousins*, would appear to me only to mean, that she was a woman moving in such a sphere as entitled her to be the familiar of her sovereign and his court. To this day, the English peerage is *cousin* to the crown. She seems to have been a lady of the provinces, and was, apparently, an heiress in her own right. But as nothing to be depended on is, I imagine, known of either Saintré or the lady, it is idle to be discussing how far the work may be founded upon fact; or to what extent it is merely an effort of the imagination. I repeat, my own impression is, that De la Salles was, as regards invention, originality, acquirement, very much such a person as Scott; and that "*Saintré*," or 'Tis one-hundred-and-twenty years since, is no better than a hodge-podge; as is "Waverley, or 'Tis sixty years since," of literary, traditional, and historical gleaning; all worked up together by a man of a high and a fine fancy and observation.

It is seldom that the moral of a work, or, at any rate, the individuality of its author, is not, at least to some degree, to be gathered from its pages. In the case before us, however, it would be a pretty difficult task to do so. Scott, as may be seen in his "Essay on Chivalry," appears to have attached a very much more serious importance to this gentleman's authority, purpose, than I have been able to bring myself to do. In fact, in my opinion, he was no better than *a wag;* and a wag of the first water too: the Fielding, or the Hamilton of his day. So far as one can guess at him, like Hamilton, he must have been a fine, and even a very fine gentleman; or, with Fielding, he probably could have been one when he had a mind: most certainly he knew what one was; no man better.

The first part of *Saintré*, looking at it as dispassionately as I am able, would hardly seem to me to be much inferior to the feebler portions of the *Grammont Memoirs;* and only to be at all so, because the subject would not permit, on the part of De la Salles, of a like display of his well-nigh unrivalled natural powers. In the general style of the two works, there is, at times, a certain resemblance:—the same straining, the same labour is observable in much of each. But however we may be divided about the opening, (for touching the *middle*, which is written without any sort of pretension, and with a charming, almost an infantine simplicity and pathos, I do not suppose that there can be much difference of opinion), I think it would be no easy matter to point to ninety or an hundred consecutive pages in any romance, French or English, ancient or modern, of a rarer, more animated, more varied or sustained excellency, than that which is evidenced of the concluding chapters of our author. The attention may not be harrowed, tortured, with all the sickening curiosity which rivets us to the pages of a Richardson; but, in return, we are quite as interested as it is either healthy, safe, or desirable to be. And where, in Richardson, or where anywhere, save in Fielding, is to be found so much nervousness with so much airiness—so much ease with so much strength—so much dignity with so much irony—so much gravity with so much humour?

Ere taking my leave of Saintré, I may be permitted to observe, that, possibly, it is to our author that the poet, Crabbe, was indebted for a hint when composing one of the most beautiful of all his tales, *The Confidant*. The parallel will at once occur to every reader, between the artifice of which Saintré availed himself to bring home to the lady all the sense of her unworthiness, and that with which the splendid fellow of a farmer confounds the "traitor friend."

Though this may not be exactly the place to launch out into any sort of digression, inquiry, touching the aspect of society in the middle ages, I may, I trust, in availing myself of the only one which is open to me, be permitted to state, that, in my opinion, there is very much misapprehension pervading all popular and received appreciation of those times; and this misconception I take to be chiefly based upon a mistaken estimate, as well of the character as the worth of politer mediæval literature. I cannot attach anything like the same importance, as authority, to old romance, that either did St. Pelaye or yet Sir Walter Scott. The latter resumes, in epitome, his conclusions thus: " We may here observe, once for all, that we have no hesitation in quoting the romances of Chivalry as good evidence of the laws and customs of Knighthood. The author, like the painter of the period, invented nothing, but, copying the manners of the age in which they lived, transferred them, without doubt or scruple, to the period and personages of whom they treated. But the romance of *Jean de Saintré* is still more authentic evidence, as it is supposed to contain no small measure of fact, though disguised and distorted. Probably the achievement of the Polish Knights may have been a real incident." Having thus delivered himself, he proceeds to lay before the reader, as deliberate statements, or rather, as authorities equivalent to such, passages from our author, which, to my poor way of thinking, to use a legal phrase, *are not evidence.* In fact, so far were the authors of that period from " inventing nothing," that it would be quite as near the mark to say, that they invented *everything.* For all that is out of nature—even unfaithful imitation of that nature, is pure invention, or the tantamount, practically, of such. And, I am sure, for any one to look for nature, (farther than occasional strokes and touches of the same), in any of the old romances previous to that of *Saintré,* would be to look for what is not to be met with. If they " invented nothing ;" then must the " *Land of Fairy* " have been somewhere ; enchantment been something ; giants and hobgoblins somebodies. This, however, I waive as captious. But if they " invented nothing," then must this idle young lady of the *Fair Cousins* have been acquainted with the Latin tongue—familiar with her Bible—well read in the classics, fathers, canon law, bulls, and decretals. It may be replied, " But, possibly, all this was but the scrapings of some contemporary, and now long-lost manual !" This I deny not. But why then should such a work have been interlarded, as this must have been, with Latin ! I may be in the wrong, but I think it would be very difficult for any man, well considering the roguery and wickedness with which these scraps are dovetailed together ; particularly if tolerably versant with contemporary lore and manners, to arrive at any other conclusion, than that the long-winded sermon of the lady of the *Fair Cousins* is one scarce interrupted burlesque, from beginning to end ; as, indeed, is a considerable proportion of the whole work. In fact, the middle part comprises all, which, to my mind, is written with any sort of conscience or sobriety. Some such education, doubtless, was bestowed upon the young gentlemen of the age; but it would require a vaster amount of credulity than, unhappily, has been apportioned out to me, to reconcile to my mind, that this was a literal or an identical course.

At the risk of being thought a little prolix, I will yet farther try to make it clear, by a reference to *Saintré*, how highly dangerous it is to accept of the old romances, and, above all, this of *Saintré*, as affording an unequivocal picture of the manners of the times. The manners, unquestionably, are there ; but it will ever require a man of an unusual research ; of no common coolness, leisure, wariness, sagacity ; of a quick and trenchant knowledge of human nature, as well in all its known and possible combinations, as in its unknown and impossible ones, to draw the line, and say, where consistency, nature ends, and where extravagance, incongruity begins.

In the first place, our author tells us, that Saintré and Bouciquaut slept together in the chamber with the King; adding, however, with his accustomed drollery, that they were, as a matter of course, turned out on certain state occasions. Yet, another time, we find several females sleeping in the room, when he expressly informs us that the King and Queen were in bed together. How is this to be reconciled? Is it at all probable that he would have called in the women at a time when he had certainly turned out the men? Or supposing, as it is almost certain, that women habitually slept in the Queen's apartment; is it likely that he would have left them there when with her himself? I am sure I cannot tell. It is only one of a score of inconsistencies which might be pointed to in his book. My own notion, however, is, that women would not be in the room; and that he simply put them there for the fun of the thing, and because they came in handy to his purpose. In fact, so thoroughly have a large proportion of us allowed ourselves to be carried away with the imagination, that it is only, or, at any rate, mainly, in the pages of old romance that we are to look for a reliable representation of the feudal world, that I hardly know to what to parallel the delusion, if not to the conviction which prevailed, with reference to the Highland clans, in the days of the fourth George. Not only do they offer but a very partial and inadequate view of the interior of society among the upper orders; but they almost *in toto* ignore the very existence of that grave and learned middle-class body, the magistracy; of all the wealthy burgher, manufacturing, and banking classes; as, consequently, the relations in which these powerful communities must have stood toward the former, each other and the state.

"But," says Lockhart, "the most striking homage, (though apparently an unconscious one) that his (Scott's) genius received during this festive period, was, when his Majesty, after proposing the health of his hosts, the magistrates, and corporation of the northern capital, rose and said, there was one toast more, and but one, in which he must request the assembly to join him. "I shall simply give you," said he, "*The chieftains and clans of Scotland; and prosperity to the land of cakes.*" So completely had this hallucination taken possession, that nobody seems to have been startled, at the time, by language which thus distinctly conveyed his Majesty's impression that the marking and crowning glory of Scotland consisted in the Highland clans and their chieftains."

I repeat now, what I advanced in the introduction to *Episodes*, that it is a very grievous misapprehension to fancy that the middle ages, all through, were anything like so corrupt, demoralized, unpolished, unsafe, as they are generally enough supposed to have been. It will be rejoined, Read the one you will, of the songs, the tales, of the troubadours; are they not one tissue of coarseness, of obscenity? are they not all rolling on intrigue, seduction, license? To this I will simply reply, by requesting my interrogator to turn to chapter one hundred and twenty-seven of the *Book of the Knight of the Tower ;* and when he has read it, to inform me whether he thinks, had such been the case, the minstrels then had swarmed in the halls of *La Gallonière*, as we have the word of the good Knight to the effect that they did? I will farther reply by asking him, if he thinks it at all probable that such a man as Landry would ever have permitted any such profanity to have been echoed, and been re-echoed within the bounds of his four walls? if he thinks that the many "good ladies, as well in France as elsewhere, who would be too numerous to tell of," were likely, any more, to have countenanced the like indecency? And even admitting that they did—as, to a considerable extent, I am prepared to concede to be the case—then must I be allowed to tell him, that such complaisance and such forbearance, on the part of these holy people, toward their comparatively low and vulgar-minded neighbours, would appear to me but as one evidence the more of all their broad and admirable charity: a charity which, this day, we are refusing to extend to them themselves. At the worst, and at the most, this literature can be only pointed to as an evidence of what people then *were willing to listen to*—what they found their entertainment in; how they *acted*, was another matter. I am no antiquary, but I am satisfied that I am possessed of as fair an insight into the spirit, the genius, and the literature of the middle ages as are most men not professedly such. And I deliberately say, that out of some hundreds of tales which have fallen under my notice, I can hardly recall a dozen that are not as unmistakeably *works of imagination;* as certainly, I say not as much, out of this world, as are *Gulliver's Travels*, or the *Arabian Nights' Entertainments*. There is no *necessary sympathy* between impurity of writing, speaking; where only coarse, pleasant, not warm; and impurity of morals or of manners. If anything, it is the other way. And it is a miserable thing for us to be allowing ourselves to draw our conclusions regarding the condition of society in the middle ages, from the extravagance of the romancers, or the licence of the troubadours. What the Knight of the Tower has recorded of his own times, the reader shall presently see for himself. What does Montaigne, if possible, even an higher authority than the Knight, tell us of the extraordinary, almost incredible virtue of the generation immediately preceding his own? the very time, too, when the lovely and accomplished Queen of Navarre was penning those ingenious tales, which, in the loftiness of our virtue, are now pointed to as an overwhelming evidence of the grossness and immorality of the sixteenth century! To the charming sketch which he has left us of that "best of fathers," the following testimony is appended:—"It is a wonder to thinke on the strange tales I have heard my father report of the chastitie of his times. * * Hee was wont to say, that in a whole province there was scarce any woman of qualitie that had an ill name. Hee would often report strange familiarities, namely of his owne, with very honest women, without any suspicion at all. And protested very religiously, that when he was married, he was yet a pure Virgine; yet had he long time followed the warres beyond the mountaines, and therein served long. * * And he was well strucken in yeares when he tooke a wife." We should have recollected that these ballads, these tales, were no other than what they *professed to be;* ballads, tales; not police reports, or yet the records of an Arches Court. With about as much justice might the *Grammont Memoirs* be appealed to, as conveying an adequate idea of the morals of the aristocracy in general in the reign of the second Charles. Yet, unconscionable a sinner as the fellow was, Hamilton has had the common honesty to admit, that it was little short of a miracle for any woman, in England, to part with her virtue before marriage. If it was a "miracle" that it should be parted with *before*, he must allow me to hold myself excused, if I consider it to have been well nigh equally a miracle to have been dispensed with *after*. I will leave it to any fair man to say, in what light will posterity, applying the same rule and compass to *Tom Jones* that we now are doing to the pages of the troubadours, romancers, almost certainly regard the age which elicited that work? I mean, what will be the impression left upon the minds of, I say not *all* men, but nine men out of ten? Surely an unfavourable one. True, a more lovely, a more bewitching creature than Sophia Western scarce ever can have flitted 'cross painters' vision, or 'cross poets' brain. A worthier old body than Mrs. Nightingale can have but rarely lived. Yet still, I say, the whole cast of this, unquestionably the noblest novel in the English, or in any other language, savours, and will savour still more, with time, of gross licentiousness. Yet what has Fielding himself had the grace to admit of the ladies of his own age? "There is not, indeed," says he, "a greater error than that which universally prevails among the vulgar, who, borrowing their opinions from some ignorant satirists, have affixed the character of lewdness to these times; on the contrary, I am convinced there never was less of love-intrigue carried on among persons of condition than now. * *. In my humble opinion, the true characteristic of the present *beau monde* is rather folly than vice, and the only epithet which it deserves, is that of frivolous." That Dr. Johnson entertained similarly exalted convictions as regarded the general respectability of the females of the upper classes in his own day, every reader of Boswell will recall. And this, too, be it remembered, at a moment when literature, if not as coarse, as naked, as that which we are considering, ten times more disreputable, warm, seductive, dangerous, was to be found on every drawing-room table, and in every lady's closet! And if, despite of all this evidence, it is still insisted on, that even to listen to, not to say relish, such a character of writing, is evidence in itself of an innately impure and indelicate turn of mind, then must Shakespeare, then must Milton, then must Johnson, then must Berkley, then must Scott, with thousands besides of the noblest and sublimest of God's created beings, have been men possessed of vitiated, perverted minds, tastes, imaginations: an implication too monstrous to be entitled to one moment of serious refutation.

I repeat, there is much exaggeration about the indelicacy of mediæval literature. That a number of the songs, the tales of the troubadours, are coarse enough, to our ears, I will not attempt to palliate or deny; but if so; they are rather tinctured with the coarseness of a redeeming, an enviable, a charming, and a primitive simplicity, than with the objectionableness of a deliberate, a conscious, or even a *possible* offensiveness. But when our levity; high spiced, conscious imaginations, are pitted with their dignity, gravity, single-mindedness, and earnestness, it is small wonder that we are at sixes and sevens. If we find three little girls, the well-brought-up, exemplary daughters of so pious, so nice, so scrupulous, so thoughtful a man; so fine a gentleman as was the Knight of the Tower, as familiar as with their garter with all those mysteries to which by wedlock alone is a woman supposed to have become initiated; if we find him opening himself unreservedly to them on topics which never now could, or, at any rate, should be touched on, save of a mother, a pastor, or a family physician: if we find in the mouth of Froissart, the purest, the most etherial, sublime of well nigh all historiographers; and even, too, under circumstances the most solemn, sad, and tragic; words which, now-a-days to be recovered, must be hunted for mid the lowest *canaille* of the back slums of Paris—in the name of all that is reasonable and unreasonable, why should we be cavilling at the same in the lay of a troubadour, or the prattle of a minstrel? Now, if there *cannot possibly* have been any sort of indelicacy in the employment of words—argue, or flatter ourselves to the contrary as we will—it only remains to be seen, does the imputed impropriety consist in the colouring? That any such freedom of colouring, as is generally supposed, is to be met with in the more reputable novels, such as *Perceforest, Launcelot, Huon de Bourdeaux;* or ballads, such as many to be seen in *Percy,* (for even in those days there were *Tom Littles, Chevalier Faublas,* and *Harriet Wilsons,*) I utterly deny. It is downright insanity to talk, *à la Ascham,* or *La Noue,* as I have often seen and heard it done, "of the unblushing effrontery with which the most barefaced intrigues are recounted." In the first place, there is hardly an intrigue in one of them, from the first to the last, such as ever *did* take place, or ever *could* take place, since human nature was constituted human nature. This remark is only made to show that these writings are not, too implicitly, to be accepted as *pictures of bygone times;* and that they are nothing better than so many miserable, primitive, childish, chalk-on-the-wall skeletons, daubings, of an age of comparative inexperience, if not innocence. So far from these pictures being drawn with the "most unblushing effrontery," I would, on the contrary, say, that they are effected with the most laudable

b

and scrupulous delicacy. The simple fact is generally all of which the reader is apprised; nothing beyond. Just compare the quietness, the consideration of the ten following words, which the reader will presently find in their place, in *Saintré*; "*and when they were come out of the secret closet ;*" without so much as a hint of, or an allusion to what, for all that, the youngest among us must surmise to have passed within; I say, compare this with the disgusting, prurient, morbid, filthy pleasure with which a Richardson trailed, through eight octavo volumes, his *one idea*, which same idea, from its very first conception, was lascivious and objectionable in the highest degree? Compare it even with the innuendo, the transparency with which, at this very hour, intrigue, the grand staple of all romance, ancient or modern, as often as not is introduced.

In support of the other allegation, that there is scarcely an intrigue in old romance; *at least as related*, that ever did take place, or ever could take place, I would point to that of the abbot and the lady, which, in its general character, is an average sample of a disclosure of the kind. To suppose that what is there insinuated to have taken place, could, under the circumstances, have done so, and remained undetected, is to suppose a simple impossibility. Hence, though a great lady *may* have committed herself with her chaplain, as well in the fourteenth century as she might in the nineteenth, the tale of *Saintré* is no evidence that this one *did*. Nature has her own ways of telling her tales; tales which, though ear of man may ne'er have heard, yet eye of man will seldom fail to reach. Though morals may be outraged; indignant nature, roused, will ever be the vindicator, the proclaimer, the asserter of her abused rights, of her insulted modesty.

Of course, when I say that intrigue is seldom or never to be met with in the old romances, under circumstances which might lead us to suppose that it had even a foundation in fact, I only speak of intrigue *with plot*, not of cases where it is merely alleged to have occurred under the commonplace, humdrum expedient of a dark night, a lantern, or a back meadow.

For several reasons, which will at once occur to the more intelligent reader, I have appended to this romance of *Saintré, The Book of the Knight of the Tower*. Some such *soberer* may not be altogether out of place, to qualify the injurious impressions which might have been left upon our minds by the perusal of this masterpiece of burlesque, of gaiety and waggery; at least, masterpiece, considering the age in which it was produced. Though but a very small, and apparently frivolous sort of an effusion; if I mistake not, it is one to arrest the attention of any thinking, or philosophic mind. It was the work of a man who might, in his younger days, have seen our hero, Saintré; and whose labours besides had clearly been in the hands of the author of the romance now bearing Saintré's name. But what chiefly induces me to lay it before the reader is this, that it contains a very ample and masterly dissertation on loving *par amour*, on which the whole moral of *Saintré* hinges. And, by the way, *en passant*, I may be permitted to state, for the benefit of the Right Honourable Lady-mothers, and their no less Right Honourable and lovely daughters, whose home is in Belgravia; that a wrinkle or two, on a certain subject which shall be nameless, well worth attending to, might be caught, even at this late hour of the day, from this somewhat primitive young lady's manual.

Now as every one, possibly, is not exactly aware of what loving *par amour* may be; and as the English compound, *paramour*, carries with it, in our times, an injurious implication, I will proceed to tell him, that, originally, it was not susceptible of any such construction. Love *par amour* simply meant, attachment between the sexes. I do not fancy, legitimately, that such a reference was applicable to the love of parents towards their children, or yet of children toward their parents. The difference would be about that which exists between the worth of the expressions, *to love*, and *to be in love*. *We love* our parents, sisters, brothers; *we are in love with* our mistresses, sweethearts. How we were supposed to love *our wives*; whether *par amour*, or otherwise, or in what that otherwise was to consist, is, I confess, a problem which, as yet, I have not been able to get to the bottom of. And as the matter, besides, is somewhat delicate; perhaps the less that is said on it the better. Love *par amour* was also honourable love; that is, when it did not degenerate, in vulgar, sensual and unscrupulous spirits, into dishonourable. In the tale of the Knight, in Chaucer, we find Palamon, when vindicating his prior claim on Emily, fiercely announcing to his rival, Arcite,

"And thou art false, I tell thee utterly,
For *par amour* I loved her first, or (ere) thou."

What character, honourable or dishonourable, the *amour* of Saintré and the lady of the Fair Cousins partook of, I am not prepared to say. Scott has unhesitatingly pronounced it to be of the latter. If, be it observed, I here speak of this amour as possibly having been of a dishonourable nature, it will, of course, be understood, that I am employing the word *dishonourable* at its conventional acceptation; for, according to their notions of these matters, such an intrigue would no more be looked on as discreditable, than would it at this day, to be the *cavalier servente* of an Italian countess. Deliberate seduction and abandonment was, unquestionably, dishonourable. But secret, loyal attachment, whether Platonic, or of a warmer complexion, was not so. I do not exactly know, myself, what to think of it; that is, assuming the tale to be founded on fact, and not a very unduly-charged representation of the manners of the times; nor, indeed, does it much signify. Doubtless such a man as Saintré was perfectly equal to all the enthusiasm, *the celestiality* (if there is such a word), idolatry, self-denial of the finest Platonic going of his age. Yet if he was, on the other hand, most assuredly he was not the man, through any straight-laced scruples, compunctions, either of conscience or of education, to stick to meet half way, if not a little beyond, the advances of the fair and frail one. If either way, I should be disposed to pronounce the connection to have been of a Platonic description; and for these reasons. Ere committing herself with the monk, it is to be observed, that the lady takes the precaution to wed him with a ring, a ceremony which, by some curious mental casuistry or other, she considered as entitling her to be a participator in the rights of matrimony. Such "left-handed," "under-the-rose" marriages seem not to have been unusual; and even to have been solemnized with some sort of religious ceremony; at least, if these knaves of minstrels, *conteurs*, are to be relied on. Now, as much to Saintré, she never did. In the next place, the pith, the moral of the tale is, apparently, a good deal the same with that of the *matron of Ephesus*. The reaction ensuing upon immoderately-prolongued and insufferable distraction threw this hitherto irreproachable woman into the arms of a soldier. Had the relation in which Madame of the Fair Cousins stood with Saintré ever been of the character of intimacy alleged, I hardly fancy that she would so readily have forgotten herself with her friend, the abbot. That she was a woman of warm and ungovernable passions is clear enough. Yet, for all that, strong as may have been the temptation to gratify them with such a man as Saintré, it might have been yet stronger with such an one as the abbot. *A propos*, in chapter twenty-five of the Knight of the Tower will be seen a very curious instance of the lengths to which even respectable women would go with men whom they loved, yet contrive to preserve their chastity, if not reputation, unsullied. It is by no means impossible that the familiarities hinted at by Montaigne, as passing between the sexes in the time of his father, may have partaken of, or have been to be traced to this character of intimacy and confidence. But enough of this; and to return to our Knight.

I have translated his book for this also, among other accounts, that, trivial and even puerile as, superficially regarded, it may appear, few works of its size would seem to me to convey a pleasanter, more condensed, more truthful, more reliable, more suggestive notion of the general face of society in the middle age world. I think, besides, that it will serve to temper more popular impression, touching the state, when it was written, of public morals and the general respectability. Nor can I gather from it that society was then, *as a whole*, in a much, if at all, a more disreputable condition than it is at this very hour. Circles, coteries were apparently more blended, confused, than they are among ourselves. Solicitations which, in our days, most unquestionably are rarely or never addressed by men of rank toward virtuous and artless females, their equals in the eye of the world; but which, as unquestionably, they do address to those beneath them, were then unscrupulously persisted in. If he tells us, that the "good and the bad ladies" all met promiscuously, in his day, in the one hall, what is this more than acquainting us, that gentlemen and ladies of a certain class—the *d' Orsay, Blessington* school—had the *entrée* of all the castles and the châteaux round? But if they had, I think, at the same time, he has made it sufficiently clear, that there was a very considerable per centage of the company toward whom they were expected to hold themselves at a pretty respectful distance. If he tells us, that when he was eighteen, he and a troop of *harém-scarém*, worthless young rascals used to go gallivanting about the world, making love to all the pretty women that they met with; what is this more than saying, that the tricks which the youngsters of a cavalry regiment, in eighteen hundred and sixty-two, will make no sort of difficulty to play with tradesmen's wives, and farmers' daughters, were at that time attempted upon young women of their own position in life? If a lady's virtue was then more liable to assault, so was it better fortified for the defence; if more exposed, it was more on its guard. But to imagine that women were less wary of the care of their chastity, in the middle ages, than they are at this day; that the penalties ensuing upon the forfeit of the same were less fearful to be contemplated, is a very grievous scandal to cast upon those who no more can stand up in their own defence. I say not, women may not have staked it oftener, for they undeniably did ;· but if they did, as the good lady de la Tour assures us, and as even she of the Fair Cousins herself admits, dearly bought were such joys; for little short were all their pleasures of the pains of hell, of martyrdom. And if the rendering up of her virtue was risky work with the lady, the game was no less a dangerous one for her betrayer or her lover. Husbands were no more complaisant in the fourteenth century than they are in the nineteenth; nor yet were fathers, or were brothers, less touchy on the score of a daughter's, or a sister's reputation. *Damages* were as liable to be incurred at that time as they are now; with this little trifling difference, however, as to payment: that whilst, now-a-days, damages mostly *go* from the pocket, in the shape of a ten thousand pound cheque upon Coutts': then, they as generally *came* in the shape of one pound upon the head, which, as frequently as not, settled one side at least of the account.

There is nothing more common, or, at the same time, more unreasonable, than to see some one passage in a man's writings pitched upon, and commented on, as a sort of *text*, in total disregard of the general tone, moral, or tenor of his convictions. If the Knight, in his old age, speaks with a pang of the licence of his own time; if he longs again for the days of *Sir Geoffrey*; be it remembered, that that self-same time which he was so ardently praying for, was the very one in which he, and all the mad young scamps with him, were galloping about the country, up to all kinds of devilment and mischief. So, we see, the world had not so very much wandered from its wonted ways in forty or in fifty years; or, as he himself expresses it, "the times present were but too like the times past." If Sir Geoffrey was dead, the Knight himself was alive, and the head of an household which must have spread an halo of purity and sanctity over fifty miles of region round. If the old lady de Belle Ville was no more; his own wife was spared to him and to the world; as were "more good ladies, in France, and beyond its metes, than he would have power to tell of." Surely this is no mean testimony to the virtue and respectability of the ages of chivalry! It should be enough to balance, and more than balance the authority of a thousand such mercenary, unscrupulous, worthless, lying dogs as were the minstrels and the troubadours.

In conclusion, I have only one favour to ask at the hands of the reader; and that is, whatever else he may be disposed to skip, that he will read the character which the Knight has left to us of "*An honourable lady.*" A more sublime, a more touching, a more affecting, a more enchanting picture of heaven upon earth, I say not, another may not have read; but this I do say, I never have. It should be written in letters of gold; "it should be bound for a sign upon our hands, and for frontlets between our eyes."

I have but one word to add; it is somewhat an ungracious one; and willingly had I spared, as well to myself, as to the reader, the expression of the same.

I am sure, when I recall the unusually kind and flattering manner in which was received, I may say, on every hand, a previous endeavour to accommodate to the public taste, some few of the more picturesque and striking passages to be gathered from the old French chroniclers and romancers; and when I still farther recall the very great indulgence (unhappily no less than was required) with which one or two somewhat salient features of an Introduction, none, at best, of the most judicious, were winked at; conscience cannot but tell me, that it were something worse than graceless, on my part, to call any unnecessary attention to the same. Nor should I now allude to the matter, did I not very clearly foresee, that, a second time, I am no less liable to be exposed to a similar character of exception. And had this objection been started but in any one quarter, I had not felt it at all incumbent upon me to attempt to remove it: on the contrary, it was a very generally prevailing one.

Here, it was said, is a man who takes upon himself the defence, in a Preface of considerable length, not, on the whole, unreasonably, though somewhat jumblingly written, of the coarseness and the raciness of our old masters; who tells us, that it is discreditable the treatment to which, one and all, we are subjecting them; that, however much is due to ourselves, something is also due to them, as, no less, to posterity; who, possibly, may be but little disposed to thank us for all this meddling; that the age is becoming emasculate, enervate; in a word, who pleads for a somewhat broader tolerance, if not of the licence, the homeliness, which our sensitiveness has now become much too crazy to put up with. But, lo, and behold, in turning over the pages of his book, where all these fine hardy propositions are to be carried out, not a word can we find which might not be placed in the hands of any "boarding-school," or "bread-and-butter Miss!" In fact, he has "shirked" the whole question. Surely, surely, there is some little thoughtlessness in all this. The charge is a true one enough; I deny it not. But if I allow to as much, may I not, in return, be permitted to inquire, " What sort of *taste* had it been for me to assume to myself the decision of any such matter; *to take for granted* that the public would be with me? Could anything have been more unjustifiable, nay, unprincipled, than to have intruded anything of the kind upon society, previously unfurnished with the *consent* of that society? Surely had I, I had merited, and richly merited, that my book had been damned. Was I, at once, to take upon myself the functions of advocate and of judge? It is the business of an advocate to plead as warmly, as closely as he pleases, or as he can; but it is *not* his business to take the law into his own hands: with the judge and with the jury it must ever abide to pronounce, Has he a reason, or has he not? Besides, it might have been observed, that if I entreated for a tolerance of, and somewhat of a return to, the homely, healthy, broad, coarse nervousness and pleasantry which were the characteristics of an Elizabethan world; at the same time the precaution was taken to suggest the only method by which I conceived it to be possible for society to retrace, in so delicate a matter, its steps. I hinted that the ground should be broken among our younger people, in our public schools. Passages, expressions, words, which it would be exceedingly distressing to me to hear from the lips of any grown-up female; a sister, a daughter, or a wife; I would, without a moment's hesitation, place in the mouth of my child; that is, always, if another, in my own position, would consent to do as much with his.

The whole pith and marrow of what I have advanced, or have to advance on this head, is this:—*that the entire matter at issue is rather a question of obsoleteness, or of non-obsoleteness; of fashion, of custom, and of manners, than of either a real or an ideal propriety*—that the bringing up, and the bringing up *alone* of our children, to consider *this* to be objectionable, indelicate; *that* to be the reverse, will, in nine cases out of ten, in after-life, be the only reason which they will be able to advance for *why* they hold the said *this* to be defended, the said *that* not to be defended—that if it can be demonstrated, that, despite of all our refining, the *even level* of the public manners, morals, remains pretty much, to this hour, what it has been for the last four hundred years, then must it be but simply ridiculous to be pandering, *on the score of a regard for the public safety*, to all this miserable fastidiousness—that it is a very hard thing that the weak are to be allowed to dictate to the strong, the ignorant to the learned, the women and the children to the men, bigots and fanatics to strong men; that the mawkishness of our fine ladies, and of our fine gentlemen is to be scraped to, and catered after, whilst the more imperious hungerings and thirstings of downright English, beef and beery blood, and brain, and nerve are to be left unprovided for: " if they are virtuous, is there, for that, to be no more cake and wine?"—that the parties who are clamouring for, and have carried all these innovations, are such as are in no way competent to form to themselves the remotest conception of all the mischief that they, and such as they, are playing with letters; and ones whose interest, comparatively speaking, is but very secondary in the matter—that no man can either foresee or foretell where all this work is to end, if, on every hand, we are to be inundated with parallel and castrated editions of our more ancient standard literature—that it is positively incredible the amount of good, wholesome, sterling, innocent, curious, characteristic, available, entertaining reading, (witness this very *Book of the Knight,*) which, to such a pass have we brought ourselves, that it is risen at of our queasy palates, as is plum-porridge of a kickshawed stomach—that there is an infinite presumption and offensiveness in any man, and I care not one fico who he be, setting himself up to be a being of a more innate delicacy than was a Shakespeare, or of a purer morality than was a Scott—that lives there the lady, this day, in this land, be she a *Portia,* or be she a *Desdemona,* yet so be, she can no more abide the jabber of her *Amelia,* or of her *Nerissa :* ay, be she fine as she who, " for very delicateness and tenderness would not so much as set the sole of her foot to the ground ;" yet for all that, must I be allowed to tell to her, as to all such like angels, or such birds of paradise, that the sooner they unbend their pinions, wing their flight to heaven, that heaven from whence they came, the better will it be for themselves, as for all those whom they may leave behind them: what have they to do with flesh, with blood, with ashes, or with dust? From all which considerations, with an hundred others, which will readily present themselves to the mind of any intelligent reader, the conclusion that I came to was this; that the sacrifice required at our hands, bears no manner of proportion to the banefulness of the remedy which is rendering that sacrifice uncalled for: that it would be much a shorter way to settle the matter, to place the whole affair in the hands of the guardians and instructors of our youth; and for ourselves, ('tis but for one generation,) to bear with any unavoidable unpleasantness incurring therefrom, just as we do with all the other little mishaps, exposés, and awkwardnesses which the necessities of children for ever are entailing on the aged, their parents, and society.

I have now done. The subject, I may be well believed when I say it, is one upon which I shall not readily return. And goodness knows, no less, it is one of which I had rather undertaken the defence, out of a sense of principle and conscience, than either with the desire or intention; supposing myself to be possessed of the capability, which I am not, to turn to account the solicited concession. I am not going to kick against the pricks; nor yet am I, to make myself ridiculous by embarking in any such crusade against the prejudices, or the manners of the age. I am no such fool. I have far too much self-respect. I know far too well what is due both from myself and to myself; if not who I am, what I am, to allow myself to figure in any so preposterous or Quixotic a light before the world. And though this self-same world will ever hold its self-same course, will wag its wonted way, despite of all that I, or any other man, can say or do to the contrary; yet still, and no less, and ever, will this eternal truth be true—" That wisdom will be justified of her children."

December, 1862.

CONTENTS.

	PAGE
Preface to Paris Edition, 1724	*xi*

CHAPTER 1.—*How Jehan de Saintré came to be in attendance at the Court of King John of France, as page of honour; he in particular waiting on the King.—And first, of my said Lady of the Fair Cousins, and of Saintré* . . . 1

CHAPTER 2.—*How in the Court of the Queen of France, there was a young Lady, who on no account would remarry, notwithstanding she was pressed by many; and of the instances which she replied touching the Ladies of the olden times* . 2

CHAPTER 3.—*How the said young Lady deliberated in her own mind, how she would cause the little Saintré to be heard of in the world; and of how she sent for him to her chamber, asking him, "Who was his lady love?"(dame par amours); and at which the little Saintré was quite put out, and could not answer her a word; except that at last he said, " he had none"* 6

CHAPTER 4.—*How the little Saintré, as in desperation, and one who had never yet experienced the sweets of love, told the Lady, that Matheline de Coucy was his lady love; which Matheline was but six years of age* 15

CHAPTER 5.—*How the Lady instructed the little Saintré in sundry salutary doctrines and matters, touching the manner in which he was to be enabled to flee the seven deadly sins* . 17

CHAPTER 6.—*How the Lady gives some further instructions to the little Saintré, touching the virtues, state, and order of nobility* 29

CHAPTER 7.—*How the Lady determined to come at the favourable or unfavourable impression left upon the little Saintré, in the matter of love par amour* 34

CHAPTER 8.—*How the Lady opened her heart to the little Saintré, showing him that it was she who was willing to love him* 36

CHAPTER 9.—*How the Lady admonished the young Saintré touching the ten commandments of the law, and in what consisted the virtues and good breeding* 37

CHAPTER 10.—*How the Lady, already smitten with the love of the little Saintré, gave him twelve écus to set himself up with, and to have himself nicely dressed* 51

CHAPTER 11.—*How the little Saintré had himself finely set out, as the Lady had desired him. And after, how the said Lady found him in the gallery, and made him follow her into her chamber; inquiring of him,—What device was that he wore? And this on purpose, so that her Gentlewomen might not suspect anything; and how she gave him yet other twelve écus in a purse* 52

CHAPTER 12.—*How the Lady feignedly menaced the little Saintré, telling him before her ladies that he would never do any good. And how, after that, the little Saintré had other clothes made with the money which Madame had given him; and how the Lady spoke to him, and he told her that it was his mother who had sent him the money with which he had dressed himself* 62

CHAPTER 13.—*How the Lady suggested to the Queen that she should speak to the King to make the little Saintré his trencher squire* 67

CHAPTER 14.—*How the little Saintré thanked the King and Queen, and Madame, for that he had been made a squire; and how he carved before the King, and how handsomely he acquitted himself* 70

CHAPTER 15.—*How the little Saintré spoke with Madame, who kissed him affectionately, in the meadow; and how she gave him a hundred and sixty écus to provide horses, and other things necessary* 71

CHAPTER 16.—*How the little Saintré provided himself with horses, as Madame had desired him; and how, when he came to thank her, she admonished him, and taught him how he was to conduct himself, as well at Court as in war, and in all other positions* 76

CHAPTER 17.—*How the Lady advised the little Saintré to read books and romances, so as to be acquainted with the manners and the achievements of the nobles of the olden time* . . 79

CHAPTER 18.—*How the little Saintré threw himself on his knees before Madame and thanked her, and how the King and*

Queen gave him money to set him up. And how, at length, Madame told him that he was to have a bracelet, enamelled, and of her device, for the first of May, and that he was to wear it for an entire year, and to defend it in the lists against one Knight or other 81

CHAPTER 19.—*How the little Saintré thanked Madame, and then had the bracelet made, as she had desired him; and after, how he came and showed it to her, at which she was delighted* 85

CHAPTER 20.—*How the Lady instructed the little Saintré, that he should announce his intention, through an Herald-at-arms. —How the best dancer, whether Squire or Lady, should have a suitable prize, and how he was to put his bracelet on his arm.—After, how Saintré gave a banquet to all the Lords and Ladies.—And how, at night, he returned to the meadow, to speak with the Lady, who told him, he should publish his Letter-at-arms in the Courts of the four Kings* . . 87

CHAPTER 21.—*How the little Saintré went to the King and Queen, to break to them his Letter-at-arms, and obtain their permission to send it; which the King consented to, though much against his will* 89

CHAPTER 22.—*How the little Saintré entered triumphantly into the lists, and of his noble equipment.—And how he carried himself so valiantly, that he was honoured and applauded of all* 91

CHAPTER 23.—*How Saintré came to the meadow to speak with Madame, and how he retailed to her, point by point, how he was equipped; what officers and parties he had provided to accompany him on his voyage.—And how the Lady wanted to know about his colours and his arms; and how they took leave of one another, 'mid piteous tears and sighs* . . 92

CHAPTER 24.—*How the Lady told the Queen, how sumptuously Saintré was set up in horses and equipage; and how the said Queen desired Saintré to bring his horses into the court, so that she might see them, which he did, and how the King and Queen saw them, and commended them* . . . 95

CHAPTER 25.—*How Saintré, as soon as he was ready to set out, came to ask the King for permission to depart, to accomplish his enterprise; which thing the King allowed to, though sorry to see him go* 98

CHAPTER 26.—*How Saintré was in the meadow, to take leave of*

the Lady, who admonished him again of all he was to do.—
And how, at last, they parted from one another; not, however, without abundance of tears, as well on the one side as the other 99

CHAPTER 27.—*How Saintré took his farewell of the King, the Queen, and the Ladies, to each of whom he gave a golden wand.—And how the Queen asked, "If there was not one for her?" On which he gave her one, excusing himself, saying, "he had not thought she would condescend to care for such a trifle"* 102

CHAPTER 28.—*How, after Saintré had taken his leave of the Barons, and Lords of the Court, he went away to dine with his companions; and how, when at dinner, the Queen sent him a rich cloth of silver; and several Lords subsidies and presents.—And how he had himself escorted, at his outset, by the heralds, trumpets, and musicians; giving them a supper at the burgh of the Queen, where he lodged* . . . 104

CHAPTER 29.—*How Saintré, being at Avignon, the Anjou King-at-arms brought him the seal, and the reply to his Letter-of-arms; and told him all how he had spoken with Enguerrant, and published the Letter-of-arms, at which he was delighted* 106

CHAPTER 30.—*How the Anjou King-at-arms told Saintré, that the King of Arragon had consented that Enguerrant should deliver him from his engagement; and how he had given him a gracious reception; at which Saintré and his companions were beyond expression delighted* 108

CHAPTER 31.—*How Saintré, being at Perpignan, the news came to the King of Arragon, who appointed him lodgings at Barcelona.—And after, how Enguerrant came out, a good league, from the town to meet him; and how honourably he received him; and of the civilities and discourse that passed between them* 111

CHAPTER 32.—*How Sir Enguerrant presented Saintré to the King, and to the Queen, who gave him a most handsome reception, and solemnly feasted him* 113

CHAPTER 33.—*How Saintré entered magnificently into the lists, surrounded by a noble assemblage of Princes and of Knights; and of the order of the day* 115

CHAPTER 34.—*How Sir Enguerrant besides entered the lists, in a like triumphant array* (omitted) 117

CHAPTER 35.—*How the King had the lances of the two cham-*

		PAGE
pions measured.—And how popularly Saintré demeaned himself, in passing before the King and Queen: they in their boxes		118
CHAPTER 36.—*How Saintré made the sign of the cross three times before he couched his lance: then, how the two champions encountered valiantly.—And how, the first day, the King made Enguerrant retire the first from the lists; saying, that Saintré had won for that day* . . .		119
CHAPTER 37.—*How the King sent for the two champions to sup with him.—And how, on the following day, they returned to the lists, performing prodigies, one upon the other* .		120
CHAPTER 38.—*How the Herald-at-arms pronounced the decision of the victory; that Saintré had gained it.—Of the prizes and courtesies exchanged between them; aud of their leaving the lists*		123
CHAPTER 39.—*How Saintré, after he had heard mass, sent by two Heralds-at-arms two axes to Sir Enguerrant, as required by the terms of his challenge.—And after, how the King sent his Herald to signify to Saintré the hour he was to be at the lists*		125
CHAPTER 40.—*How the two champions entered, for the third time, solemnly into the lists*		126
CHAPTER 41.—*How they issued from their tents to perform their Arms*		128
CHAPTER 42.—*How they marched one against the other; each doing valiantly*		128
CHAPTER 43.—*How Saintré took leave of the King and Queen, and of all those of the Court; and of the presents that were made* (partly omitted)		135
CHAPTER 44.—*How Saintré, accompanied by all the Lords, departed from Barcelona, on his way for France* (omitted) .		136
CHAPTER 45.—*How Saintré and his companions came; and of the good reception which they met with from the King, the Queen, Madame, and the rest*		136
CHAPTER 46.—*How Saintré, by dint of journeying, made his appearance before the King, and of the honours and good cheer which were made him; and how Madame's heart was cured*		138
CHAPTER 47.—*Here tells how Saintré became Chamberlain to the King, and of the alliances between him, and Myngre, otherwise Bouciqualt*		140
CHAPTER 48.—*How Madame desired Saintré to deliver the*		

	PAGE
Polish Baron from the enterprise he had undertaken (the first portion of this Chapter is omitted)	142
CHAPTER 49.—*How Madame bemoaned herself to Saintré, and of the tender things she said to him*	146
CHAPTER 50.—*How the Lord de Loiselench and Saintré came into the lists, to perform their arms on horseback: present, the King, the Queen, and many Lords and Ladies* (the opening portion of this Chapter is omitted) . . .	148
CHAPTER 51.—*How the Lord de Loiselench and Saintré entered the lists, to perform their arms on foot* (the account of this combat is omitted)	152
CHAPTER 52.—*The manner the King ordered the prizes to be distributed* (partly omitted)	153
CHAPTER 53.—*How the Lord de Loiselench supped with the King* (omitted)	154
CHAPTER 54.—*How the Lord de Loiselench took his leave* (Several passages in this Chapter are omitted) .	154
CHAPTER 55.—*How Sir Nicolles de Malle-Teste, and Gallias of Mantua, Squire, came to the Court to perform their arms*	156
CHAPTER 56.—*How Saintré and Bouciqualt went in search of the two champions, to bring them to the King of France; and of how they fought with them*	159
CHAPTER 57.—*How Saintré tilted against the Baron de Tresto, and they were adjudged equal* (the opening portion of this Chapter is passed over)	161
CHAPTER 58.—*How the Lady asked Saintré to set out for Prussia, against the Saracens, and he promised to go; and how the King made him the head of five hundred lances* (the opening and concluding portions of this Chapter are passed over)	161
CHAPTER 59.—*How, when the time was come, that they were to set out for Prussia, the King gave his standard to Saintré, constituting him his Lieutenant.—And after, how the said Saintré and the other Lords took their leave of the King, the Queen, and the Ladies; and of the great mourning there was at their departure; especially on the part of Madame*	163
CHAPTER 60.—*How the Saracens were in a greater number of Turks and infidels than had ever been seen together since the time of Mahomet* (the order of the battles omitted) .	169
CHAPTER 61.—*How, in the battle of the Saracens, Saintré, at*	

	PAGE
the very first onslaught, slew the Grand Turk, and did so well his work, that all the infidels made way for him.—And then, of how the Emperor of Carthage, the two Soldans of Babylon, and Mabaleth, the Grand Turk, were killed; with many others, as well on the one part as the other (omitted)	171
CHAPTER 62.—*How the news were blown about everywhere, but especially into France, how Saintré had performed prodigies; and of how, in particular, among other things, he had killed the Grand Turk, and trampled on his banner; at which the King was greatly delighted, and thanked God, and all the Saints, in great solemnity.*	172
CHAPTER 63.—*How Saintré and all his noble host of French Christians, after the overthrow of the infidels, returned to Paris, where they were joyfully received of the King, the Queen, and all the realm*	173
CHAPTER 64.—*How Saintré told the King that, to show that he was really glad to see him back, he should let him sleep with the Queen; which the King promised him.—And how the Queen, quite tickled, asked him, "What, on earth, had put such a piece of assurance into his head?"—And after, how, at midnight, he went to speak with the Lady alone; who gave him the kindest reception in the world; not, however, without many kisses and embracings*	176
CHAPTER 65.—*How Saintré deliberated with himself to wear a golden vizor for the space of three years; and how the King consented to it, though much against his will*	179
CHAPTER 66.—*How Saintré went to speak with his Lady in the meadow, and how he told her of his enterprise; at which she was horribly vexed and displeased.—But how, being passionately entreated by Saintré, at last she gave him her consent, placing his ensign on his shoulder*	183
CHAPTER 67.—*How the ten companions came, in the morning, to see the King* (partly omitted)	186
CHAPTER 68.—*How the King spoke with Saintré; and of the presents that he made to him, and his companions* (partly omitted)	190
CHAPTER 69.—*How Madame arrived at her country house; and of how she was received*	194
CHAPTER 70.—*How Madame and Damp Abbot fell into discourse, and of how she thanked him*	201
CHAPTER 71.—*How Damp Abbot was extolled*	202

x *Contents.*

	PAGE
CHAPTER 72.—*How Madame found herself compelled to take part in the collation*	204
CHAPTER 73.—*How Madame and her Women praised Damp Abbot, the one to the other*	205
CHAPTER 74.—*How the Queen wrote, the first time, to Madame*	210
CHAPTER 75.—*How Madame, without waiting for any further explanations, made her answer to the Queen*	211
CHAPTER 76.—*How Madame handed her letters to Master Julien, and gave him his instructions*	213
CHAPTER 77.—*How the Lord de Saintré and his companions came to the Court of the Emperor; and how, to their great honour, they were delivered by the Lords, hereinafter named; being all noblemen, and men of fame and reputation* (omitted)	216
CHAPTER 78.—*How the French arrived, and of the honours were paid them* (omitted)	216
CHAPTER 79.—*How the battle went, and of the ordnance of the Emperor* (omitted)	217
CHAPTER 80.—*How the Imperial King-at-arms distributed the prizes, and what he said to the champions* (omitted)	217
CHAPTER 81.—*How the Lord de Saintré and his companions returned to Paris, and came to see the King*	217
CHAPTER 82.—*How Damp Abbot appeased the Lord de Saintré*	235
CHAPTER 83.—*Of the state in which Madame, Damp Abbot, and all their people were left*	249
CHAPTER 84.—*How Madame returned to the Court*	250
CHAPTER 85.—*How Madame came to the Court, and of the good reception she met with*	252
CHAPTER 86.—*How the Lord de Saintré, without, however, naming any one, gave them the history of Madame, Damp Abbot, and himself; and how he gave Madame back her belt: present the Queen, and many other Ladies and Gentlewomen*	253
NOTES	259

PREFACE TO THE PARIS EDITION OF 1724.

IF the rarity, and the price of a work, are to be any index to its merit, one would think that that of *Saintré* should be caught at with avidity. A copy was sold for ninety-seven livres, ten sols, at the sale of the library of the late M. Bulleteau, first Secretary to the King. And the one from which the present impression is taken cost the publishers one hundred and eighty livres. It is a little octavo, in double columns, and Gothic character; and was printed at Paris, by Philippe le Noir, in 1523. It also seems that the author, who was one ANTOINE DE LA SALLES, as appears by his Preface, addressed to my Lord of Anjou, Duke of Calabria and Lorraine, and Marquis de Pont, wrote it in the year 1459. This may be gleaned from the end of the book, where is a letter addressed to the same Duke of Anjou, to whom he further promises some other matters, to be gathered from the chronicles of Flanders.

However much diligence I may have applied to discover what the author of this romance was, the simplicity of the style of which is altogether so remarkable, I have been unable to arrive at any certain conclusion. As far as one can conjecture, he was a gentleman of quality, and attached to the Court of Lorraine. And this is to be inferred from the

Preface, which is prefixed to the history of *Sir Floridan and the fair Ellinde*; the author of which, *Race de Brinchamel*, addresses him; and in which Preface he observes, that he has just finished, according to his instructions, a book entitled, *The Little Nuptial; treating of Marriages, according to the Statutes and Laws*. Again, as much is to be concluded, from a passage, not far from the close of the same history, wherein the author demeans himself towards Antoine de la Salles in the following manner:—" *So, my very redoubted Lord, as humbly as I am able, and with joined hands, I have to beg and entreat of you, that you will take, of a little owner, a little offering, of a poor servant, the good wishes—from one ever tendering himself to the loyal, honourable, and desirable services of your noble orders, &c.*" Now, it is hardly to be supposed that Brinchamel would ever have expressed himself in terms of so much submissness, had not Antoine de la Salles been a man of some condition.

But to return to our novel. If the author has made us acquainted with all the persons of quality, and left us the names of all the nobles of the times of which his history treats; and if he describes to us, exactly, their several arms, (which, in itself, is no mean merit,) he does not, the less, avail himself of the licence common to almost all romancers; for he takes, for his foundation, an anachronism that would be unpardonable in any work pretending to seriousness, or truth. He lays the scene of his romance at the Court of King Jaen, and of the Queen, Bonne, (as appears by his second chapter); now this Bonne, of Bohemia, was never known by the rank of Queen.

This is the manner in which Mezeray speaks of them: " *We are not to reckon Bonne, of Bohemia, the first wife of Jaen, among the number of the Queens; inasmuch as she died before her husband succeeded to the crown. In reality, she married Jaen when he was but Duke of Normandy, in* 1332. *She died in January,* 1349; *and Jaen only came to the crown* 22nd *August,* 1350.

At his second nuptials, the 13th *February,* 1349, *he married Jeanne de Boulogne, widow of Philippe de Bourgogne.*

He was taken prisoner at the battle of Poitiers, in 1356; *and died, the* 8th *April,* 1364; *having reigned but fourteen years.*

So that it is clear, that all we are told of Saintré cannot possibly have taken place under the reign of King Jaen. Hence, to give an air of probability to his story, it was necessary for the author to lay the plot under *Charles VI.*; or, at any rate, *Charles V., called, The Wise*. And this appears the more clearly, because the Dukes of Anjou, Berry, and Bourgogne, and styled the King's brothers, were, in reality, brothers to Charles V., and sons of King Jaen; who had only one brother, namely, Philippe, Duke of Orleans, who died childless.

As regards the little Jehan de Saintré, it is only with the greatest difficulty that I have been able to discover who his family were. This is what I found about them, in a manuscript endorsed, *Notes as well Historical as Genealogical, vol.* 279; *and the* 3rd *of the Governors of the Provinces, chiefly those of Anjou;* and borrowed from the cabinet of M. de Clerambaut, genealogist of the various orders of the King, and who kindly has lent it to me, as well as thrown what light he could upon the matter. *Jaen de Saintré, or otherwise, Xaintré, Knight, Seneschal of Anjou and of Maine, enjoyed, along with the authority of this charge, that of Lieutenant to the Lord de Craon in the year* 1355; *and, under him, commanded thirty men-at-arms. In this same year, the same Lord de Craon, Pierre de Craon, the Lord de la Suze, Guillaume de Craon, Viscount de Chateaudun, and him; that is to say, Saintré, joined in an attempt to clear out one called Rennequin, captain of Blain in Bretagne, on the part of the Lord de Clisson, one of the principal chiefs of the Bretons, then in rebellion. Apparently on his own account, we find Saintré endeavouring, by every means in his power, to render himself master of the castle of Chautocé. To this end, he tampered with Lambert de Guerard, Gerardin de la Fontaine, and Jean de Saintonge; and the price of their defection was to have been ten thousand florins of gold, in écus. Six thousand he was to hand over as soon as he got the place. But they broke the matter to the four Lords, and made another treaty with them, which the king (Jaen) confirmed in* 1355. *By it, it was secured to them, that, in the event of the stratagem succeeding, they were to have six thousand écus; besides which, they were each to receive a thousand écus from the King next coming Lent; that they were to have the four most considerable prisoners, with a third of the expenses of the expedition; that Lambert Gerard was to be recompensed with a grant of* 100 *livres of rent, in land, with the office of Sarjeant-at-Arms; and, besides that, they were to keep any prisoners they might have already made; and that Guyard, the German, and Pierot, the Bourgignon, were to be liberated out of prison, free of all ransom.*

This Lord de Saintré held different appointments in the various wars; and deservedly is paralleled with the Mareschal de Boucicaut, with this difference only, that if he was inferior to him in point of tact, address—in all matters of stratagem, negotiation—he surpassed him as invariably in the open field; nor did any man ever hazard himself more daringly, either in single combat or to the thickest of the assault.

He was of an ancient Vendômois house, the fame of which he enhanced, not a little, by his exploits; and the memory of which will be for ever preserved in the Romance of LITTLE JEHAN DE SAINTRÉ. *It is an extraordinary medley of fact and fiction; most pleasantly written, considering the age, of which it represents the tone, the temper, the manners, and the customs, with a naïveté altogether the most arch and surprising.*

He had, for his arms, guelle à la bande d'or, brisée d'un lambel d'or, de quatre pièces, et pour cimier, un bois de cerf; and this answers, as far as regards the bend and the crest, to the seals attached to the original documents and deeds, which I have seen at M. de Clerambaut's; especially to a quittance, in 1355, given by Jean de Saintré, Seneschal of Anjou and of Maine, for 450 livres; being the wages received of himself and the 30 men-at-arms, from Amaury, Lord de Craon, and Lieutenant of the King, in the departments of Anjou and of Maine.

I discovered, besides these, an extract from the Parliamentary register, bearing date the 20th of November, 1386, in virtue of which the patrimony of Jeanne de Thoüars, wife to Sir Jean de Saintré, and then dead, was adjudged to her husband.

We have now to examine, if the Saintré referred to in the manuscript of M. de Clerambaut is the one who figures in our romance. There is every reason to believe that he was not; and that this latter was the son of the one of whom I have just spoken, and on this ground: because we see, from different evidences, that, in the year 1355, he assumed the rank of Knight; whereas the Little Jehan de Saintré was only made a Knight, by the King of Bohemia, the day of the great battle with the Saracens; as appears by Chapter LX. Up to that time, he had enjoyed no other title than that of Squire, which, as being a Knight's son, he had a right to. That his father was a Knight, appears, in fact, from the terms in which the Lady of the Fair Cousins, at the commencement of the 58th chapter, addresses him; "*and, for these reasons,*" says she, "*I have been thinking, that really, it is time you should be as all your predecessors have been:* that is to say, I think you have, at length, sufficiently distinguished yourself to warrant your being made a Knight, as all your ancestors have been. Besides, it was customary, at that time, for sons to charge their father's arms, in the lifetime of the latter. It was apparently, for this reason, that Saintré charged with a *lambel*. Hence, there is every cause to believe, that those which I have just described are those of Little Jehan de Saintré, and not of his father, who, according to all appearances, was this Sir Jean de Saintré, Seneschal of Anjou and of Maine; and who had the hero of our romance by Jeanne Chaudrié, as is alleged in the manuscript of M. de Clerambaut; as is also, that this Jeanne de Thoüars, who died in 1386, was the wife of Little Jehan de Saintré, to whom her goods were consigned by an order of Parliament.

However all this be, the families of Saintré, in Vendômois, or Touraine, of which I have given the arms; and those of Saintré, Lords de Breviande and de Dizier, whose arms were, *de sable, au chef d'argent,* are now extinct.

The house of Saintré, which still is to be found in Normandy, is not descended from any one of those stocks which I have named. Their arms are, *de guelles à trois coquilles d'or*. They are Lords de Grand-Pré, in the parish of Vatteville, election of Ponteau-de-Mer, and generality of Alençon. Their name is *Cintray*.

Touching the *Lady of the Fair Cousins*, I have not been able to find, in our histories, so much as a glimpse, to throw the slightest light upon the subject of her identity. She calls, in the 18th chapter, the Dukes of Anjou, Berry, and Bourgogne, *Fair Uncles*. If they were her uncles, then must she have been niece to the King. In which case, the Queen would hardly have addressed her, as *Fair Cousin;* unless, indeed, as a term of toying, or endearment. But allowing, a moment, she were of some other relation, let us see on whom our surmise then would light:—

The King Jean had but four daughters; so of one of them she must have been born—

1. Jeanne, born the 24th June, 1343, was married to Charles, the wicked King of Navarre, towards the beginning of 1351, and died in 1373.

2. Marie, born in 1344, was married to the Duke de Bar, in 1364, and died in 1404.

3. Marguerite, was born in 1347; became a nun at Poissy, and died in 1366.

4. Isabeau, born in 1348; was married to Galeas, Duke of Milan, in 1360; and died in 1372.

It is clear, from this genealogy, that the heroine of this romance could only have been one of the daughters of Jeanne, Queen of Navarre; who had two:—

1. Marie, who married, in 1394, Alphonse of Arragon,

d

the first of the name, Duke of Gandie, and who died without issue.

2. Jeanne, married to Jean, the valiant Duke de Bretagne, in 1386; and who died in 1399. She married, afterwards, in 1404, Henry IV., King of England.

If the adventures of the Little Saintré really took place under Charles VI., who came to the throne in 1380, one might imagine Marie, when widow of Alphonse of Arragon, to have been the Lady *par amour*, in as much as she was only married in 1394. But however this may be, as the whole affair must have been so recent, (that is, supposing it to have any foundation in fact,) I am of opinion that Antoine de la Salles acted very discreetly in merely identifying his heroine by the designation of *The Lady of the Fair Cousins*. The manner in which she forgot herself with the Abbot, and which appears from the 69th chapter to the end; as well as the way in which Saintré avenged her infidelity, and divulged his resentment, all demanded that her name should be concealed from the times; especially in an age when "true love" was so much the order of the day.

All that remains for me now to inform the reader of, is, that I have not spared any pains to render the perusal of this romance as well instructive as entertaining. I have, as far as was in my power, (thanks also to the co-operation of one well skilled in our old literary lore,) given the meaning of all the more obsolete words; which, otherwise, would have nonplused him. I have diversified it with occasional historical incidents and anecdotes, in themselves sufficiently curious. I have added all the Christian denominations of the chiefest of the French nobility, whose names are encountered, and, to conclude,

I have to hope, that the public will at least thank me for having presented it with this edition of a chronicle, which all persons of taste and judgment have so long and anxiously been looking for.

THE HISTORY AND PLEASANT CHRONICLE

OF

LITTLE JEHAN DE SAINTRÉ,

AND OF THE LADY OF THE FAIR COUSINS;

Without being any otherwise named.

CHAPTER I.

How Jehan de Saintré came to be in attendance at the Court of King John of France, as page of honour; he in particular waiting on the King.—And first, of my said Lady of the Fair Cousins, and of Saintré.

IN the time of King John of France, the eldest son of Philip de Valois, there was at his Court a certain Lord de Pouilly, in Touraine, who had living with him, in his hotel, an exceedingly comely and graceful lad, named Jehan, and eldest son to the Lord de Saintré, also of Touraine. And this Saintré, such was his witchery, came to be so pleasing to the king, that he determined to have him near him, child as he was. So he appointed him to be his page, making him always to be with him when he rode abroad, and at other times to wait about the Court, as might the other young people and pages of honour. But of all the pages, there was none stood higher with him than Jehan de Saintré, or who attended on the king more frequently at table; or who showed himself more handy, or ready to oblige, in anything that might be required of him, whether it were business or sport; nor was there any who made himself more useful to the ladies, that is, as far as he was able. For the rest, for his years, which were XIII., he was an uncommon hardy and forward lad;[1] whether it was to ride upon the high horse, to play at tennis, to sing, to dance, to run, to vault, to leap; nor was there any sort of pastime, in which he saw his seniors to delight, to which he did not naturally take. And although, of his person, he was little and frail, his heart was great, and, among its other virtues, firm as the whin and the steel. By all which rare conjunctions, virtues, graces, accomplishments, he arrived to be so loved and extolled, as well of the King, the Queen, the Lords, the Ladies; in fact, everybody; that all were of accord, that assuredly, some day, if he lived, he would come to be one of the most renowned gentlemen of France. And certes, as they foretold, so it fell out; for, of all her knights, he was admitted to be the flower, and it is of a portion of his exploits that the following history is to treat.

CHAPTER II.

How in the Court of the Queen of France, there was a young Lady, who on no account would remarry, notwithstanding she was pressed by many; and of the instances which she replied touching the Ladies of the olden times.

THE AUTHOR.

ABOUT this time, there was in the Court of the Queen Bonne of Bohemia, wife to the said King John, a lady, sufficiently young, a widow, and who was come of the kindred of the *Fair Cousins*. But of her name and family, history has forborne to speak, and for the reasons which will afterwards appear. This lady, then, from the death of her late lord, her husband, whether it was from causes which are not sufficiently explained, or that it was in imitation of those widows indeed, of which the Roman Gestes, that are so famous, make so many and such glorious mentions—but which, to be brief, I pass—once come to be a widow, on no account would allow any man to address her. Apparently it was her determination to follow, in all things, the examples of those widows of the olden time, and of which her histories spoke. For from them she learned that there was practised among the Romans, a highly commendable custom of honouring and countenancing widows; that is, those who, upon the deaths of their first husbands, refrained from any farther, and who, out of the sincere and devout regard entertained for their memory, were content to preserve a pure and unspotted chastity. And as much the apostle tells us, in his first epistle *Ad Timotheum*, and in the second chapter, —to honour widows. For those are not real widows who are only so because they can find no one to have them, or yet who remain so, simply that they may the more easily carry on their wicked ways, or for their advantage, or for any other account than out of a love to God, or to their first husbands; as are those others who will not accept of any, whether for better or worse, as says Virgil in the fourth book of his Eneas; which Eneas so loved Dido, that he died of it. But to love again, would Dido take no heed; for, as she had loved him living, so did she, dead; nor could she forget him. And to Anna, her sister, when she would urge her to remarry, she would only give her, for an answer, thus,

> Ille melos primus qui me sibi junxit amores,
> Abstulit, Ille habeat secum, servetque sepulchro.

Of which the meaning is: "He who first was joined to me, having now left me, has carried all my affections with him. I will that they be always his; with his ashes let them lie." And like as the Romans honoured with crowns, those that accomplished feats of arms; for instance, as he who, the first, would break into the camp of an enemy, was crowned with a wreath of laurel; and as he who would soonest mount upon a ladder or scale the walls of a city or tower, was rewarded with a mural crown, and so, proportionally, for other achievements; likewise did they solemnly crown those women, widows, who, out of love and honour to their first husbands, steadily persisted to refrain themselves from marriage; determining resolutely to guard their chastity. And through these crowns, they came to be more considered than the other widows were. And on this head, Saint Jerome, writing to Juminien, puts before him the instances of many widows, who would have nothing to say to second husbands; as that of Marcia, the daughter of Cato, who never ceased to deplore her husband. For when her friends, thinking to comfort her, would say, "Alas, alas, when will all these lamentations be over?" she would tell them, "But with my life!" And besides her, he speaks of another, named Lucia, who, neither day nor night, for one moment ceased to weep; for ever recalling the memory of her husband; and whose father, to divert her, when alluding to another husband, could get no other answer from her, than, "Alas, sir, for God's sake, forbear!" And when her father told her, that it was wrong for so young a woman to remain a widow; for all reply, she told him, "Sir, so fully did he possess and fill my heart, that even ever so little, never could I love another. And if, in my unhappy inexperience, it were my lot to fall upon one who were kind to me, never, for an instant, should this poor heart know peace, for fear of losing him; and if on one that were unkind or cruel to me, soon should it bring me to my grave: and so, sir, for these reasons, I shall remain as I am." And many other beautiful and touching instances are alleged by the same blessed Saint Jerome, but which I omit, as any one may find them there who pleases. Among other matrimonial ensamples, he notices one, that in effect, is risible enough; which is to be found in the IIII. XX. XVI. of his epistles. It is of a woman of Rome, who was not, however, exactly of the sort of widows we are speaking of, for she had had XXII. husbands. And it so happened, that the people of the town, coming to hear how there was a man alive who had had XX. wives; they so managed that they were brought together. And it was amid all sorts of merriment, feasting and pleasantry, that the marriage was consummated; the whole town of Rome remaining on the tiptoe of expectation, to see on which side the victory would be declared. And as fortune would have it, it was the woman who succumbed. And as soon as it got to be publicly known, all the gallants came together, and placing in his hand a branch of laurel, in token of the victory that he had attained over her who had discomfited XXII. husbands, and on his head a chaplet of green leaves; in this state they conducted him through the town, to the clamour of trumpets and of horns; crying before him, as they went, "Long live Paulo; the overthrower of the overthrower of XXII. husbands!" And with this we will make an end of his examples, and return to our history of Madame and of little Saintré.

CHAPTER III.

How the said young Lady deliberated in her own mind, how she would cause the little Saintré to be heard of in the world; and of how she sent for him to her chamber, asking him, "Who was his lady love?" (dame par amours); and at which the little Saintré was quite put out, and could not answer her a word; except that at last he said, "he had none."

THE AUTHOR.

THIS young lady, however, as has been already said, having resolved, from whatsoever consideration or considerations it might be, never again to marry; for all that, had many imaginations in her head; and, among the rest, it had oftentimes occurred to her, that she could not do a better thing than to make the fortune of some young gentleman, or squire. And with this conclusion, at length, all her speculations ended. And accordingly, for some little time, she kept her eyes abroad, among the more conditioned young gentlemen of the Court, to see which were the most likely to prove an eventual credit to her choice. And at last she pitched on the little Saintré. And so it was, as well to satisfy herself as to his likelihood, as for her own entertainment, that she would openly start him, and talk to him, on all sorts of subjects; and from all which it arrived, that, the more she saw of him, the more she liked him. But it was on other matters than love that their talk was; for, as yet, she neither would, nor even dared farther to discover herself.

[2] At length, it came one day, after Madame had been amusing herself with him, as indeed was warranted of her position, and conventionality permitted, that she retired to put the Queen to bed. And on returning, in passing through the gallery, her squires, ladies, and gentlemen about her, there she saw the little Saintré, who was

looking from a window, at his companions, who were playing at tennis in the court below; and who, as soon as he saw the train of Madame, incontinent fell upon his knees, making his obeisance; which, when Madame saw, she was delighted, and stopping before him, said to him, "Saintré, what is it you are doing here? Becomes it a squire, in such a wise as this, to see his lady pass? On your feet, young master, and fall in with the rest." On hearing this, the poor little Saintré, his face like a furnace, and all out of countenance, got up upon his legs. And as soon as Madame saw him to be before her, she and her ladies, all tittering, continued as they were going; Madame saying to them, "Just wait a moment, till we get by ourselves, and you will see some rare sport!" Then said Madame Jehanne, "And of what, Madame?"

"Of what!" said Madame; "you shall presently see the famous battle there will be between the little Saintré and me."

"Alas, Madame," said Mistress Katherine, "and what has he done? he is such a good lad;" and whiles she was yet speaking, they had come to the door. Then said Madame to her people, "You may leave us, all you men." On this, they were all retiring; and, among the rest, the little Saintré fell on his knees, to make his reverence. But when Madame saw him thus about to retire, she said to him, "You are to remain where you are. Young master, I have accounts to settle with you." And as soon as the door was shut, and she had seated herself on the foot of the little bed, she called him to her, bidding him to come and place himself between her and her ladies; enjoining him, on his oath, to tell her the truth of whatsoever matters she should ask him. The poor child, who could not so much as conceive to what it was that Madame was driving, gave her his word, all the while bemoaning himself, "Alas, and what have I done; what is to become of me?" And presently, seeing him in all this agony, Madame, smiling the while upon her ladies, begins, "Now, master, look at me, and on the troth of that faith you pledged me, tell me, how long is it since last you saw your lady love?" (*dame par amours*.) And no sooner did he hear speak of lady loves; as one who never before had heard of such a mystery, than the tears came rushing to his eyes; his face so pale, and heart so sick, that never a word could he find to reply. Seeing this, Madame began to say, "How now, master, what is the meaning of this;" and the other ladies who were with her, "Ah, Saintré, good friend, why do you not tell Madame how long it is since last you saw your lady *par amours?* It is no such great a matter, that you must be making all this secret of it: besides, you have passed her your word." And so miserably did they badger him, that at length he said, "I have none."

"Have none!" said Madame; "heh, who then is to be the happy fair one, when you do have one? It may be, that you have none; but her whom you like most, and best could wish to have for your lady; how long is it since you saw her last?" The little Saintré, who, as yet, as has been said, had neither heard of nor experienced the gentle intimations of the god of love, still remained silent; fumbling, all sheepish, with his fingers in his belt. And when Madame saw that he had not a word to say for himself, she said, "Ha, fine sir, what sort of behaviour is this? Is it that you refuse to answer me? Am I hurting you, that I simply ask you, when last you saw her whom you most desire to be yours?" On this, Mistress Jehanne, Mistress Katherine, Isabelle, and the rest, who all the time had been laughing, began to be sorry for him. So they said to Madame, "Madame, you see clearly that he has not come prepared to satisfy you on a such a head; allow him time to collect himself. And if you will but be good enough to forgive him this once, he will let you know to-morrow."

Said Madame, "I will have it from him, or ever he leaves the room." Then they all commenced with one accord, to say; the one, " my son ;" the other, " my friend ;" the third, " dear little Saintré, now do tell Madame when it was you last saw your lady, or otherwise you are her prisoner." Finding himself thus hotly pressed, and now half desperate, he sharply asked them, " What is it you are wanting me to tell, when I tell you that I have none. If I had, I would tell you willingly."

"Without another word," said they, " tell us then who you love best ?"

"Who I love best!" said he, "I love my mother best, and after her, my sister, Jacqueline."

Then, said Madame, " What is this, Sir Stripling, are you out of your wits ? it is not of mothers, or of sisters, that it is now question. Love of one's parents, kindred, is quite another thing from love *par amours*. I am asking you, of those who are nothing to you."

"Then of those, on my faith," said he, "I do not care for one."

" And you do not care for one," said Madame, " don't you ? Ha, caitiff knight, so you care for none! Poor chicken heart, well see I, by this, never will you come to any good. To what are we indebted for the valorous achievements, the imperishable memories, and the ever-glorious feats of a Launcelot, a Gauvain, a Tristan ; of Biron, the courteous; and of the other heroes of the Round Table ; also of Ponthus, with so many countless other valiant squires and knights of this kingdom, whom, had I time, I could easily name ; if all was not the price, the wages, of their love, and that they might be confirmed in the graces of their ever-to-be-adored mistresses ? And I know of more than one, who, through having been true lovers, and loyally acquitted themselves to their ladies, came to be had in the highest consideration, and who will never cease to be heard of as long as they live. And if it had not been that they were lovers, they would no more have been thought of than the veriest gaukey going. And yet, sir, you say, that you neither have a lady, nor want to have one! By your own confession, you are a pitiful fellow, so you may be off, for I will have nothing more to say to you." And though Madame repeated all this sternly, for all that, her ladies knew well by her smiling, that, however much it had an air of earnest, it was only said in jest. And when the poor little Saintré thus heard his cruel sentence, at the hand of Madame, he began to cry most piteously, thinking himself to be for ever dishonoured, and undone. Then began Mistress Jehanne, Mistress Katherine, Mistress Isabelle, and all the other gentlewomen, to be really sorry for him. So smiling as they came, they all fell on their knees before Madame, praying that, for this once, he might be pardoned, and pledging themselves for him, that ere two days were over, he should have made his election, and be prepared to name his lady.

"Hush a bit," said Madame; "you are simpletons to suppose he has half the pluck in him."

"But he will, Madame," said they; "will you not, sir?"

"You are dreaming," said Madame; "are you capable, sir, of what they say?" On this, the poor little abject, plucking up heart, said, "Yes, Madame, since such is your pleasure."

"And you will promise it to me?"

"Yes, Madame, on my honour."

"We shall see," said Madame; "now you may go; and mind you so manage matters, that, to-morrow, you are forthcoming in the gallery, about the same time I found you to-day, so that I may find you; or otherwise, make up your mind that you are to see your mother." On this, the poor unfortunate, on his knees, was given his *congé;* all Madame's ladies reminding him, "Now mind, Saintré, you are as good as your word: now remember, we are pledges for you." And no sooner did he discover himself to be out of their reach, than he set too to scamper, as if fifty wolves had been at his heels; whilst Madame and her ladies, who should by rights have taken their sleep, never ceased for a moment to laugh, and make themselves merry with the fright they had given Saintré: so that it was vespers before they knew what they were about, and they had to rise without having ever closed an eye. And when Saintré had got to the other children, his playfellows, God knows how he regaled them all with an account of his adventures. However, such was the contentment came over him to find himself once again at liberty, that, by little and little, all his fine promises got out of his head; excepting only when he stumbled on Madame, or her ladies, when he would make off as fast as his legs could carry him, which made them nearly kill themselves with laughter. At last, at dinner time, one day, the two ladies, seeing him here and there, and everywhere, waiting on all the ladies and gentlewomen, as heretofore, saving only themselves, bidding him come to them, said, " Ha, Saintré, fair sir, by what unlucky mishap have we come to fall into your ill graces? You used to attend on us as on the rest; but now, you run away at the very sight of us!"

"Ladies," said he, colouring all over, and making off as he said it, "with your permission——"

Madame, who was at the lower end of the table, where the King and Queen were at dinner, happening to see the little Saintré, and also the two ladies, how they were amused; as soon as the boards were removed, asked them,

"What it was the little Saintré had said to them which seemed so to have tickled them?"

Then they told her how he helped all the other ladies, but would not come near them.

"Just leave him to me," said Madame, "I'll quickly bring him to his senses."

So, as soon as the wine and desert were handed round, Madame, who saw the little Saintré with a cup in his hand, called him to her, and said, "Saintré, go to the gallery and wait for me there; I want to send you on a commission into the town. I know you would like to oblige me, and will be my friend."

The little Saintré, hearing Madame address him thus softly, feeling as if a weight was taken off his shoulders, and thinking, surely Madame has forgotten all about the promise, said at once, "Most willingly, Madame."

By this, the King and Queen had both withdrawn, and the little Saintré had gone to the gallery. And as soon as the King had lain down, as Madame was returning to her chamber, she found the little Saintré in attendance, as she had desired. So she said to him, "Fall in with the rest." And as soon as she had gotten to her chamber, and had seated herself on the foot of the little bed, she told the squires, with the rest, "that they might retire." Then calling the little Saintré to her, she thundered out, "And so, sir, do I see before me the man who, in two days, was to have fulfilled his oath, and now for four has been eluding me! What vengeance, what punishment were too terrible for the man who is at once a traitor and a perjurer?"

On hearing this cruel and this dreadful charge, the little Saintré gave himself up at once for dead; so, falling on his knees, and with clasped hands, he cried,—"Mercy, Madame, mercy, mercy!" protesting that he really had not had a moment to himself to think of what he had promised.

Madame, who, over his shoulder, saw all her ladies in fits, was, all this time, at her wits' end to keep her countenance. However, she managed to say with tolerable firmness, "Well, sir, admitted it be as you allege, in these four days have you made your election?"

To have again this horrible question put to him, he had as leave been dead as alive; so with his eyes all full of tears, and a face as pale as death, he began to plead for time, as if he had forgotten all about it, or could think of no other way of getting out of it.

Then Madame, delighted to see him in such a strait, turning to, and all the while smiling on her ladies, said to them, "What are we to do with a faithless squire like this; who, two times, has passed his word to a lady, as well you know, and in so light an affair has broken it; what punishment does he not merit? And you, Madame Jehanne, I ask the first."

And when the poor young gentleman heard himself thus attacked by Madame, he thought that surely this time, at any rate, he was lost, and for ever undone. So, with joined hands, being still on his knees, he cried out to Madame, "Mercy! mercy!" and then turning to the other ladies, implored them to intercede for him.

Madame, all this time, however well pleased; and who, the more she saw of him, thus simple and innocent, the more she liked him: and though imagining, that could she but once by fair means win him over to her, she should easily mould him to her wish, nevertheless was determined that Madame Jehanne and the rest, should give her their decision.

Then Madame Jehanne, beginning to be really sorry for him, nor perceiving any more than the others the inward drift of Madame, said to her, "Madame, you must allow, if he has failed in his word, he has at least given you for his excuse the multiplicity of his affairs ; and you now see, how, on his knees, and with how much humility, he craves your pardon for his offence, as do we all."

"And you, Madame Katherine, what have you to say?"

"Alas, Madame, I do not well know what to say, except that he regrets what he has done; and that you see he is really and heartily sorry for it ; and so I must intercede for him."

"And you, Isabelle, you are the eldest ; what have you to say?"

"Alas, Madame, I do not well know what to say except that he regrets what he has done ; and that you see he is really and heartily sorry for it ; and so I must intercede for him ; and, besides, you hear the poor prisoner has of himself confessed, that he had not, as yet, settled on any lady, to be her servant ; and I do think, he is to be believed. Besides, Madame, it is easy to understand of a lover so inexperienced as he is, and one determining religiously to devote himself to the service of his lady, how it is no easy matter to select a lady *par amour*. By my faith, Madame, methinks love is a matter of which he knows precious little, and has never heard mention. Is it not so, my child?"

"By my faith, good mother, yes," said Saintré, "I never spoke to any such person, nor saw one."

"Now, see there, Madame ; your poor supplicant never saw nor heard tell of lovers ; how then, in goodness' name, could he choose his lady? And if even those who are the most initiated in these mysteries, have many a sorry cogitation ere they will expose themselves to the risk of a refusal ; much more might he. And, for all these considerations, I do think, Madame, that this time he should be forgiven."

"And what say you, Margaret, and the rest of you? I want to hear what the whole of you have to say."

But they all, with one voice, gave it for the opinion of Isabelle, as being the eldest among them, and the one who had had the most experience of the world.

CHAPTER IV.

How the Little Saintré, as in desperation, and one who had never yet experienced the sweets of love, told the Lady, that Matheline de Coucy was his lady love; which Matheline was but six years of age.

"NOW," said Madame, "I have heard all your opinions about this shameful breach of faith, and it seems you are all for forgiveness; so, for all your sakes, for this once, he is pardoned. But, one thing, mark you well: he has not done as he ought, seeing he was to have made choice of his lady, and he has not done it."

"Ha, Madame, but yes," cried they all, laughing.

"But no," said Madame.

Then said they, "Think you, Madame, he would have taken all these four days, had it not been that he was determined, without fail, to fix on some one?"

"But no," said Madame.

"But yes," said they; "we will answer for him."

Then they asked him, "Is it not so, my lad?"

On this the poor little wretch, half frightened out of his wits; all taken at unawares, was constrained to say, "Yes."

Then, said Madame to him, "Now are you really the man I took you for?"

Seeing that there was nothing now for it but that some one was to be named, his tears began to flow afresh; his colour to come and to go, as one who was at his wit's end what way to escape.

Then said Madame to her women, "Ha, is it not as I told you? All he wanted was to get himself out of his scrape."

Then said they all, "Alas, now, Saintré, do tell it certainly to Madame; and you, Madame, take him on one side, and certainly he will tell you all. No loyal lover can ever be expected to publish, in this way, the name of the lady of his choice."

Then said Madame, "Leave us by ourselves."

And when they had drawn on one side, she said, "Saintré, good friend, there is no one now here but you and me; so tell me faithfully."

And when the little Saintré saw that there was no way of getting out of it, he said, "Alas, Madame, let me be forgiven, since you are determined that I must confess. And as he was turning over in his head whom he should mention, as nature might prompt him, and will ever, sympathetic, draw kindred unto kindred, it came into his head that he would name a little girl, who was about the Court, and which girl might be some six years of age. So he said, "Madame, it is Matheline de Coucy."

And when Madame heard mention of Matheline de Coucy, she perceived that it was only some childish and foolish attachment. Nevertheless, she thought not proper yet to relax her severity; so she said, "Now see I clearly that you are nothing better than a poor craven-hearted squire. I do not, by this, mean to say that Matheline is not a good-looking girl enough, nor yet come of a good house; for, indeed, she is of a better than you should pretend to; but what good, what profit, what honour, what assistance, what advantage, what comfort, what aid, what counsel, can she ever be of to you? How is she to make your fortune, render you famous, or heard of in the world? What means, furtherance, can you ever have from Matheline, who is but an infant? Sir, you should choose some lady of an high and a noble blood; one discreet, and who will have wherewithal to assist you, and to supply your necessities. And you should so dedicate yourself to her, and so undividedly love her, that, let you be called upon to undergo, or suffer what you might, she should still know that all was supported out of the pure and holy love you bore to her. And do not be taking it into your head, that there is any in the long run, be she whom she will, unless it be some more cruel fair one than any I ever yet heard of, who will not notice, pity, show grace and mercy to you; or from whom you will not meet with a kind reception. And by this means you will become a somebody—a man of consideration. By any other course, I would not give one rush for you or your chances; as sings the old master:—

* (A short ballad is here omitted; having no sort of value.—*Translator*.)

CHAPTER V.

How the Lady instructed the Little Saintré in sundry salutary doctrines and matters, touching the manner in which he was to be euabled to flee the seven deadly sins.

NOW, upon this head, I must farther tell you; that whoever would lay himself out to serve devoutly any such Lady, I say, he may be saved in body as in soul, and I will tell you how. As regards the soul, you are to know, that if he abstains from mortal sins, he is saved; and as for the other, mere venial ones, by a sincere confession they are wiped out, and are atoned for by some slight penance.

And first, as regards the sin of Pride, that the party loving may acquire the much longed-for grace of his Lady, he will so master himself, as to be ever gentle, humble, courteous, affable; so that nothing unhandsome can at any time be laid to his reproach. As much says Thales, the Milesian sage :—

Si tibi copia, si sapientia formaque detur,
Sola superbia destruit omnia, si committetur.

That is to say, my friend, "Though you may have riches, as the sand; though you may have wisdom, though you may have rank, though you may have every bodily perfection; let but all these be dashed with pride, and the whole is spoiled." And on this head, says Socrates:—

> Quantumcumque bonus fueris essendo superbus,
> Totum depravat te sola superbia dampnat.

That is to say, my friend, "However good you may be, if you are proud, the whole is marred. Your pride alone damns you."

And that your pride may be damped, you have but to remember that you have to die. Bethink you whence you came, and whither you will have to go. That will arrest you. And on this point, again, says Trimiges, the philosopher:—

> Ut non infleris memor esto quod morieris.
> Unde venis cerne, quo vadis, te quoque sperne;

with so many other authorities, that too long would it be to rehearse them; and so at present I leave them, to come to what I have to say, which is, that a true lover, such an one as I speak of, will follow them all, to purchase the ever-to-be-desired grace of his ever-beauteous Lady; and for which he will banish this horrible and abominable sin of pride, and all that pertains to it, and will make to himself provision of this delightful virtue of humility. By this he will be absolved and freed from the sin of pride.

THE LADY.

And as regards the second sin, which is Anger. Certes, no true lover ever was irascible. It is true, I have known many a sore trial to have been put upon them; but then it was only to prove them. No lover ever gave way to anger, if not under the influence of some other passion besides love. And so, my friend, if this sin is offensive in the eyes of God, so is it also derogatory to the honour and the person of him who is overtaken with it. And for this reason, you must flee it with all your might, and follow the counsel of the philosopher, who says :—

> Tristitiam mentis caveas plus quam mala dentis.
> Seigniciem fugias nonquam piger ad bona fias.

That is to say, my friend, "Fly melancholy as you would the toothache. Also, fly indolence, if you would banish care: and always be doing some good." And on this head, says Pittacus of Mitylene :—

> Effugias iram, ne pestem det tibi diram
> Juris delira, nutrix est schismatis ira.

That is to say, my friend, "Flee rage and anger, so that they may not infect you with their cruel pestilence; for they are the ways which lead astray, and the nurse of every discord and division." And on this point, says the gospel :—

> Non odias aliquem sed eum potius tibi placas;
> Quisquis odit fratrem censetur ab hoc homicida.

That is to say, my friend, "That you are to bear ill-will to none; but to forgive all; for whoever hates his neighbour, he is a murderer," as says the evangelist. And on this head, says Saint Augustine, in one of his epistles, "That even as sour wine will taint and corrupt the vessel in which it is placed, if it remain any time, so likewise will anger taint and corrupt the breast into which it enters." And with this conclusion agrees the apostle, who says :—

> Sol non occumbat super iracondiam vestram.

That is to say, "Let not the sun go down upon your wrath." And farther, says Cato :—

> Impedit ira animum, ne possit cernere verum.

That is to say, my friend, "That spite and anger dissipate and blind the understanding of a man, so that he cannot see the truth that is before him." And, from all this, my friend, you will gather, that the true lover, such as I speak of, always is, and will be joyous; hoping by his faithful and acceptable service, to find all mercy at the hands of his much-to-be-desired Lady. And in this confidence, he sings, and dances, and makes merry, as Solomon tells him, in his last book, where he sums up all by saying, *Bene vivere et letari*; that is to say, "Live well and jollily." But this good living which he speaks of, does not simply mean to eat good victuals, to drink good wine, to lie abed of a morning, or on downy mattrasses; in a word, to wallow in all delights; but it means, to live, firstly, as in the eye of God; then in this honourable voluptuousness and tranquillity of mind. So, to this end, I say, that all true lovers, who aspire to acquire the ever-to-be-desired good opinion of their ever-lovely Ladies, must shun, as the pest, this pernicious sin of pride, loathsome alike to God and man; and take up with this amiable and desirable virtue of patience; by this means they will be freed from this disagreeable and envious sin of pride.

The Lady.

As for the third sin, it is Envy. This true lover, such an one as I speak of, never is envious of any one. For if such a taint once come to the knowledge of his Lady, infallibly he would lose her for ever; for never could any Lady of honour love a man capable of jealousy; except, indeed, to be jealous of well-doing; as, at church, the most devout; at table, the most hungry; in the company of Ladies, the most courteous and engaging; in the field, the most terrible; in justing, the most gallant. In all such matters, you are indeed to be jealous; but in no others. And on this point, says Seneca:—

Quid melius auro? jaspis. Quid jaspide, sensus. Quid sensu? ratio. Quid ratione? modus. Omnibus adde modum, modus est pulcherrima virtus.

That is to say, my friend and son, "What thing is better than gold? jasper; than jasper? sense; than sense? understanding; than understanding? manner, for manner is the crown of every other virtue." And again, on this article, says the philosopher:—

> Filius ancillæ morosus plus valet ille.

That is to say, my friend, "That the son of a charwoman, well brought up, is worth again the son of a King, ill bred and ill mannered." And again, while on this head, as a farther countenance to good manners, I will tell you a saying of Solon of Athens, which is as follows:—

> Per vinum miser, per talos, et mulieres.
> Hæc tria si sequeris, semper egenus eris.

That is to say, "That by wine, by dice, haunting the company of lewd women, you will be always poor, miserable, unfortunate, and shunned of all honest persons." And farther, on the sin of envy, says Plato:—

> Invidiam fugere studias, et amore carere.
> Que reddit sicum corpus faciens corinicum.

That is, "Seek to shun envy, for envy mates not with love; dries up the flesh, blighting and corrupting the heart." And from all this, my friend, fly all such vices, and all evil company, for love enjoins as much, as do all Ladies of honour to their lovers; following the injunctions of the philosopher, who says:—

> Malo mori fame quam nomen perdere fame.

That, good friend, is to say, "Let me starve sooner than I will forfeit my fair renown." So, to conclude, my friend, remember well this saying which says, "I had rather starve than lose my good reputation;" and again, this other, of the philosopher, the wise Chilon, of Lacedemon:—

> Nobilis es genere, debes nobilis magis esse.
> Nobilitas morum pluris est quam genitorum.
> Nobilitas generis mortem superare nequibit.

That is to say, my friend, " Though you be come of
noble birth, seek farther to be ennobled of your virtues;
for the nobility that comes of good breeding is of infi-
nitely more account than that which comes of birth;
nor can this latter, be it ever so famous, so notable, survive
beyond the grave." So that, to be this perfect lover,
which I wish you, you must eschew this miserable sin
of envy, and array yourself with this right glorious virtue
of charity, which is the daughter of God, and which he has
so urgently recommended to us. Do so, and so will you
be cleansed from, cleared, and quit of this sin.

The Lady.

And as for the fourth sin, which is Avarice. Assuredly
avarice and true love cannot lodge, at once, in the one
breast. And if the avaricious man, by any hazard, is
amorous, it is not to be supposed but it is of some vile
hag or other, and by which he will not be called upon
to spend. But the true and loyal lover will aspire to be
liberal, and honourably to serve his Lady; and out of self-
respect, will always keep himself well dressed, well mounted,
and all his people as beseems his state. And if any
attempt to do more, he will be but a fool for his pains,
and will come to trouble. For lovers and Ladies of
honour care for no such prodigals or spendthrifts. But
they love those who carry themselves as is becoming;
that is to say, who appear in arms, at tilts, at tourna-
ments, and on all honourable occasions, as befits their
rank, without any effort at idle display; who give according to their means, and for the love of God, in the most
necessitous directions; as says the gospel :—

*Beati misericordes : quoniam ipsi misericordiam consequentur.
—Mathei, v. cap.*

That is to say, my friend, " Blessed are the merciful, for

they shall obtain mercy." Something to the same point, says Periander of Corinth :—

> Et sis preclarus non sis cupidus nec avarus.

That is to say, my friend, "Once come to be considered, and you will have riches enough." Hence, be not either covetous or avaricious, for all such dispositions are hated of all, nor can be loved of any. And this is confirmed to you by what the philosopher tells us :—

> Furtum, rapina, fenus, fraudem, simoniam, causat avaritia, ludum, perjuria, bella, radix cunctorum sit nempe cupido malorum.

That is to say, my friend, "that avarice is the root of larceny, of rapine, of usury, of fraud, of simony, of perjury, of brawls; in a word, of every mischief." And Bias, of Prienne, allows as much :—

> Plus flet perdendo cupidus quam gaudet habendo,
> Et magis est servus cum plus sibi crescit acervus.

That is to say, my friend, "The covetous man undergoes a greater agony in losing than did he ever prove of joy in receiving, and the more he amasses, the more beggarly and cowardly he becomes." And, as Saint Augustin says, "The bosom of a miser is no better than a hell;" for never was hell so full, that it cried, Enough; so is it with the avaricious, for if all the riches of the earth were his, never would he consider them to be sufficient. And on this head the Scripture says :—

> Insatiabilis occulus cupidi, in partes iniquitatis non saciabitur.—*Ecclesiastici*, viiii. *cap*.

That is to say, my friend, "That the eye of the covetous is insatiable, and never will be glutted to its fill." And many other authorities are there, which are too long to give you, and hence, I pass. So, in order that the true lover, such an one as I am speaking of, may acquire the ever-to-be-desired grace of his ever-beauteous Lady, he must practise every virtue, and renounce this ugly sin of avarice, and betake himself to this delightful and winning virtue of generosity, at once loved of God, and honoured of the world; and by means of which he is saved.

THE LADY.

And as for this fifth sin, which is Idleness; certainly, my friend, no true lover ever was idle; for the ever gentle and passionate desire, which, day and night, possesses him, to acquire the ever-to-be-desired grace of his ever-beauteous Lady, never would permit of it. For, whether to sing, to dance, above all the others he is the most indefatigable, the most ready to rise betimes, to say his prayers, to hear mass, to be off to the chase, when the poor crippled, slugabeds of lovers are asleep; this will ever be his way. Wherefore flee this sin, after the counsel of Epicurus, the philosopher, who says :—

> Otia, vina, dapes, caveas ne sint tibi labes ;
> Vix homo sit castus requiescens, et benè pastus.

That is to say, my friend, "Fly boozing, superfluity of wine, excess at table, so that you come not to be drowned in luxury; for it is next to impossible for any indolent person, well filled, to contain themselves within the bounds of chastity." And, again, concerning this miserable vice of indolence, says Saint Bernard :—

> Vidi stultos se excusantes sub fortuna, vix autem diligentiam, cum infortuniis sociabis.

That is to say, my friend, "Fools will ever lay their troubles to the door of fortune; and whilst you will hardly ever see an industrious person unfortunate, as assuredly will you ever find idleness and misery packing hand in hand." And on this head, Saint Bernard adds :—

> Revidere quæ sua sunt, quomodò sunt, summa prudentia est.

That is to say, my friend, "That to see to one's affairs, how they are, and what they are, is prudence." And, you see, he does not simply say, "look to your affairs," but "look twice," by which he would mean, that you cannot too often look. And as much adds Atheneus, the poet, where he says :—

> Ocia sunt juvenum menti plerisque venenum,
> Et juvenum corpora, viciorum maxima causa.

That is to say, my friend, "That idleness, for the most part, is a canker to the minds of the young; for in young persons, almost all viciousness takes its rise in the flesh." And on this head, says Seneca :—

> Pigritiam linque quæ dat mala tedia vite,
> Tedia virtutis fuge, nam sunt damna salutis.

That is to say, my friend, "Have nothing to say to idleness, for it renders life tedious and insipid; and fly everything that is opposite and irksome to virtuous and arduous achievement." And for this reason, my friend, seeing that all true lovers, such as I speak of, are, by their virtues, saved; abandon, I beseech you, this miserable and discreditable vice of indolence, and give yourself up wholly to the thrice illustrious virtue of diligence, and so will you come to be accounted among them that do. And thus will you be, from this wretched vice of indolence, saved and free.

THE LADY.

And as for the sixth sin, which is of the belly, or of Gluttony. Certainly the true lover has no business either with eating or drinking, further than to satisfy nature; as says the philosopher, "that we should only eat and drink to live, not live to eat and drink, as the pigs do." And on this head, Tulles, the Milesian sage, says :—

> Pone gule frenum ne sumas inde venenum,
> Nam male digestus cibus extat sæpè molestus.

That is to say, my friend, "Put a padlock on your mouth,

so that this poison may not get into you; for superfluity of food, half digested, is, above all things, injurious to the system. Again, on this head, says the sage Solon, of Athens:—

> Ne confunderis, nunquam vino replearis.
> Vilis diceris, nisi vino te moderaris.

That is to say, my friend, "See that you are at no time addicted to wine, so that you may never be brought to confusion; for you will be looked on as scandalous, if you do not as well use wine moderately, as it you." And on this head of gluttony, says Saint Bernard, in his Moralities, "that when once this vice comes to be master of a man, he forfeits all the good repute in which, till then, he was held." And when the belly is not kept within bounds by a rigid enforcement of abstinence, all the other virtues are choked. And on this head, says Saint Pol:—

Quorum finis interitus: quorum deus venter est, et gloria in confusione eorum, qui terrena sapiunt.—*Ad Philip. tertio capitulo.*

That is to say, my friend, "That those who savour of earthly things, their end is death. Those who make of their belly, their god; their glory will be their shame, their confusion, whether in matters of love or of arms." So, I do beseech you, that you will not be of them; but follow the counsel of the ancient; to avoid all which, he says:—

> Sic semper comedas, ut surgas esuriendo.
> Sic etiam sumas moderatè vina bibendo.

That is to say, my friend, "Always partake in such a manner that, when you rise from table, you may be still hungry. Also, let your drink be moderate," for by so doing you will, in the course of nature, be longer spared; besides, you will be had in the grace of God, of all true lovers; and, above all, in that of your Lady. So, you are to abstain from this graceless and beastly sin of gluttony, and take up with that benignest of virtues, abstinence, and the flower of every excellence. And, by this means, you will be, from this sin, freed and saved. And I will now have done to speak of this sovereign remedy, for all true and loyal lovers, touching this sixth mortal sin, which is gluttony.

THE LADY.

And as to the seventh sin, which is Incontinence. Verily, my friend, in the breast of the true lover, this sin is even dead. For so terrible is his apprehension that it might cost him the loss of his Lady, or that she should resent it, that so much as a dishonest thought will not cross his mind. But he will, in all things, follow the counsel of Saint Augustin, who says:—

> Luxuriam fugito ne vili nomine fias.
> Carni ne credas, ne Christum nomine ledas.

That is to say, my friend, "Flee lust so that you may not be sullied with an infamous renown. Also, trust not too much the flesh, lest you come to offend Jesus Christ." And with this agrees Saint Peter, the Apostle, in his first epistle, where he says:—

> Obsecro vos, tanquam advenas et peregrinos, abstinere vos à carnalibus desideriis qui militant adversus animam.—*Prima Ep.*, ii. *cap.*

That is to say, my friend, "I beg of you, as strangers and as pilgrims, that you will abstain from fleshly delights, for, day and night, are they at warfare with the spirit." And on this head, further, says the philosopher:—

> Sex perdunt vere homines in mulierum; animam, ingenium, mores, vim, lumina, vocem.

That is to say, my friend, "That the man who haunts the company of loose women, loses six things; of which, the first is his soul; the second, his wits; the third, his manners; the fourth, his strength; the fifth, his eyes; the sixth, his voice. And, for this cause, fly, my friend, this sin, and everything connected with it. Cassiodorus, on the Psalter, says, that it was wantonness which first brought the devil, from an angel, to be a devil; induced death into the world, and robbed the first man of that blessedness which was prepared for him—that wantonness is the nurse of every evil, the well-spring of every vice; that perverted path which estranges us from the grace of God. And on this head, says David in his Psalter, as he cries to God:—

Odisti observantes vanitates supervacuè.—*Ps.* xxx.

That is to say, my friend, "Thou, my God, hatest, and hast ever hated those who follow vanities." And many other like injunctions have been left of the blessed doctors of the holy church; and not only of them, but of the philosophers, poets, and other wise pagans, who had never even heard of the true knowledge, the most holy and surpassing affection of the true God, the Holy Spirit; and who had, one and all, this sin in such abhorrence, that, to rehearse you all, would be impossible. And so, excepting only one of Boethius, I will pass them over to come to other matters. This is what he says:—

Luxuria est ardor in accessu, fœtor in recessu, brevis delectatio, corporis et animæ destructio.

That is to say, my friend, "That lust is fire at the beginning; loathsome when done with; a very nothing, for its duration; perversion, as well of body as of soul." And inasmuch as this, my friend, is, of all sins so shameful a one, the true lover, such an one as I am speaking of, out of the dread that his Lady should be displeased, and to win her by every means in his power, will flee it. And if, by any chance, by some uncontrollable impulse of his nature (*contrainte d'amours*), he comes to be a forfeitor therein; such, and so great are the agonies and apprehensions to which they are subjected, viewed all the terrible perils and mischiefs that may come of it, and which the tortured breasts of loyal lovers are exposed to, that it will not be accounted unto them for a mortal sin. And if so be that sin there be, truly it is amply atoned for of the aforesaid penalties, which, unhappily, they must undergo. So, from all this, I may safely say that the true lover, such an one as I speak of, of this sin, and of every other sin, is absolved, quit free, and saved.

CHAPTER VI.

How the lady gives some further instructions to the little Saintré, touching the virtues, state, and order of nobility.

THE LADY.

AND as to the salvation of the body, I have already said, that such a lover can be saved in body and in soul. After the preservation of the seven deadly sins, which regard the soul, of which you have already heard, I will now speak to you of the saving of the body, and that in different ways; and first, in the matters of love, (*faict d'amours*).

The true and loyal lover is one who is a gentleman, sane and sound in body and in mind; and who, day and night, dedicates himself to the unwearied service and grace of his ever-beauteous Lady; and this, by the seven opposite applications to the seven mortal sins which I spoke of. And this lady must be, in point of honour, the *nonpareille* of her sex. I embrace all, for all are presumed to be ladies *par amours;* even supposing that they may be in no way inclined to love either him, or anybody else. Again, right reason and nature ordain, that she should, above all other earthly things, esteem and interest herself in him, and in such a manner, that in his welfare, honour,

and advancement, would be all her delight; and, contrary,
with all his misfortunes should be her sympathy. And
let her be what lady she might, and he what gentleman;
if both such as I speak of; of her means, in his necessity,
he never should be unprovided. And under any other
course, she would be to be despised, contemptible, and
would merit to be banished from the society of all right-
minded persons; and to be cast, body and soul, into the
filthy and bottomless abyss, receptacle of ungracious souls.
However, I never yet heard tell that any such have been.
And by this means, the true lover, who is saved in body,
is saved also in soul.

THE LADY.

And as for the rest, touching, more particularly, the salvation of his person; the true accomplished gentleman lover,
who is neither designed nor suited to the study of the
right prudent and holy sciences of theology, of the decretals, the laws, or other learned professions, but only to
the most noble and illustrious science and occupation of
arms, and whereby he may purchase to himself the grace
of his ever-to-be-desired Lady, is he who is ever foremost,
is outdone of none; and, above all his fellows, causes
himself to be heard of. When he is at mass, he is the
most devout; at table, the best conducted; in the company of lords and ladies, the most accomplished. With
his ears, he will never so much as hear an indelicate word;
nor will he allow his eyes an indiscreet regard; nor from
his lips an unhandsome word to escape; with his hands,
he will never venture on squeezing or dishonest liberties;
nor, with his feet, wander into forbidden quarters. What
need I add more? In a word, no other will be equipped
like him; as for his armour, it will be of the best, and
after the latest ordinance; he will be well mounted, and
have his caparisons of the richest; and, for the love of his
Lady, will ever be in the foremost of the fight, as well on

horse as on foot. And although it may be said, that all these wagers are but vanities, and are forbidden by the Church, as is to be seen in the decretals, as I have heard; and first, where it is said,—

> Et alibi non tentabis Dominum Deum tuum.

For one must know, God will be only for him who is in the right—

> Item Prædestinationes xxiv., quæstione iv.

Wherein they say, neither law nor reason warrant these extremities. Besides, they allege that it is to tempt God; for the clerks say, that to go through with anything unnatural is either monstrous, or tempting God. And again of Purgatory;—

> Vulgari per totum, in capitulo, consuluisti ii., quæstione v.
> Item capitulo, prædestinaciones xxx., quæstione iv. Et notabiliter in capitulo gloriosus de veneratione sanctorum, libro sexto.
> Item capitulo, ut nemo, in propria causa jus sibi dicat, per totum, capitulo de gladiatoribus tollendis, lib. vi.

And other decrees, without number, forbidding all wagers of battle, and those combats that I speak of. But the emperors, kings, with the other princes of this world, conformable to the rights and customs of their temporal regalities, have authorized and commanded such combats, upon all such occasions as circumstances may have called for them. And, upon this head, there was a furious struggle between the Holy Father Pope Urban, the fifth of the name, and the good King John of France, touching a wager of battle which was between two knights; the one French, the other English, at Ville Neuve, near Avignon. And although the Pope was determined to put in force the weight of his decrees, and had placards attached to all the church doors, forbidding any, under pain of excommunication, to be present at the same; yet, for all that, the most Christian king, for the maintenance of his royal privileges, refused to put a stop to it, and resolved, as a temporal prince, to support the temporal laws; which speak thus:—

> Et ejus, ff. Si quis homines eadem lege et jure, ff. Si quis alium, ff. Lombarda quæ incipit si quis, ff. Ultimo l. Lombarda de consti, ff. l. similiter, ff. Ultimo Lombarda de homicidio, l. si quem inLomb arda de parriti,ff. Ultima in Lombarda de homicido, l. Liber homo in Lombarda de fur l. Si quis alium in Lombarda de adulterio. l.

And there are many other occasions, provocations, on which they are permitted by the laws, known as *The Lombard;* where they may be found at length, and their different natures. However, they are strictly forbidden now-a-days, by the statutes of the most Christian king, Philip, excepting in four instances only, not more.

The first case is, that it be certain, evident, uncontested, that the mischief has been really compassed; and to this effect is the clause:—

> Il apperra evidament hommicide, trahyson, ou autre vray semblable malefice par evidente soupeceon.

The second case is; that the occasion be such, that natural death would come of it. The third, that none can be punished, except by wager, in all cases of murder, or when charged of treason: in both which instances, he who is impugned must defend himself at the risk of his person. The fourth is, that he who is challenged be defamed of the fact, circumstantially, or by presumption tantamount to conviction. And this is what is said on the head of evidence. But notwithstanding that these wagers of battle be thus prohibited, and these disputes, reserved for the decision of the church, which, by its decretals, has pronounced a contrary course to be wickedness, tempting God, and vanities; returning to my point, the true lover is in no way guilty of any of these sins, as he is only actuated for the increase of his honour, without any sort of quarrel, or to the prejudice of any. And I will answer for him, that even in the thickest, he does not so much wish any sort of overthrow or dishonour to his antagonist, as reputation to himself. And in testimony of this, he should call God to his vindication, and to be his witness. And that God may be the better disposed to hear him, he should go absolved and repentant, on account of all the perils that may ensue. Of the oaths which they take, and the ceremonies that they go through, to be short, I shall say nothing at present. But when the true lover leaves his tent, all armed, as he should be—equipped with his shield, and all the armour which pertains to knighthood— he first makes the major sign of the Cross, then he lowers his pennon, then they hand him his lance or his sword, which he takes in his right hand, wherewith to defend himself, or assault, as best he may. After that, he is seated on a stool, or else waits, erect, till such time as he is called upon by the judge, or umpire of the field. Then this true and loyal lover arises, and puts himself in motion, sternly, and proudly, as though he would eat his adversary up; and he will, above all, have a care that his first blows are directed coolly and cautiously. As much advances Valerius Maximus, in his fifth book, when he says, "that it is insufferable for a general or a soldier to have to say, I never thought this would have happened!" For as there is nothing in this world which can ever be a second time done; so, especially, in all matters that are to be decided of the sword, and are, of all others, the most perilous, it behoves those who are committed to them, to carry themselves with an infinite wariness and apprehension. And conformable to this is what Vegece says, in his first book on the Secret of Chivalry—that errors in most matters are to be retrieved, saving only such as fall out upon the field of battle; to these no remedy can be applied, for, incontinent, the penalty ensues upon the forfeit. And for this reason, my friend, the wise, true, and devoted lover is loyal, and should be, in all his ways and deeds, cautious, wary, and advised. And it is commonly they, albeit they may neither be so rudely built, nor so terrible in the fight, or to slay, as many another, who expose themselves to the cruelest assaults; conformable to the words of the sage, of whom I spoke to you before :—

Malo mori fame, quam nomen perdere fame.

That is to say, my friend, "Rather let me starve of hunger than lose my fair renown." And in addition to this, the perfect lover follows, every day, toward all those who have done him any kindness, or are disposed to do it, whether as to counsel, reprehension, or regard, the inculcation of Aristotle, who says :—

Diis parentibus et doctoribus non possimus reddere equivalens.

That is to say, my friend; "that to the gods," for which you will understand, God; "our fathers, mothers, as well as others of our kindred and instructors, we can never return a sufficient recompense for all that they have done for us."

———•◦•———

CHAPTER VII.

How the Lady determined to come at the favourable or unfavourable impression left upon the little Saintré, in the matter of love *par amour*.

THE LADY AGAIN.

"NOW, my friend, I have put before you, and showed you many things, which, I pray God, all, or most part, you have attended to and understood. What say you? Do you feel as if it was in you; that, with time, you would ever come to be capable of all this? Tell me, what do you think of it?"

THE AUTHOR.

And when Madame had thus finished her sermon, Saintré, like a child as he was, and all bewildered with all these fine doctrines, had not a word to say. Then said she to him, "Fair Sir, what think you; have you the heart to attempt all this?" On this, the poor little fellow, raising his eyes to her, and with a low voice, replied, "Yes, Madame, willingly."

"You will, my friend!"

"Madame, yes; with all my heart. But who is the Lady, such as you speak of, who would accept of my services, or care, Madame, for me?"

"And why not?" said Madame, "Are you not a handsome young fellow? Have you not eyes to see; ears to hear; lips, tongue, to speak; hands and arms to make use of; feet and legs to walk; a body and a heart to carry you through, and loyally to dedicate to all that she may enjoin of you?"

"Madam, I have!"

"And why then do you not come out of your shell? However much you may be worth, do you really fancy that any Lady is to be so far unmindful of her honour as to take upon herself to court you? No. But when they are compelled, as it were, of an invincible inclination toward those they love, to allow it to escape them; then, by that means is the true lover shown in what manner he may proceed. So why do you not make a push? Besides, however high or worthy may be the Lady, in proportion as you make her condescension gracious, so proportionately will she be indebted to you."

SAINTRÉ.

"Madame, I had as leave die as once offer myself and be refused, only to be laughed at and twitted for my pains. And, for this reason, Madame, I had better remain as I am." And when Madame heard this, and all his way of reasoning, and how he was unable to catch her drift, she could no longer stifle what was upon her breast, so she said to him :—

CHAPTER VIII.

How the Lady opened her heart to the little Saintré, showing him that it was she who was willing to love him.

THE LADY.

"NOW, listen to me as a good Christian, and as a gentleman, which you are; will you swear to me; by God, on your faith as a Christian; and on your honour as a gentleman; none now being present, or who can hear, save you and I; that, of all the things which I am saying to you, or that I may have occasion hereafter to say to you, or may already have said to you; to no manner of soul, that can either live or die, will you in any sort reveal them. Will you put your hands in mine, and swear to me this?"

"Yes, Madame," said he, "on my honour."

THE LADY.

Then said Madame to him, "Now, Saintré, supposing it were I, would you like, for my sake, to serve me loyally, play a noble part, and come to great honour? Would you obey me?"

THE AUTHOR.

To this, the little Saintré, who had never yet turned in his head what it was to be the servant of a Lady, *par amours*, knew not well what to reply; so, falling on his knees, he said, "Madame, I will do whatever you require of me."

"And then, with your hands in mine, you will promise me this?"

"Yes, by my faith, and my loyalty. Madame, as I

promise you, I will perform, and will do whatever you may desire."

"Now, you may rise, and listen well to what I am about to say to you, and remember it."

CHAPTER IX.

How the Lady admonished the young Saintré touching the ten commandments of the law, and in what consisted the virtues and good breeding.

THE LADY.

FIRST of all, I will and require that, above everything, you love God with your whole heart, according to the commandments of Holy Church; the best that you can, or are able. Farther, I will and command you, that, next to God, you love and obey the blessed Virgin Mary; above all other considerations, the most that is in your power. Also, I will and command, that you love and commend yourself to the ever-blessed and true Cross, on which our Saviour, Jesus Christ, died and was impassioned; and which is our true talisman and defence, as well against our enemies as evil spirits. Also, I will and command that, every day, you observe your *pater-noster*, or some other form of prayer, and that you recommend yourself to your good angel, into whose keeping God has committed the safety and the charge as well of your body as your soul; that he will direct you, keep you, and defend you, when he may not be by you; and that he will be with you, in life as in death. I also will and command you, that you will ever have St. Michæl, St. Gabriel, or some other angel, saint, or saintress of Paradise present in your memory, so that they may be, toward our Lord and our Lady, your advocates, ambassadors, and intercessors; as are those who are mostly to be found in the courts of kings and of great princes, towards such as cannot, of themselves, see, speak with, or find access to them. Also, I will and command, that, for the ten commandments of the law, you keep and fulfil them. And these are they :—

First; you will neither worship idols, nor any kind of false god.

You will not falsely swear, in God's name.

You will keep Sundays, and all appointed feasts.

You will honour father and mother.

You will not commit murder.

You will not commit adultery.

You will not steal.

You will not bear false witness.

You will neither desire nor covet your neighbour's wife; and also will not covet anything of another.

The Lady.

I farther will and command, that you, in everything, subscribe to the Twelve Articles of the Faith, which are virtues in divinity, nurses to a rectitude of mind; as says Cassiodorus, in his exposition of the *Credo;* " that faith is the light of the soul, the gate of Paradise, the key to eternal life; for, without faith, none can please God. And on this head, says St. Peter, the Apostle :—

Sine fide impossibile est placere Deo.—vi. cap.

That is to say, my friend, that, " Where there is not faith, it is impossible to be acceptable unto God." Of faith, six heads regard the divinity of God, the Father; and the other six, the humanity of Jesus Christ : which six, pertaining to the Divinity of God, the Father, are these :—

Believe in God, the Father, omnipotent, Creator of Heaven and of Earth.

Believe in his true Son, man also; Jesus Christ, our only Saviour.

Believe in God, the Holy Spirit; the true and fervent Love (*vray zel et amour*) of God, the Father, to God, the Son; and of God, the Son, to God, the Father.

Believe in Holy Church, and in her Commandments.

Believe in the Communion of saints, and the Remission of sins.

Believe in the Resurrection of the flesh, and in the Life Eternal.

And the six pertaining to the Humanity of Jesus Christ, are these:—

Believe that the second person of the Trinity, that is to say, Jesus, the Son of God, the Father, was conceived of the Holy Spirit, and born of the Virgin Mary.

Believe that he was crucified, died, and was buried, under Pontius Pilate.

Believe that, as soon as he was dead, he descended into Hell, to liberate the holy Prophets, and just persons, who were there.

Believe that, the third day, he arose of his own proper power, from death to life.

Believe that, forty days after he had risen, he ascended into Heaven, his body glorified; and that he is there seated at the right hand of God, the Father.

Believe, that he will come to try the living, and the dead, at the terrible day of judgment.

Farther will I, and command, that the seven Cardinal virtues are to be in you; of which three are divine, and four moral.

The three that are divine, are Faith, Hope, and Charity.

And the four moral are, Prudence, Temperance, Vigour, and Justice.

I farther will and command you, that, the seven gifts of the Holy Spirit, you are to credit and pursue. That is to say, the gift of awe, the gift of pity, the gift of knowledge, the gift of fortitude, the gift of judgment, the gift of understanding, the gift of wisdom.

I also will and command you, that the eight Beatitudes you are to cultivate and rely in. And first, humility of spirit, gaiety of heart; towards yourself, tears for your sins; towards others, a desire to do a rigorous justice. Be compassionate, and merciful; seek to be pure at heart; be at peace with all, and be patient.

Also, I will and command you, that in the four accomplishments of the person, you are to take your delight. That is to say, in intelligence, in subtlety, in agility, in facility.

I farther will and command you, that the seven spiritual and godly virtues may be ever manifested on your part. That is to say, to instruct the ignorant, to correct the faulty; to put in the way the lost and the erring; to hide the failings of another; to put up with injuries; to comfort the comfortless, and to pray for all sinners.

I farther will and command you, that the corresponding seven virtues of a more material compassion, be likewise evidenced of you. And above all, to feed the hungry; to give to the thirsty drink; to house the poor, to clothe the naked, to visit the sick, to ransom the prisoners, to bury the dead. And on this head, says my lord, St. Gregory, in his epistle to Nepotian, "I cannot recall to have ever read or heard tell of any coming to an unfortunate end who had sufficiently abounded in works of charity; for so many mediators will be found for such an one that it is impossible but their prayers must be effectual." And, to the purpose, says our Lord, in the Evangel:—

Beati misericordes, quoniam ipsi misericordiam consequentur.—*Mathæi*, v. cap.

That is to say, my friend, "Happy are the merciful, for they shall obtain mercy; so many entreaters will they find."

Farther, I will and command, that you will firmly believe in the seven sacraments of Holy Church; that is to say, in the holy Baptism, in the holy Confirmation, in a sincere Penitence, in the holy sacrament of the Altar, in the holy Orders, in the order of Marriage, and in the holy Unction.

And I farther will and command, that you use all your might to avoid falling into the six mortal sins; and first, pride; next envy; then laziness; after gluttony, anger, and incontinence.

The Lady.

I farther will and command you, that you have a care, let what will overtake you, of falling into any of the seven sins against the Holy Spirit; which are despair, presumption, a denial of the truth, to harden oneself in the sin of brotherly envy, breach of charity, despair in the ultimate virtues of penitence. With this, I command you, that, when in your power, you will be present at the sermons and ceremonies of Holy Church. And, to be short, whatever Holy Church wills and commands, no matter what any one may say, you are to attend to. I farther will and command, that, at the beginning, or at the middle of Lent, at Easter, at Pentecost, and at the five feasts of our Lady, at All-Saints, at Christmas, you confess, and put yourself in the hands of some discreet physician of the soul, just as you would your body. I farther will and command you, that, be you in the company of whom you may; King, Queen, Lords or Ladies; or where you list; in the field, in the street, or in the doors; whenever you shall see the images of our Lord, our Lady, however homely they may be, or yet the Cross, or any of the angels, saints or saintesses, to whom all worship is due; incontinent you will raise your hat or cap; and this, regardless of what any one may either say or think. And if so be that you have not got one on, then let your salutation be made within you, and from your heart. And it is to be the same with the poor. If they ask you for alms, give it, if you have to give; if you have not, let your own conscience attest its own willingness, and call on God to witness of the same. And if, through any apprehension of being ridiculed, you refrain from these things, then, I have to tell you, you will be guilty of as mortal a sin as if you had fallen into the other extremes of hypocrisy, of ostentation, and of vain glory.

THE LADY AGAIN.

I farther will and command you, that when you shall be grown, so as to be a participator in the noble feats of arms, as men of war are wont; in battles, in sieges; by land and by sea; in strife of death, whether singly or with the companions; in mines beneath, or on the battlements above; on the ladder, at the barrier, on the sally, in the ambush, or wherever else you may be; you will ever have on your lips that most holy invocation which our Lord gave to Moses, to be by him passed to Aaron, his brother, the high priest of the law, and wherewith-all he was to bless the sons of Israel; as is said in the Bible, in the book of Numbers, fourteenth chapter:—

Benedicat tibi Dominus, et custodiat te, ostendat tibi faciem suam Dominus, et misereatur tui.
Convertat Dominus vultum suum ad te. Et det tibi pacem.

For this supplication, proceeding, as it does, from the very mouth of Our Lord, appears to me to be more laudable and efficacious than any other that I know of. And, for this reason, I would recommend it to you, as well when you rise, as when you go to rest. But, as it seems to me, that, in making use of it, you rather bless others than yourself, I would have you, when you make the sign of the cross, to say as follows:—

> Benedicat michi Dominus et custodiat me.
> Ostendat michi faciem suam Dominus et misereatur mei.
> Convertat Dominus vultum suum ad me et det michi pacem.

And, whatever you do, do it cheerfully, and so will no trouble ever come nigh you. And this benediction, my lord, St. Francis, put upon brother Lyon, his companion, overtaken of a devilish provocation, and which never after troubled him.

The Lady.

I farther will and command you, that, when you shall be in the wars, and in the fight, and shall have come to be triumphant over your adversaries; or when vengeance, or when wakened ire shall fire you, that you will call to mind the words, where it is said in the first book of the Bible, Uteronomy:—

> Quicumque fundet sanguinem humanum, furdetur et sanguis illius.

Again, says he, in his passion:—

> Qui gladio percusserit, gladio peribit.

Again, says he, to David:—

> Non edificabis michi domum. Quia vir sanguinis es.

Another time, says he, by the mouth of David,—

> Vir sanguinum et dolosus non videbit dies suos.

That is to say, my friend, "That the man of blood shall not live out all his days." And what he said before, my friend, was, "That, who kills with the sword, shall perish with the sword." Again, says he:—

> Virum sanguinum et dolosum abominabitur dominus.

That is to say, my friend, "That the man of blood, and

the spiteful, is an abomination to our Lord." Again, says he, by the mouth of David :—

Si occiderit Deus peccatores viri sanguinum declinate à me.

That is to say, my friend, "Though thou, Lord, mayest slay the sinners; let not blood be under my hand." And so many other minor charities has he put upon us, and enforced by his own example, and of which the Scriptures are full, that it would not be in the power of the greatest clerk so much as to rehearse them. And, for this reason, my friend, from this unnatural vice, as from every other, I will and command that you preserve yourself clean and quit; and that you will, to the best of your power, abstain from offending either God, our Lady, or any of the court of Paradise; and that you will take up with those never-enough-to-be-admired words of Seneca, who was a heathen, yet who says :—

Si scirem Deos ignoscituros, et homines ignoraturos, non tamen dignarer peccare propter vilitatem ipsius peccati.

That is to say, my friend, "Though I might know, that neither gods saw me, nor could men espy me, yet, for all that, would I not sin." Fancy, then, my friend, if Seneca, who was but a poor heathen, thus held vice and sin in abomination, how much more should we, who, by the precious rite of baptism, are become members of the holy faith of Jesus Christ? So, all these things I have to require that you will do your endeavour to accomplish.

The Lady again.

And as for the other matters, which regard your person; I desire and command that, every morning, as soon as you arise, and every night, before you lie down, you will bless yourself, making, most scrupulously, the sign of the cross, this way, and not sideways, or crooked, as I warned you of, in the devil's characters; commending yourself to

God, to our Lady, to the true cross, to your good angel, and to all the saints and saintesses, your intercessors. And you will rise betimes, and you will dress yourself cheerfully, and as nicely as you can, and without making any noise. And as soon as you have got your doublet laced, and your stockings nicely on and tightly drawn, and your shoes well rubbed, then you will comb yourself, and wash your hands and face; then clean your nails, and, if necessary, pare them. You will then put on your belt, and draw your frock down. And when you are all ready, or ever you leave your room, make the sign of the cross, to our Lord, and to our Lady; and to them, and to your good angel, and to all the saints and saintesses recommend yourself. Then, do this, as Saint Augustin requires, when he says :—

> Primo quærite regnum Dei.

Which is to say, before you proceed to do anything else, be it what it will, go first to the chapel, and take of the holy water; and if mass is going on, attend to it; and if it is not, you are to get on your knees before the images, or the pictures of our Lord Jesus Christ, and of our Lady; and, with your hands clasped, and without any gazing either here or there, you are to say your prayers and orisons, with all the devotion you are capable of; not, however, to them, but out of a love to him who is in the heavens. And, after that, you will go into the great hall, and there, with all the knights and squires, you will wait till my lord the King, and madame the Queen, or either of them, may be going to hear mass, when you are to accompany them. And if you have not yet heard it, then, without looking about you, you are to fall on your knees; taking care, however, not to be in the front of any lord or lady, who, in honour, are to be preferred before you. But neither are you to put yourself among the grooms, at the back; for, in all things, the mean is to be preserved, as says the philosopher, in his Ethics, to this effect:—

Virtus consistit in medio.

That is to say, my friend, "That virtue consists in a medium state, and the Versifier says, on the same head:—

Medium tenuere beati.

That is to say, my friend, "That those are blessed who, not seeking after things too high, are to be contented with reason." And you are then, unfeignedly, and from your heart, whilst mass is being said, to repeat your prayers, or other lessons which you may be in the habit of saying, whilst it is going on. And, that over, you will then worshipfully reconduct my lord and madame. Then, if you happen to be either hungry or thirsty, by all means go and breakfast; but see that it is sparingly, and not for the mere sake of cramming, as I charged you before. You are to put off eating, if you can, till dinner-time; as says the philosopher: "that one ought only to eat and drink to live; not live to eat and drink." And true is it, what poor folk say of us, their masters; "that guzzling kills more of us than does the sword." And I farther forbid you to be quarrelsome, or a liar, or a tattle-tale, for these are things that carry no good with them. Cassiodorus, in his book on the Extollation of St. Pol, says, "that wickedness, from its very nature, and even though there be none to expose it, will expose itself. But, on the contrary, such is the character of virtue, so fixed and unassailable is it, that, more it finds of calumniators, more and more will it vindicate itself." And on this head, says the Holy Scripture;—

Super omnia veritas secundum.—*Esdras*, iij. cap.

That is to say, "That truth is above all things." And

for this, my friend, be always firm and truthful, and fly the company of scandal-mongers, the noisy and the idle, for with them harbours neither peace nor safety. Also, have clean hands, as clean lips: do all the good you can to all, without grudging; nor think yourself too fine for, or above, anything. Seek the company of none but the wise; attend to, and treasure what falls from them. Be humble and courteous. You are not to speak of yourself at any time; nor yet too much of anything at all; for the old adage says, "of too much babbling, one comes to be taken for a fool;" or, again, too little. And you are to have an especial care, that no lady or gentlewoman, nor any female whomsoever, comes to trouble on your account. And should you happen to be in the company of any who so far forgets herself as to address you unbecomingly, you are to show her, civilly but firmly, that such familiarities are unpleasing to you, and to withdraw.

The Lady again.

I farther will and command you, that you will be merciful toward the poor, and that you will never make light of the misfortunes of another; and that, to the utmost of your ability, you will distribute to the necessitous. And you will remember the words of Albertus:—

Non tua claudatur ad vocem pauperis auris.

That is to say, my friend, "Let not your ears be closed to the cry of the distressed." And I farther will and command you, that, should it ever come that God, in his graciousness, shall have raised you to be famous among men, on no account are you then to forget, for the transitory and unsatisfying joys of earth, the ever-glorious and imperishable riches of the sky. On this head, I have already told you the words of the poet, which are these:—

Quando dives moritur in tres partes dividitur: caro datur vermibus; pecunia parentibus: anima demonibus: nisi Deus misereatur.

That is to say, my friend, that "As soon as the rich man is dead, he and his goods are parted. And this is the disposement—his body to the worms; his gold, his silver, his jewels, with all he had, to his successors; his soul to the devil; that is, if God has not mercy on it." And on this head, my friend, remember that beautiful passage in Aristotle, where he says:—

> Vir bone quam curas res viles res perituras.
> Nil profuturas damno quandoque futuras.
> Nemo diù mansit in crimine: sed cito transit.
> Et brevis atque levis in mundo gloria peris.

That is to say, my friend, that Aristotle, in his general doctrine, says, "O, whoever thou art, that, by overweening might seekest to scale the highest heights of riches and of honour, have a heed lest, by the vain attempt, you be precipitated into the depths beneath. For, great enterprise, great risk. And when all is done, and what is worse than all, you will have to die."

The Lady.

I farther will and command you, to be carried in your memory, that, in all your prosperity, you will be mindful of the words of Seneca, in his last book, on Benefits, in the XXI. Chapter, where he says, "That those in place are in want of nothing, save only of some one from whom they can hear the truth." And on this follow sundry recapitulations of the vyings and the heart-burnings which are ever at the courts of great lords, as to who will be the most obsequious toward them, and the most cunningly shall flatter them. And on this head is written, in the Politics, in the third Book, and in the ninth chapter, "that the sycophant is an enemy to all right-mindedness; that he instils himself, as it were a bung, into the right eye of his lord, who may be listening to him. Thus are great men blinded; by which means they lose, as well the love of God, as all self-respect and knowledge of themselves. For the most part, they neither know what it is they should follow, nor what it is they should avoid; and look to be right roundly praised, for what, in reality, they should be as right roundly blamed. And all this comes of no other fault of theirs, than that they cannot abide to hear the truth. And for this reason, my friend, above every other thing that I have told you, or may have to tell you, observe and remember, you are to avoid that most pestilent of all followings, the following of flatterers. And, trust me, if ever you come to be any one, or to be possessed of anything, you will have enough of them. And these things, I urge upon you, that God may be your true friend, and that you may arrive to be a man of renown, in your generation; that your name may be heard of, not only in this kingdom, but throughout the length and breadth of Christendom. And so it cannot be otherwise, but that by an obedience to the service of our Lady, and of your Lady *par amour*, you will be in the long-run saved; not only your body, but body and soul together. And this is enough for the present. And as soon as I see that you are conforming yourself to all that I have told you, or, at any rate, doing so to the best of your capacity, I will then love you, and show you kindness, and you will be my friend. Now, tell me, faithfully, what you think of all this; do you feel an inclination in you to obey me?"

SAINTRÉ.

Then the little Saintré threw himself on his knees, and presently said, " Madame, for all you have told me, I am obliged to you; and, if it please God, it shall be obeyed."

THE LADY.

"You will!" said Madame; "we will see how you go on. Now, be of good heart, come what will; and do not

be distressing yourself about what you have heard. And
remember, I would not have you to laugh, or appear to
understand anything, lest my women should at any time
misgive us. But, before them, you are to look sheepish,
and put out, just as you did before. Now, wait for me,
for I will come to you again presently."

THE AUTHOR.

Then Madame, who was seated, arose, and said aloud to
her ladies, "Heh, what are we to think of this young
ne'er-do-good? Though he has been all this hour at confession, I have not yet got out of him who his Lady is?"
Then, as in a fury, she said to him, "Away with you, for a
sot; you will never come to anything!" And as she was
going into her closet, she turned, still as in a rage, and
said, "Wait where you are, I will make one more trial of
you." Then, right tickled in his own mind, after all
Madame had told him; pretending to be in the sulks, he
remained, as she commanded him.

And when, in a little time, Madame had returned, she
called him to her, and said out loud, so that all might
hear, "So, young master, am I never to know who this
Lady is? If I guess her right, on your faith, will you
tell me? Now, is it not So and So, or So and So?"

"Madame, indeed, no." "Then it is So and So, or So
and So, or So and So? Now, ladies, see the affront he
has put upon you; for did you not go guarantee for him,
that, by this time, he would have elected his Lady, and
you see, it is none of all these?"

"But," said they, "it cannot be but he has one; and,
such being the case, take him apart, and if she is such as
she should be, he will tell it to you, and thus he will be
quit of his oath."

Then Madame, all laughing, and as if it was a capital
joke, took him aside, and quietly said to him:—

CHAPTER X.

How the Lady, already smitten with the love of the little Saintré, gave him twelve écus to set himself up with, and to have himself nicely dressed.

THE LADY.

(3) "MY friend, I give you this purse, such as it is, with the twelve écus that are in it. And it is my wish that the colours of which it is made, and that the motto which is on it, from this day forward will be yours. You are to adopt and wear them for my sake. And the twelve écus you will lay out on a doublet of damask, or of crimson satin; two pairs of fine stockings, the one of a rich scarlet, the other of a copper black, of Saint Lo; and they must be all embroidered, and of the colour and of the device of the purse. And besides, you will get four pairs of linen collars, and four kerchiefs, nicely smoothed, and shoes and slippers, neatly fitting you. And when you have done all this, let me see you, in your new trim next Sunday, and be sure you do everything discreetly and warily; and soon, please God, I will do more for you than that.

THE LADY.

Then the little Saintré, like an innocent little thing as he was, and all out of countenance, could not be brought to accept the purse, telling Madame, "that he was obliged to her, but she must not be offended at his refusing it; for, as yet, he had done nothing for her."

THE LADY.

"Nothing for me!" cried Madame. "I know well you have done nothing for me. It would be very odd if you had; but, if it please God, you will yet do plenty for me. So I request and desire you to take it." And, saying this, slyly and quietly wrapping it up in a cloth, she slipped it into his sleeve, telling him, "Now, you may be off, and mind you do as I told you, and that I never hear anything but good of you. So, God be with you, and remember, you are not to be seen in the gallery again till you have on your new clothes. And for the present, I will add nothing, save that I will pray God you may be found answerable to all, or, at any rate, the most part of what I expect of you. Then continued Madame, in a gruff voice, and aloud, "Off, out my presence, for a craven wretch! For this once you are safe; you have yet to be absolved; another time, you shall meet with no such mercy."

THE AUTHOR.

And when he had taken his piteous leave, and was out of the chamber, she said to her women, laughing, "I do verily believe we are but losing our time over him; he has not got it in him to choose his Lady, nor do I believe he knows what it is to be in love. At any rate, he is good enough to laugh at, so we will keep him to it."

Then Madame had herself undressed and went to bed, as did the rest of them; by this time well wearied of the unconscionable parley of Madame and of Saintré. And now I will forbear to speak of Madame and her women, and return to the little Saintré.

CHAPTER XI.

How the little Saintré had himself finely set out, as the Lady had desired him. And after, how the said Lady found him in the gallery, and made him follow her into her chamber; inquiring of him,—What device was that he wore? And this on purpose, so that her Gentlewomen might not suspect anything; and how she gave him yet other twelve écus in a purse.

THE AUTHOR AGAIN.

THE little Saintré, as soon as he had got well away from the door, looking about for the nearest corner, and that nobody was by, presently made for it. And, first, he draws his purse from out of his sleeve, and laying it out, considers it. And when he saw it all so nice, and the twelve écus in it, it is not to be questioned, but he was enchanted; for the King, himself, he did not take to be more rich. And in turning over with himself how best he was to carry out the instructions of Madame, and how fine he was to be on the following Sunday, he fell to dancing and capering at the thoughts of it. Then straight he went to Perrin de Solles, who was the King's tailor, and said to him, "Perrin, my friend, for how much can I have, for Sunday next, a doublet for myself? but it must be of damask, and as crimson as it can be."

Perrin, having thought a little, and taken his measure, said to him, "Have you any money?"

"Yes, Perrin; but it must not be too dear."

Then Perrin, seeing what a graceful little fellow he was, said to him, "Saintré, my son, on my faith you cannot have it for less than six écus; but it shall be of the very finest."

Then Saintré, all young and generous, without another word, put his hand into his purse, and taking out the six écus, handed them to him. And as soon as the affair of the doublet was settled, he went to John de Busses, who was stocking-maker to the King; and with him he made a bargain for two pairs of stockings, that, one with another, were to cost him two écus, and which he paid for down. Then he went to François de Nantes, embroiderer to the King, and showed him the purse to embroider by, as Madame had devised; and the bargain was for two écus. So that there were only two left. Then he went to a good wife of the town, of whom his father, the Lord de Saintré, had oftentimes spoken to him, and said to her, "Marie de Lisle, my good mother, can I have two pairs of fine linen collars for Sunday first, and for one écu?"

"Yes, that you can," said Marie.

"Then, my mother, here it is; and manage so, that

next Sunday I can have one for certain." Then drawing his purse out of his sleeve, he opened it out, and showed her the two écus.

"But, my son," said she, "who gave them to you?"

"Troth," said he, "Madame, my mother, sent me twelve; one, you must take as the price of the two pairs of linen collars; and the other, with the purse, will be my own."

And when Marie saw the purse looking so pretty, she was well pleased for his sake, and said to him, "God requite the Lady who cares in this way for her son!" Then she said to him, "And the other ten écus?"

"My mother," said he, "they are already laid out."

"Alas, my son!" said she, "have you not lost them, or spent them as you should not?"

"No, my mother, I have not; but, Sunday you will know all about it." And so the whole week went away, till the Sunday morning, when who should come in, together, into the chamber of Jacques Martel, the first equerry of the stable of the King, and where Saintré and the other royal pages slept, but our said Perrin de Solles, tailor to the King; Jehan de Busses, stocking-maker; François de Nantes, broiderer; and Guillaume Soldan, shoemaker; all of the King; carrying, one the doublet; another, the embroidered stockings; and the third, the shoes and the slippers! And when Jacques Martel heard that they were all at the door of his room together, he ordered it to be opened. And when they were all come in, and he had seen what it was they had with them, he asked them, "Who all this was for?"

"My master," said they all, "we are for the little Saintré; we are all for him."

Then Jacques, turning to the little Saintré, said to him, laughing, "Faith, Saintré, you must have been getting in your rents!"

"My master," said he, "it is Madame, my mother, who

has settled for all this, for she sent me money, as well to amuse myself with, as to get what I might want. And it seems to me, that, except to keep myself dressed, as I should be, I have but little call for money."

"Now, truly," said the equerry, "I loved you well before, but from this day forth, I will love you yet more." Then turning to the other gentlemen and pages, he said to them, "Ha, worthless lads; when will your pocket-money be spent as Saintré's," instead of fooling it away. at cards, at dice; in taverns, cellars, and in brothels! What have I not done to keep you from them?"

Then said Saintre, "Now, my master, dress me; and mind you make me fine."

And when he had everything on, the little Saintré, who had already settled for all, gave to his playfellows the one half of the remaining écu, and the other to the grooms of the yard, who, all along, had loved him more than any other of the pages, for he had always let them have their part in any luck that came to him.

And when the equerry, with the rest, were dressed, and they had heard mass, they went to the audience-hall to wait upon the King; but it was not without many a heart-burning, and a surmise, on the part of the other pages, that they kept looking at Saintré. And as soon as the King had come out of his chamber, and had seen the little Saintré in all his new equipment, he began to laugh, and to ask the equerry, "How comes it he is so fine all of a sudden?"

"Sir," said he, "to my amazement, this morning, in came Perrin de Solles, Jehan des Busses, François de Nantes, Guillaume Soldan, with their varlets, into my room, all carrying his clothes. I verily thought I was in for the bailiff."

On hearing this, the King and all his courtiers began to say, "that he had well done."

Then said the King, "I would be well content he had some three or four of my years, he should be my trencher varlet." And with this, he went to mass, together with the Queen. And as soon as mass was over, and they were coming back, Madame saw the little Saintré, a little way off, looking so nice and graceful. Then, as they were proceeding, she stepped forward, and said to the Queen, "Hey, Madame, look here; just see the little Saintré, how dear a little fellow he is."

"Ha, fair Cousin," said the Queen, "you are right; it is really a pleasure to see him."

On this, they were going into the great hall to dinner. Madame, who could never so much as take her eyes off him; so as to be able to get closer to him, and speak to him in private, making for some other ladies, said to them, "Supposing we have a look what device it is the little Saintré has got upon his stockings? Things have come to a pretty pass when such young whelps as this are setting up their devices, and announcing themselves for squires of dames!"

"Hey, Madame," said one, "it shows the gentleness of his nature;" another, "Hey, 'fore God, let us see what it is!" and a third, "Madame, come, let us go look."

Then Madame, and they all, went to a window, and having made him come to them, she said, as if she knew nothing of the matter, "Ha, master, ha, we want to have a look at, and make out this wondrous device of yours upon your stockings."

Then the little Saintré, who was upon his knees, began to entreat that they would spare him. "But no," said they, "for most assuredly we will see it, and at once, too; so, no more about it, for the King is going to dinner."

Then one of them caught him by the arm, another by the shoulder, a third by the legs; and when they had whipped him off his feet, they laid him on his back. Then

Madame, with the ladies who were with her, together with many others whom they called, kneeling down over him, examined all these fine devices. And when Madame heard all the admiration of the devices, such was her delight, that it set her altogether, as well body as mind, in a tremble and a flame. And as soon as the boards were removed, and grace had been said; brief, when the minstrels and the tabours had struck up, and the dancing and the singing been prolonged, till the King, who was about to retire, had called for the spicery, and the parting cup: Madame, who all the time had never removed her eyes from off the little Saintré, so well and so nicely did he sing and dance, began to think that she would like to see the devices a little nearer, and speak to him again. For, the more she saw of him, the more she liked him; nor, indeed, was there man or woman in the Court who did not foresee that, sooner or later, he would come to be heard of. And as he was handing to this one, and to that, the cups, Madame, as he was passing, said, " Wait for me, little Saintré, where we were the other day." This, he perfectly understood; and presently after the King withdrew, and the Queen retired to rest. And as Madame was returning to her chamber, she found the little Saintré in the gallery, as she had ordered him. So she said to him, as if half surprised, " Hey, master; how fine you are! get on before. Where have you been these five or six days? You must give an account of yourself." Then, turning to her women, she said, " We must see this young fellow's devices; and, if we can, make out of him how he came by them, and all about it; for I never will believe that he either has the wit or the spirit to be in love." And in gossiping this way, she reached her chamber, where she dismissed all her gentlemen, excepting only Saintré. Next, she made him close the door. Then, placing him in the centre, Madame told him she was determined to know about the devices; so she said to him, "Ha, master, master, you tell us you have no lady, and yet you make yourself fine, this way?"

"Madame," said he, "thank God, it was Madame, my mother, who made me this way."

"And how can that be?" said she, "she lives in Lorraine, nor do I believe she was ever at the Court in her life."

"Madame," said he, "it is twelve écus, she sent me in a beautiful purse of gold and silk, that have made me fine."

"Now, certainly," said Madame, "we must see this purse, and know where the twelve écus have gone to; for if they have not been spent as they should be, I will write to her, that she sends no more."

Then the little Saintré drew the purse from his sleeve, and took it out of its cover. Madame, who knew for a certainty that none of her women had ever seen it, took it, and looked at it, before them all, as though it were for the first time. And when she had compared the device upon the stockings with that upon the purse, and seen that they were the same, she said to him, "Now, young master; first, What did this doublet come to?"

"Madame," said he, "I gave for it, to Perrin des Solles, six écus." "And the stockings," said Madame; "who made them, and what did they cost you?"

"Madame," said he, "these scarlet stockings, and another pair, of fine copper colour, of St. Lo, cost me two écus, with Jehan de Busses. And, for the embroidering of the stockings, I gave two other écus to François de Nantes."

"And what became of the remaining two écus?"

"Madame, of the one, with three sols, I got two pairs of fine linen shirts; and with twenty sols, I had three pairs of shoes, and three pairs of slippers. The remainder I gave to my companions, to the varlets who came with the things, and to the laquies of my master, the equerry, to drink with."

Madame, who was well pleased to hear all this, and saw how much this courtesy and generosity would tell for him with the world, said, laughing, to her women, "He has pocketed the half of it."

"By my faith, Madame, saving your grace, there is not a denier of it left."

"Then," said Madame, "this time, at any rate, I will have out of you who your Lady is? Come here and speak to me."

"Nay, Madame," said they, "you are too hard upon him, persecuting him, this way, about such matters."

"Do not you be troubling yourselves," said Madame; "just fall a little back, for I am determined to know it."

And as soon as they had withdrawn, Madame said to him, "Now, hear me, my friend; up to now, I am well satisfied with you. Strive still to do what is right, for you are perfectly equal to it. But, above all things, I have to charge you, from one and all, be it the dearest friend you have on earth, keep what is passing, and has passed between us."

"That I will, Madame, for I have leaver die."

"Now, my friend, you must get two other robes, of which the one will be of fine black cloth, of St. Lo, and is to be lined with marten. And the other is to be of a fine gray, of Montivilliers, and will be lined with fine white flannel, for every day's wear, excepting when you will be out with the King. And you will also have a doublet of satin blue, and two other pairs of fine stockings, kerchiefs, shirts, and slippers. And you must also provide yourself with clothes to play in; for this you must do to keep yourself in health; as also with bows and arrows, and bats and raquets for tennis. And in order to all this, and to support you in your new state, I give you sixty écus, and I will then see how matters go on. And as you have not yet got any valet, you are to get Gillet, who is a steady, and to-be-depended-on servant of the equerry, to look after your wardrobe, shoes and things; and for his wages, you will give him eight sols the month. And if you carry yourself discreetly and warily, you shall have collar and chain, belts of Bohemia, robes of damask, and everything you can wish for; but all, provided only you prove yourself to be a man of honour, close and loyal."

"Madame," said he, "with God's permission I shall be all that."

"And, my friend, mind this. However displeased I may appear, or however heartlessly I may treat you before my women, you are not to vex yourself."

"No, Madame, I will not, since such is your wish."

"Let nothing put you out."

Then began Madame, incontinent, to rate him bravely before her gentlewomen, as if she was in a horrible rage with him. Then she went to her garderobe, and taking out of her coffer sixty écus, she put them in a purse. Then she returned, and calling him to her, said, "Ho, Sir, ho; are you still coming the obstinate; am I never to be trusted in? And if you will not tell it to me, then tell it to Madame Jehanne, or to Madame Katherine, or to Isabelle, or to the one of them you like."

"And what, Madame, would you have me tell; when I have none?"

"Have none! and yet you have devices, and initials among them, Sir sniveller! A pretty fellow, too, to want to make himself pass for a lover!"

"Madame, on my faith, I have told you whom I love, in this world, best, and who it was that ordered me to wear the devices."

"Ha, master, master, you take us for simpletons, so you

do, to be talking to us this way about your mother. I can easily understand that you love your mother, and that it is she who supports you; but don't you tell me, it is her devices you wear. Come here; I have just bethought me of another, whom I do verily believe it is."

Then she took him apart, and said to him, "Take this purse, and mind you do not lose it; there are sixty écus in it, and be careful what you do with it. And, for the future, you are to remember to keep clear of the galleries, at the hours when I mostly pass, and you are not, too frequently, to stop to talk to me. But whenever you see me pick my teeth with my bodkin, thus, you are then to understand that I want to speak to you, and immediately to rub your right eye; for by this, I will know that you have caught my meaning to a certainty, and will expect you. Now, mind you do what is right, so that I can love you; and as soon as I see that you are conducting yourself as you should do, then will I adopt you for my friend, and you shall be equipped as you deserve."

"Madame," said he, "with God's grace, all shall be done."

"Now, you may go: I want to sleep; and remember, however much I may chide you, rate or laugh at you, before the world, you are not to take it to heart. Put up with it, and go through with it."

CHAPTER XII.

How the Lady feignedly menaced the little Saintré, telling him before her ladies that he would never do any good. And how, after that, the little Saintré had other clothes made with the money which Madame had given him; and how the Lady spoke to him, and he told her that it was his mother who had sent him the money with which he had dressed himself.

THE AUTHOR AGAIN.

THEN Madame, as in an anger, said to him, "Off with you, young man, off, for you will never come to any good!"

"Alas, Madame," said they all, "surely you are not in earnest? you will not for ever banish him?" and, "Saintré, surely it would be better to tell Madame the truth."

Saintré, who well knew what was going on in the heart of Madame, now, in his turn, pretending to be angry too, fell on his knees, and without so much as rejoining, took his leave. Then they all set to, to make themselves merry with all the terrible assaults of Madame, saying, "Faith, we have seen the last of him: depend upon it the sport is spoiled; we will not catch him in a hurry again." But they little knew the pleasant understanding that there was between Madame and him.

"Tush," said Madame, "he is not going to get off that way. The best of the joke has yet to come."

"Alas," said Isabelle, "it vexes me to see the poor child tortured this way!"

And now I will forbear a while, to speak of the tricks and merriment that Madame and her women were permitting themselves, and begin to speak of how he spent the sixty écus.

THE AUTHOR.

And as soon as the little Saintré had parted from Madame, he began to count his treasure. And when he came to see all the money in his hand, he was so aghasted that he neither knew what to do, or what to make of it. And the whole day was spent in deliberation, where or how he was to hide them; for neither to the equerry, nor yet to anybody else durst he intrust a sight of them; inasmuch as Madame had expressly forbidden him to let any one know of it. So at last, he resolved to keep them in his pockets, at least till the morning, when he would lay them out. And when the morning was come, which he thought would well nigh never be, so long and tedious seemed the night, he arose. And when he had heard mass, he went to Perrin des Solles, and ordered the three furred robes, as Madame had desired him; one of which he wore the Sunday following, with the damask blue doublet. And, for all this, he found the money to suffice; and to spare.

THE AUTHOR.

And when Madame saw the little Saintré, dressed in his robe of black, and lined with marten, and his doublet of damask blue, she was enchanted more than words could tell; so, taking her pin, she made him her signal, to which he replied. And when Madame, in returning to her chamber, perceived him at a distance, in the gallery, she said to her women, "Look, if yon is not our young joker; we have yet to settle with him!" And as soon as he saw them he turned on his heel, and was making off another way. Then Madame sent after him, and when he was come, she said to him, "Ha, master, master! is that the thing, to gallop off as soon as you see the ladies coming? Where are your manners? Go on before."

And when Madame had gotten to her chamber, she

dismissed all her people, save Jehan de Soussy, equerry to the Queen, and Thibault de Roussi, her own; two of the most circumspect about the Court, so that they might learn what she thought it was, perhaps, as well they should know. So she said to them, "I have made you men to stop, too, that you may have a laugh with us." Then Madame began to say to the little Saintré, "So, master, so; after all the times that we have begged of you to tell us who is your Lady *par amours*, never yet, for prayers, for entreaties, for menaces, for affronts, have we been able to get it out of you. And since it is clear that you will not trust it to any of us, at least tell it to Jehan de Soussy, and to Thibault de Roussy; or to whichever of them you may choose."

"But, Madame," said Jehan de Soussy, "why should he tell it to us, seeing he refuses to tell it to you?"

But to this the little Saintré, who, in himself, was under no sort of alarm, and perfectly understood the drift of Madame, would not reply a word, pretending to be huffed. And when Madame saw that he would not confess, she said to Jehan and to Thibault, "See this master, with his robe furred in marten, his doublet of silk, his stockings broidered, and all this fine set-out, and yet he will have us to believe he has no Lady! and what is more shameful still, that he does not want one. By my faith, now that I see him close, many a one would be willing enough to have him." And then turning to him, as in high displeasure, she said, "How is it, Sir, that you, who are but a page, albeit you are come of a good house, have all these costly clothes?"

"Madame," said he, "since it is the pleasure of madame, my mother, that I am to be nice, and she has desired me to be so; it is but meet that she be obeyed."

"And how much did she send you?"

"Sixty écus, Madame."

"Sixty écus! then you fooled away the half of it?"

"No, Madame, by my faith, I have not."

"And this robe, and this cap, these stockings, and this doublet, came to sixty écus, did they? I should just like to know how?"

"Not so, Madame. I have, besides what you see, another robe of a rich blue, lined with fine lambs'-wool of Romanie, also another of fine gray, of Montvilliers, lined with nice white flannel, two caps, and two pair of fine stockings, one of which is striped. And I have four écus left."

"And who was it put you in the way of getting all these fine things?"

"Madame, no one, except Perrin des Solles."

Says Madame, "I know well that he is an honest and a safe man; your affairs show it; for your money, as it seems to me, has been very properly expended. And did you not tell me a little ago, that she had sent you before twelve écus, with which you made yourself so nice, at the first?"

"Madame, yes."

"Then may God long preserve to you such a mother, and see that you continue the son you are to her. And now you may all go, for we want to sleep." And with this they all withdrew. And as they were going, Jehan de Soussy and Thibault de Roussy stoutly took the part of the little Saintré, and told him, "that he was not to be put out with the words of Madame;" and, on the other hand, they as strongly blamed Madame for the authoritative manner in which she meddled in matters that no way regarded her; prying into other peoples' affairs.

"Faith, you are right," said he, "it is anything but pleasant, to be badgered with all her impertinence; and all because I will not tell her, or yet her women, who is my Lady *par amour*. Nor will they believe my word, though I swore to them that I neither have one, nor will have one, nor want one. And, by my faith, even if I had, they should be the last to know it, for the way they have pestered me." And then they all began to laugh. And when it was told after to Madame and her women, what Saintré had said of them, they could not keep from laughing either. And so, in a little time, it came to pass, as Madame had intended, that all the words of Madame and her Ladies, and the recriminations of the little Saintré, were sown up and down the Court; as would also have been certain other matters if they had but known them, to the no less entertainment of the same. And so this true and faithful attachment came to be long and covertly entertained; even till Fortune, with her wonted mutability, thought proper to turn her back upon them, as you shall in the sequel hear.

THE AUTHOR.

And this loyal and secret understanding continued till Saintré was in his XVI. year. About which time, Madame, that it might be carried on yet more warily, said to the little Saintré, "My friend, it is time the dance should begin; but everything must be done with an eye to appearances. And seeing that I have, quite as often as is the thing, sent for you from the gallery to this place; and however you may have insisted on it, that it was your mother who sent you the money, and set you up; for all that, strange things may come into peoples' heads; and let but one come to guess how matters stand, and the whole is noised abroad. And, for this reason, I have come to the conclusion that, for the future, I will not send for you any more to the gallery. But whenever you may want to speak to me, or I to you, we will make our signals, as I showed you, and then you will come and open the door of my garden, as soon as you shall have seen me return at night to my chamber. Here is the key, and there we can chat, and amuse ourselves together, to our hearts' content.

CHAPTER XIII.

How the Lady suggested to the Queen that she should speak to the King to make the little Saintré his trencher squire.

AND when they were come to the third year of their amours, which was the sixteenth of Saintré, Madame began to think, that he was at last big enough to leave off to be a page, for he was well able to carve; and that he could not do better than become trencher varlet to the King or Queen, if it was but to be managed. So she began to beat about her brains, and thus she reasoned with herself, "If you set on the equerry; on account of the twelve écus, and putting one thing with another, he may not unlikely think it comes from you; and if you speak of it to this lord, or that, odds are but they will suspect something. Yet, for all that, he must be pushed; Saintré cannot, any longer, be left a page." And, for conclusion, what she decided on was, to petition the Queen to make the request to the King. Then she made her signal with her pin, to which the little Saintré rejoined.

The Author.

And when they were in the meadow together; kissing him at the same time tenderly, she said to him, "Joy of my heart, you are now XVI. years of age; so that you are too big to be any longer page. Now, I have been thinking, to get you forward, that I will contrive to interest madame, the Queen, in you; so that, by her influence, you may be appointed carver to either her or to the King. For, at the very first, he promised as much, when he saw you all so smart; for he said, laughing, "Had he but four or five of my years, he should carve before me." So I give you notice, that you may be prepared, in case Madame in any way refers to it, to thank her most humbly for her kindness. She is not to fancy I told her an untruth.

THE AUTHOR AGAIN.

On hearing this, the little Saintré was delighted, and most humbly thanked Madame, who, tenderly kissing him again, gave him his discharge. Then as soon as Saintré had gone, Madame quietly closed the door, and went to bed.

THE AUTHOR.

Madame, who, to advance the suit of her most humble servant, never omitted to be, day and night, about the Queen, said to her, one morning, smiling, as she was rising, "Madame, I must clear myself, while I bethink me, of what I had undertaken, but had slipped clean out of my mind, a dozen times over; and that is, to be your solicitor, on the part of a bashful young Squire; for, so modest is he, that he dare not be his own."

"And who is he?" inquired the Queen.

"Madame, it is the little Saintré."

"And what is it he wants?" said the Queen.

"Madame, he says, he is ashamed to be any longer page; that he is now XVI. or XVII. years of age; and what he wants is, that you would be pleased to entreat the King that he might be appointed his trencher varlet. If you will, he says he will write to his father and mother that they provide him with horses, and establish him as he should be."

"And, truly," said the Queen, "his request is reasonable and allowable enough. I will make it with pleasure, for I know well, my Lord loves him mightily. He is an exceedingly graceful little lad, and I hope, fair lady, that, some day, he will be a man of renown."

And this request, the Queen was not long in making to the King; and the King, out of his natural good-nature, and from all he had heard of him, told her, readily, "It should be," and, that there might be no time lost, on the next occasion the Queen saw the steward of the household, in the presence of the King, she recalled it to him. Then the King told him, that the little Saintré was to be his trencher varlet, and that he was to begin that very day, and to provide himself with three horses, and two grooms in livery. The steward, who knew how well the King was disposed toward him, and saw the Queen so pleased, as soon as he perceived the little Saintré, among the other gentlemen, he called him to him, and said, "Little Saintré, good friend, what is your name?"

"Mister Steward," said he, "my name is Jehan."

"Jehan," said he, "from this day forth, you cease to be page. The King has appointed you to be his carver; and you are to have three horses, with their livery, and two grooms. And for this reason, my son, if you have well done till now, for the time to come do better; for it is the much the King has heard to your advantage, and the little to your discredit, that makes him love you as he does. Now, do not you be too much elated for all this good luck; and, doubtless, he will do more for you later. Keep your hands and nails clean, and the rest of your person as proper as you can; for, if there is one officer more than another who is called upon by his proximity to the King to have himself sweet, it is you." And there was not one in the hall, or who heard of the advancement of the little Saintré, that was not delighted. So may we see what a laudable and advantageous thing it is for all young gentlemen to study to oblige, to offend no one; to be patient, humble, gentle; for by such means will they come to be held in the grace of God and of all honest people; as says the proverb:—

> Who cannot ill and good alike support,
> Is not the man to thrive in hall or court.

CHAPTER XIV.

How the little Saintré thanked the King and Queen, and Madame, for that he had been made a squire; and how he carved before the King, and how handsomely he acquitted himself.

THEN Jehan Saintré, to show himself humble, gentle, and grateful, as he was, cast himself at once upon his knees before the King, and thanked him for the great honour that he had done him. Then the King, like a wise, gracious, and condescending prince as he was, said to him, "Saintré, only do what is right, and you shall see that we are aware of it." And then Saintré turned to the steward of the household, who was present, and thanked him before the King and every one, for the good word he had been pleased to say for him. And he felt no sort of shame, as many another would have had, to do this publicly. Then he left, and went in search of the Queen, who was in her chamber. Then aloud, before all the company, without appearing to take any notice of Madame, he thanked her humbly, upon his knees. On which the Queen said to him, "Saintré, your services and your readiness to oblige us all, especially the Ladies, have, happily, somewhat docked your apprenticeship of page. You are now become Squire to my Lord and to myself. And, for this reason, my friend, strive always to do what is correct, and to make yourself agreeable to all; for, one day, it will be returned to you, tenfold." Then the tables were laid, and the steward came to summon them to dinner; Madame, all the time, pretending to the other ladies and gentlewomen to have no sort of curiosity as to what had befallen Saintré; carelessly remarking, "He seemed a handy-enough sort of a little groom."

THE AUTHOR.

And when the King and Queen were seated; and Madame, at the end of the table, then the Steward of the house took the bread-basket, and gave it to Saintré, and laid the napkin on his shoulder; after which, he began his new office of carver varlet, and so creditably did he acquit himself, that, both King and Queen, and all the company, expressed their admiration. Madame, who was seated at the end of the table, and who could scarce keep her eyes off him, began to think to herself, Surely he now fully deserves his three horses, which he is to have, and his two grooms. Then she drew her pin from her breast, and, as if occupied with her teeth, she made him her signal, and so often, that at last Saintré perceived her: which, as soon as he did, as well as he could manage, he replied to.

CHAPTER XV.

How the little Saintré spoke with Madame, who kissed him affectionately, in the meadow; and how she gave him a hundred and and sixty écus to provide horses, and other things necessary.

AND as soon as it was dusk, he went to the meadow, and there awaited Madame, who was not long in coming. And then was there such caressing between them, as none, save he, or she, who has proved the like, can form the lightest imagination of. Then she said, "My only friend—my heart's content—we cannot long be here; kiss me as if you loved me. See here, take this bag, which I give you; there are one hundred and sixty écus in gold in it. And you will buy yourself a handsome, dashing, and showy horse; and mind he is fiery and spirited; let him cost what he may, be it eighty écus. And you will get a second, of a commoner sort, on which you are to ride on ordinary occasions, and for about twenty écus; and, besides these, a hack, to carry your valise and your groom. This will cost you thirty écus. You will then have xxx. écus over; these, you will lay out upon appropriate harness and trappings for your horses, and liveries for your servants; and if there remain anything after, you can spend it as circumstances may require. And whenever you are in want of anything, make your signal; that is all you have to do. And now, adieu, my hope, my joy, my everything to me; adieu, adieu!"

"And, adieu, Madame, my only mistress, and whom I ought to, and will obey!" And with these words they both separated.

The Author.

And for this night, the little Saintré returned to sleep in the chamber of the equerry, who said to him, "Saintré, my son, though I am more sorry than I have words to express to lose you, I am right glad to see where it is you are going to. Then, turning to the other pages of the King, who were about Saintré, he said, "Now, my children, see for yourselves; is it not a winning thing to do the thing that is right,—to be gentle, courteous, humble, affable, obliging and conciliating to all. See here, your playmate, who, through being such, has come to be in the good graces of King and Queen, and everybody. Whilst as for you, who have not a thought in your heads but quarrels and noise, and cards, and dice, and how to sneak to your low and pothouse associates, and from which neither prayers nor blows will keep you; despite of all your rank, your birth, or your money, the older you get, the more miscreant and contemptible will you become." And by the time he had said this to them, they were all undressed, and in bed.

The Author.

The little Saintré, as he could not break to any one the adventure of the hundred and sixty écus which he had in his pockets, for that night could not sleep a wink out of fear of being robbed. God knows, if he thought the light would ever come, so that he could buy himself his horses. ⁽⁴⁾ But when, at last, it came, and he had dressed and heard mass, he went straight away to the burgess, Marie de Lisle, and said to her, " Marie, good mother, news for you !"

" And what are they, my son ?"

" Marie, the King, of his good pleasure, has determined that I am not any longer to be page, and he made me, yesterday, carve before him. He has put me on the footing of three horses and two varlets; and he has sent me privily, by one of his household, one hundred and sixty écus, with which I am to mount and equip, as well myself as the varlets, and get myself everything I want. But he has strictly forbidden me to speak of the money to any one, for fear of the jealousy that would come of it. So I have to pray of you, good mother, that it comes to the ears of none on earth."

" Ha, fair son," said Marie, " Now, God be praised. Never shall mortal know of it, if you do not mention it yourself; for, assuredly, I will not. But how are you going to manage it? You must consult some one who understands horses, and can put you in the way of finding servants."

" My good mother, and friend, I have been thinking that I would write to my lord, my father, to send me one or two. And as for the horses, our master, the equerry, would be but too happy to oblige me; and there are more besides, if I were only to ask them. But I do not intend to be in any hurry, for fear people might begin to suspect something."

What need I say more about it? Before a month was out, he had his varlets, and was well mounted; he and they with everything they wanted. And every day he came to be more and more in the favour of the King and Queen, and more and more to be talked of in the Court.

And when Madame saw how he was in the good graces of the King, she took her pin, and made the appointed signal, which, when Saintré saw, he rejoined to. And as soon as it was evening, and they were in the meadow, the Lady said to him, "My friend and heart; thank God I now see clearly you are safely grounded in the love of my Lord and Lady. It is now time to bethink ourselves, how best you are to be continued in your present prosperous gale, which is no easy matter in Courts. Great men, and great men's servants, first and foremost, must be gained, if not by gifts, at least by promises. You cannot give to all, at once; hence, necessarily, expectations must be dealt to some. But whatever is promised must religiously be performed. For, presents and expectations, when it is in your power and inclination to dispense them—a good turn, good cheer, please people, flatter them; each, in a different way; and fairly take them captive; so that you have everybody at your disposition. To the officers of the wardrobe, you should give liveries, so that they might all become your friends; to the Queen, from time to time, a pretty ambling cob, or a handsome horse for her litter, or her chariot. To the other ladies you will give, according to their rank, to one a head-dress; to another a belt of silver, nicely gilt; to some, only fine stuffs; to others, rich furs or diamonds; to others, again, gold enamelled rings. To the inferior gentlewomen, good marketing purses, baskets, laces, pins, or caps will suffice. It all depends upon their position. And thus, by your generosity and liberality, you will come to be had in the love, grace, and esteem of all. And if you ask me, How are you to give away the thing you have not? I reply, So long as you shall continue to serve me faithfully, so long shall you want for nothing. And as soon as your body and your members shall be firm and set, I will then have you to engage in feats, by courtesy, of arms. And whatever enterprise I

may send you on, you are to go through with it. And
that you may be still further advanced, and yet more in
the graces of my Lord, and of Madame, and of all; and
as a foundation to all your prosperity, here are, in this
purse, four hundred écus, of which one hundred will be
for a nice little mare, or a pretty horse, which, first of all,
you are to present to Madame, thanking her for the honour
that my Lord did you, at her request. And another
hundred will go to make over-coats, in livery, for their
valets-de-chambre. They are to be all of one cloth and
colour, and with your own device. And, to please them,
you had better wear one yourself, on All-Saints next. And
when the feast of Christmas has come about, you will have
made for each of the other officers a robe of the same
device, but of another coloured cloth. And the remaining
écus are to be laid out in purchases for the rest—ladies,
gentlewomen, and others—and which you are to have ready
for New Year's Day. You will also give coats to the
Kings-at-arms, the heralds, trumpets, and minstrels.
And now, as it is time to part, my heart's content and joy,
my most faithful servant, kiss me, and that God may keep
you!"

THE AUTHOR.

Jehan de Saintré, who now clearly saw all that Madame
had done for him, and was yet willing to do for him, young
as he was, threw himself on his knees, most humbly
thanking her, saying, "Ah, my most redoubted Lady,
perfect in perfection; in whom is every virtue, honour,
worth; alas, how am I ever to repay you the thousandeth
part of all I owe you. However, my very trusty Lady,
what I can do, I will do; and God, who knows my heart,
and my heart's desire, he it is who will acquit me of the
rest." Then Madame made him rise, and then kissed him,
wishing him adieu.

CHAPTER XVI.

How the little Saintré provided himself with horses, as Madame had desired him ; and how, when he came to thank her, she admonished him, and taught him how he was to conduct himself, as well at Court as in war, and in all other positions.

THE AUTHOR.

AND when the morning was come, and mass was over, Jehan de Saintré went in quest of the grooms and farriers of the King's and Queen's stables, and he had them to breakfast in his room. And presently he said to them, " I have eighty or a hundred écus by me, and I have half a mind to lay them out on a handsome and a serviceable sort of a mare, if I could but find one."

Then said they, " Nothing easier." And to oblige him, they despatched the liveliest and most knowing of the stable boys, telling them to go the round of the marts, and bring them word again, where the likeliest horses were then standing. Which, when they had done, one that they went to see was bought. And it he made a present of to the Queen, telling her : " My sovereign Lady, let me first present to you my humble duty, and then grant me, that I may be permitted to thank you for the obligations and the honours which, you yourself first, and the King after, at your request, have conferred upon me. And, as some little acknowledgement on my part of the same, will you be pleased, Madame, to step to the window and you will there see a little mare which I should like to give you ; entreating you to take it as it is meant ; for, you know—*little merchant, little packet.*"

At first the Queen, though gently, excused herself. However, at length, being entreated but simply to look at it, she consented. And when she had gone to the window, and seen what a nice and pretty little thing it was, and how it was all covered with a furniture of silk, and of her own colours and devices, she agreed to accept it. And as soon as he was gone, the Queen began to say all sorts of things to his advantage, to those around her, and to Madame among the rest; who, however, seemed to pay but little heed to what was going on; albeit, in her heart, she was enchanted to see how handsomely he was spoken of. And when Christmas came, all the valets-de-chambre, as well as the officers, King's-at-arms, trumpeters, and minstrels, had their clothes, and the Ladies their New Year's gifts. And Madame chose for hers, one of the plainest of the whole, a ruby. And so, throughout the entire Court and kingdom his fame began to be blazed abroad; not, however, without the malice and the heartburnings of many, as it will ever be in Courts. However, so incessantly was his praise the theme of the wise and good, that every day he increased more and more in the good graces of the King and Queen; and every day brought with it some new friend, or some new gratification on the part of the King. Nor yet, for any one thing that befell him, did he ever allow either petulance or haughtiness to escape him; but, even forced himself to be condescending to those whom, at heart, he well knew to be his concealed enemies. And in this manner passed away some three or four years. At length, Madame, who clearly saw, and followed all that was going on, thought, one day, that she would like to speak to him, so she took her pin, and made her signal, to which he replied. And when they were in the meadow together, she said to him, "My only friend, praise be to God, there is neither King, Queen, Lord, Lady, nor Gentlewoman; man nor woman, high nor low, who is not at strife who most or best can praise you; and all this, because you have shown yourself to be, and are, humble, gracious, courteous, affable; and besides, by your liberality, is yet everything more blazed abroad. And so I have to pray and beseech of you, that, without running into any idle, or uncalled for expense, and which will redound rather to your shame than to your credit—to your damage than advantage—your gratuities will be judiciously distributed, seeing such are the returns that come of them. For, first, you see, it will impart unto your name an imperishable glory. Next, it will confirm you in the love of all, and gain you friends on every side. It is the secret and the key to all advancement; it quenches all the fires and heats of strife, and is the only path to safety; for, of the enemy, it will make a friend. And, for this reason, my friend, I enjoin it to you. And if it so be God's good pleasure that your circumstances will permit of it, let your days be dedicated to feats of arms. And whether you shall be employed in the service of great Lords, or Princes; or, contrary, they shall be serviceable to you; even let it be your end, to increase in the love of God, and to gain to yourself allies. And however much fortune may stand your friend, put not that faith in her immutability, but that you shall remember the words of Alanus, in *Articladiano*, where he says:—

> Tempore felici multi inveniuntur amici.
> Cum fortuna perit, nullus amicus erit.

That is to say, my friend, that, "Let but fortune once take any man by the hand, and set him up among men, and incontinent will he be blessed with friends enough, and to spare. But let her turn her back upon him, and sorry a one will he find." And, for this reason, he is worse than a fool who puts his trust in her.

CHAPTER XVII.

How the Lady advised the little Saintré to read books and romances, so as to be acquainted with the manners and the achievements of the nobles of the olden time.

THE LADY.

I FARTHER wish and pray of you, that you will often make it your pastime to read delightful chronicles; but above all, the marvellous and authentic means by which the Romans acquired for themselves the sovereignty of the world. Read *Titus Livius*, or *Berosus*. When you want to know about the twelve Cæsars, read *Suetonius*; and about the conspiracy of Catiline, read *Sallustius*. If you would like to hear about the cruel war of Pompey, and also of the decisive battle wherein the said Pompey was overthrown, read *Lucan*. And if you want to know about the kings of Egypt, read *Macrobius*; if about the Trojans, *Dares Phrigius*. If you would like to know about the diversity of languages, read *Arnobius*; or about the Jews and the destruction of Jerusalem, *Josephus*. And if you want the relations about Africa, read *Victor*. But *Pompeius Trogus*, according to *Valerius*, is the one who has written most fully of times preceding his own; for he treats of the origin, as of the locality of all countries.

THE LADY.

And now, I will forbear to speak of ancient history, to which, I do beg and pray that you will, of your own accord, devote and turn your attention. You cannot better occupy your time. It will instil into your breast the seeds of every noble and illustrious aspiration; as says the poet,—

> Ut ver dat flores, flos fructum, fructus odorem.
> Sic studium mores, mos sensum, sensus honorem.

That is to say, my friend, "As the springtime brings

the flower; the flower, fruit; the fruit, odour; so study brings knowledge; knowledge, tact; tact, consideration." And so it will come, that by reading and retaining in your memory noble histories, incidents, passages, you will arrive to attain to the never-ending joys of Paradise; wealth in arms, wealth in understanding, wealth in riches. Live tranquilly and honourably. And when your Lord, or any other, shall ask you honestly for your advice, let it be like to that of Claudian, the poet, when he counselled the Emperor Honorius; for said he to him,—

> Te patrem, civemque geras, tu consule cunctis.
> Non tibi, nec tua te moveant, sed publica vota.

That is to say, " As father and as friend, let all you do be wisely done. Support your people. Let self ever be the last consideration. Love God, and the commonwealth." For this was the manner of the old Romans; by this means they mastered the world, and gave the laws, which, to this day, are in ure among us. And on this head says St. Augustin, in the fourth book of his City of God, and in the twelfth chapter, out of Sallust recalling the words of Cato, where he says—

> The things which make us, Romans, so powerful, are our indefatiguableness, and that everything is done upon deliberation, and by consultation.

And hence, my friend, I press upon you, that the matters of your Lord, or of anybody else who may confide in you, be faithfully and secretly kept. For these are things which will mightily effect your honour, one way or another.

And now, my friend, I have said enough to you, for this time; and I pray God, that all, or the greater part, it will be in your power to attend to."

CHAPTER XVIII.

How the little Saintré threw himself on his knees before Madame and thanked her, and how the King and Queen gave him money to set him up. And how, at length, Madame told him that he was to have a bracelet, enamelled, and of her device, for the first of May, and that he was to wear it for an entire year, and to defend it in the lists against one Knight or other.

THE AUTHOR.

AND when Madame had made an end of what she had to say, Jehan de Saintré fell on his knees, and humbly thanked her, saying, "My ever gentle lady; her, of all the world whose influence is most upon, and sweetest unto me; with all the acknowledgment I am able, I thank you." Then, as it was growing late, she kissed him, and bid him to be off, saying, "Off with you; I do not know what it is you mean. Leave the rest to me."

THE AUTHOR.

In the morning, as soon as it was light, Saintré arose; and when he had heard mass, he made such haste, that he was the first in the robing-room. And in a little time, the other Knights and Squires began to appear. And when the King came to mass and saw Saintré so well and handsomely arrayed, he called to the Lord d'Ivry, and said to him, "Or I am much mistaken, this Saintré will, one day, be somebody. But how comes it, he manages to be always so nicely dressed?" "Sir," said the Lord d'Ivry, "I have heard that it is his mother who provides everything for him; but, I fancy, it is done with the consent of the father, who allows her the credit of it."

THE AUTHOR.

On hearing this, the King stopped short, and thought with himself, how he would do something for him. And, as soon as he was again in his chamber, he sent for his treasurer, and desired that Saintré was to have five hundred écus. And when the Queen heard of it, she had him given three hundred, and a piece of damask. And such was the grace in which Saintré was held by King and Queen, that there was not a Squire in the Court stood higher in their estimation than he. And all this was owing to the solicitousness of Madame, who for seven years had loved him. And when he was in his twentieth to his twenty-first year; and in which he received many kindnesses from the King; of the other times when Madame met him, I will skip; for it would be too long to rehearse.

The Author again.

And when Saintré was of the age that I have said, Madame, whose only imagination was how to make him all he should be, and to be heard of, thought with herself, Surely he is now big enough, and has spirit enough, to make himself heard of in the world. And when they were together, in the shade, and they had told to each other all their hearts, Madame said to him, "Ever dearest friend, joy of my soul, seeing that, through God's grace, you are at length confirmed in the good opinion of my lord, the King; of madame, the Queen, and indeed, for that matter, of everybody else; I have bethought me, you are now man enough to do something in the way of arms; so that, as well in this realm as beyond, you may be spoken of; and, to this end, I wish you, this first coming day of May, to wear, for my sake, a bracelet of enamelled gold, with our old devices; and it is to be set with six fair diamonds, six fair rubies, and six large and handsome pearls, of four or five carats, and all which you will find in a bag, enclosed in this handkerchief; and there are also in it two thousand écus, to help to set you out, and to go towards the expenses of your voyage and residence abroad. For the remainder, be under no sort of apprehension. I will so manage it, my Lord, Madame; and my Lords, my fair Uncles, of Anjou, Berry, and Bourgoyne, with the other princes of our blood, one and all shall aid you; and even supposing that they do not, as long as ten thousand écus will hold out, don't you be making yourself uneasy."

THE AUTHOR.

And when Saintré perceived the sacrifices which Madame was willing to make for his sake, and her anxiety for his advancement, and the infinite love she bare to him, such was his amazement and delight, he could not find a word to return. However, he flung himself upon his knees, and, as well as he could, he thanked her. Then Madame, who had not, by any means, the same difficulty in expressing herself, said, "My friend, I, who from among all others selected you to be my servant, have now to require, that, from this day forth, you will away with all anxiety, and take to you but one thought—to live joyously, and to be of good cheer. Of gold, silver, furniture, to set you up, now, at the commencement, I will provide you sufficient. And when your bracelet shall be mounted, you will come here to me, the evening before the first day of May, which will be shortly, and I will, for the first time, attach it to your arm; and, from the following day, you are to wear it for a year. And if, within that time, you have not met with Knight, or Squire, of name and renown, withouten soil or reproach, who, to deliver you from your vow, shall have had the better of you on horse, or on foot, it is to be yours. And he must also have the better of you on foot, after, supposing him to have won it from you with the lance. And after this manner are the arms to be. First, on horseback, in full tilt, one against the other; in war-saddles, and in complete harness, till one or other shall have fairly broken his lance. That is to say, between half a foot from the spear's point, and one foot above the grip. And to the one of you who shall have the first broken it, his companion, while still on his horse, and in the presence of the judge, shall present a diamond of the value of three hundred écus, or above, which he is to give to his lovely Lady. And on the following day, should God have preserved you from hurt, as from all craven-heartedness; or, if not, the eighth day, at latest, at the hour appointed by the judge, you will again combat, but on foot, one against the other, with battle-axes only; and this is to continue, till one or other of you be thrown from his legs, or have lost his axe from both his hands. And if at the end of these assaults of arms it is your companion who comes off the victor, I will and require that, there and then, you present him with the bracelet. But if, with God's permission, it is you that have the better, he is to get off simply with the loss of the axe which he then shall have in his hand; and, for one day only, of his armour.

"Now, my friend, albeit you are but young, and neither large nor strongly built; for all that, be not you afraid of any one, for often it will happen that the weak will have the better, in the fight, of the strong, the few of the many; let but God be for them. For men, indeed, it is who fight, but it is God that giveth the victory, and to whom he will; and, for this reason, seek, if to a happy issue you would look, for the counsel, aid, and help of God. But, should fortune prove to be your foe, which, God defend, do not on that account allow yourself to be cast down; I shall ever be what I was to you; nay, I will even love you more dearly than before; for, according to the laws of chivalry and of honour, double praise and double courtesy is ever to be the meed of the less fortunate. So that, whichever way it goes, you cannot come off but with success. All I have to hope is, that God will keep you from all faint-heartedness; which he will, if, from your heart, you put your trust in him. And I would rather prefer you to have to do with some one already known than a young person like yourself. And in order to ensure this, before they can have seen you, I wish and require, that, one month sooner than you may be ready to set out, you will send a king or herald-at-arms, first, to the court of the King of Arragon; next to that of the King of Navarre, for these are the most considerable of the Kings of Spain. He will after go to the Court of the King of Castille, and then to that of Portugal. These are, all four, Christian Kings. And if at any of these Courts, he shall find Knight, such as I speak of, or Squire, who will seriously undertake to release you from your engagement, then is the King to meet you, on his return, with an undertaking to that effect, given under his hand and seal. And if God will but be all, or even in part, for you, dear friend and heart, you will be a famous Squire; and, heaven knows how of my Lord; and madame, the Queen; and of all noble men and women you will be loved; the very thought of which should brace you up to overthrow a giant. And so, my friend, to conclude, be valiant; and in all your doings have recourse to God; seek his counsel and his aid, and never shall you have call for any other. And now I must break off; this is all I can say to you at present."

CHAPTER XIX.

How the little Saintré thanked Madame, and then had the bracelet made, as she had desired him; and after, how he came and showed it to her, at which she was delighted.

The Author.

THEN Saintré dropped on his knees, and said, "Ever redoubted Lady, my deity below, my sovereign friend; as humbly as I am able, as I can find words to express myself; for all this I thank you. And as for the arms that you have laid upon me, 'fore God; my lord, St. Michael, the angel, never, after your grace and your love, was there anything on this earth I more passionately longed for. Depend upon it, with God's grace, you shall hear such a tale of me as you, my Lords, and every one will be contented with." Then he wished her good bye; and when she had passionately kissed him, ten, fifteen or twenty times, she said, "May God be with you!"

THE AUTHOR.

"And in turning over this new project Saintré spent the night. And when it was day, and he had heard mass, he sent for Gilbert Lorin, jeweller to the King, who was well known, as to be trusted, and said to him, "Gilbert, my friend, I want a bracelet of gold, enamelled after my own colours and device, and it is to be set, on either side, with two diamonds, six rubies, and six pearls; and here they are." And when Gilbert had looked at them, he said, "They are of the finest." And, to be short, in two days the bracelet was made. And when next Saintré was in the company with Madame, he rubbed his right eye, which was the signal they had between them, to which Madame replied with her pin. And when they were together in the evening, in the meadow, to arrange, Saintré showed her the bracelet, by the light of the moon; but as she could not see it distinctly, Madame said to him, "I will see it by torchlight, and also to-morrow. You shall have it back to-morrow night, when we will be here again, and entertain one another to our hearts' content.

CHAPTER XX.

How the Lady instructed the little Saintré, that he should announce his intention, through an Herald-at-arms.—How the best dancer, whether Squire or Lady, should have a suitable prize, and how he was to put his bracelet on his arm.—After, how Saintré gave a banquet to all the Lords and Ladies.—And how, at night, he returned to the meadow, to speak with the Lady, who told him, he should publish his Letter-at-arms in the Courts of the four Kings.

AND when Madame, on the following day, had examined the rich and beautiful jewel, she was enchanted; so she immediately made her signal to Saintré, to which Saintré at once rejoined. And when they were together, Madame said to him, "My friend, here, take your bracelet; so handsome is it, I hardly fancy anything could be more so. What I wanted to say to you is this: it came into my head, when at dinner, that, as to-morrow will be the day before the first of May, you should give a grand supper to a number of the Knights, Ladies, Gentlewomen of the Court, and others; at which, however, I am not to be, though you will invite me. And that your enterprise may be more appropriately inaugurated, by the King-at-arms, or the Herald, you will have it cried, That the Lady or the Gentlewoman, Knight or Squire, then present, who should be adjudged to dance the best, or to sing the best, should have, the Lady or Gentlewoman, a fair diamond; the Knight or Squire, a fair ruby. And you will have, all ready, a grand and splendid banquet, at which will be served entremets, and dishes of every kind. [5] Then you will have the peacock brought in; and then the Lords and Ladies, Gentlewomen, Knights, and Squires shall make their vows; and when they have been made, then you will vow to the Ladies, to the peacock, to your Lady elect, or to be elected, that, to-morrow, the first day coming of May, you would fasten the bracelet, which you will then show them, on your left arm, and that you will wear it there for a whole year: that is, always provided you do not meet with Knight, or Squire, of name and reputation, who is to take it from you, as I told you; and also, provided always it be the King's good pleasure to allow the same. And when you shall have done all this, and reconducted the Ladies to their chamber, you will then come to me, and bring the bracelet with you, so that I may be the first to fasten it on you."

"Madame," said Saintré, "may God, the giver of every earthly good, return all this to you, and give to me the grace to requite the same; for other thought, or desire, this day, have I none." Then Madame, as was her custom, gave him his dismissal.

THE AUTHOR.

The following day, which was the last of April, as soon as it was light, Saintré was busy getting together cooks, and viands of all sorts. In a word, the banquet and the supper were prepared, as Madame had suggested. Then he invited Lords, Ladies, Gentlewomen, Knights, Squires, citizens and their wives of Paris; with a quantity of others. And when the dances, supper, and the banquet were over, and Saintré, with the rest, had seen the ladies home; and the King and Queen had taken the parting cup; and, in fact, all were gone, Saintré, as Madame had desired him, went to the meadow, and in a little time Madame came to him. And then, for the first time, she put the bracelet on his left arm; but, inasmuch as it was late, and it was time to part, she hardly remained a moment. However, in fastening it on, she said, "It is my prayer to God, and to our Lady, that from the day and the hour when you are to leave me, wherever it may be your fate to be called, to the day of your return, all praise and honour may be yours. And, that this may be, I now vow to them, that, so many Fridays and Saturdays as you shall be abroad, so many Fridays and Saturdays shall not linen touch my naked flesh."

"Ha, Madame," said he, "and what have I ever done for you, that such a Lady should make any such vow for me?"

"Yes, my friend," said she, "you have done enough; for are you not the man I love? And I think you cannot do better than, as soon as you can, having first obtained the permission and free consent of my Lord, to despatch your letters to the four Courts of the four aforesaid Kings, by an herald, or batchelor-at-arms, who will meet you, on his way back, on the road." And with these words, Madame allowed him to take his leave. And then with breaking hearts, and tears streaming from the eyes of each, they parted from one another.

CHAPTER XXI.

How the little Saintré went to the King and Queen, to break to them his Letter-at-arms, and obtain their permission to send it; which the King consented to, though much against his will.

THE AUTHOR AGAIN.

THE following day, which was the first day of May, Saintré appeared in a new suit, as did all his people, and the bracelet was on his arm. Then, having ordered a mass of the Holy Spirit to be said, as soon as he had heard it, he got together all his friends, as Madame had desired him. And all with one heart, they went in a body to the King; many of them protesting they would be with him in his voyage. And when the King, who, on the occasion, was accompanied by his brothers, and others of his blood, came out of his chamber; Saintré, with his friends, threw themselves on their knees before him. Then he began gracefully to enlarge himself, and said, "Our sovereign

Lord, it is usual with those who are nobly born, to seek to acquire unto themselves renown, by the right noble science of arms, and in divers ways. I, among others, being one of these aspirants, yesterday evening, at a little banquet, where were present these, my most redoubted Lords and Ladies, Knights and Squires now about you; with sundry others, made a vow, that I would, this morning, put on my left arm this bracelet which you see, to be only removed under the conditions which, if you will be pleased to look on this paper, you will perceive."

Then the King took the challenge, and had it read aloud before him; but it was long before he would give him any answer, turning over in his mind, as well the riskiness of the arms as the tenderness of Saintré, and the great affection he had for him. And when Saintré saw, by the time it was coming, the misgivings of the King, he began to be fearful of a refusal; so he said to him, imploringly, "Sir, it is the first request of the sort I ever made to you; for the love of God let it be granted to me!" Then my Lords, his brothers, and all the company, seeing how passionately his heart was set on it, all supplicating for him together with one voice; at length he consented. Then the King went to mass; and Saintré, after he had thanked him, seeing the Queen to be approaching with all her train, went to meet her. Then, when on his knees, he said, "Our sovereign Lady, the King has been pleased to grant me permission to proceed with my proposed passage of arms, as this, my bracelet requires; with the assistance of God, of our Lady; and of my Lord, Saint Michael the angel; and according as the tenour of my cartel runs. So, I have to entreat of you, my sovereign Lady, that your consent I may also have."

"And what, my friend," said the Queen, "have you, at your years, to do with arms; who put this into your head?"

"Madame," said he, " God and a thirst of honour have set me on."

" Then," said the Queen, " If so be they set you on, I sincerely trust and pray they will also bring you off with credit."

Then said several to Madame, " Madame have the letters read, so that you can understand their nature. We can hear them after mass." During this Madame came forward, looking on him wondrous pleased, as also were the rest, to see what was going on. Then the Queen said to him, " Saintré, seeing my Lord has thought proper to be content; it is meet that I should be so likewise. So I pray to God, to our Lady and to my Lord, Saint John, since you are determined to go, that all may redound to your honour and advantage." Then the Queen went to hear mass, and on coming back, she called for the challenge, wanting to hear it. And when she had heard it, she said, " Alas, this young fellow, who is little better than a child, how can he ever fancy himself equal to such an undertaking? it must come from a marvellous spirit and ambition. If he return, with God's permission, sound and safe, there is nothing that he may not, and will not attempt." And when the Queen had said this, she went to table, to dinner.

CHAPTER XXII.

How the little Saintré entered triumphantly into the lists, and of his noble equipment.—And how he carried himself so valiantly, that he was honoured and applauded of all.

THE AUTHOR.

AND as soon as the tables were removed, the King, the Queen, and the Ladies, and all the company withdrew to the balconies, to see the justings, which were about to begin. Then came Saintré upon his war-horse, covered with a caparison of white damask, all powdered with *fleur-de-lys*, and bearing for his device, *Forget me never*. Next began the tiltings, as well within as without the barrier; which, to be brief, I shall omit to speak of, as also the names, saving only that of Saintré, who shivered lances, drove one of his opponents to the ground, right over the crupper of his saddle; as did he two others, horses and all; and of all the combatants he was the last to unlace his helmet, or to quit his seat. If Madame was content, you need not ask. And indeed, so were the King, the Queen, and all the Court; each one vieing with the other, who loudest could extol his handsome justing. And for this, his maiden essay, he had a magnificent diamond, which he gave to Madame.

THE AUTHOR.

The next day he appeared again in the lists; caparisoned, he and his horse, with new furniture, of green satin, sowed with pansies. What need I say more? he acquitted himself so admirably that it was the marvel of all. But the King, considering how well he had already done, and to cut off all chance of accidents, forbad him to take any farther part, and so he did not again enter the lists.

CHAPTER XXIII.

How Saintré came to the meadow to speak with Madame, and how he retailed to her, point by point, how he was equipped; what officers and parties he had provided to accompany him on his voyage.—And how the Lady wanted to know about his colours and his arms; and how they took leave of one another, 'mid piteous tears and sighs.

THE AUTHOR AGAIN.

AND when the feast was past, Saintré set about collecting powerful chargers, and also beating up Knights and Squires, his friends and kinsmen; Kings-at-arms, Heralds,

Trumpets, Minstrels, and two drummers; as also the preparation of robes, embroidery, harness, trappings, feathers, and other things necessary; so that he could speedily set out on his voyage, and accomplish his arms. And when all things were in readiness, he made his signal to Madame. And when they were in the meadow, in the evening, together, he told her how everything had been done and ordered; how he had three Knights, Such an One, Such an One, and Such an One, with XIII horses; and IX Squires with XXIII horses; a chaplain with two horses; the Anjou King-at-arms with two horses; the Heralds, Touraine and Lusignan, with four horses; four trumpets with six horses; two drummers with two horses, together with four magnificent and powerful chargers, mounted by four little pages, and followed by two grooms, on horseback, to have the care of them. Besides these, how he had two cooks with three horses; a farrier, and an amourer, with four horses; eight sumpter horses—four for himself and four for his people—beside twelve varlets on horseback, to wait on him when he halted, with a steward who had three horses. In all, ninety horses, and all mounted with her colours, and with her device. But all this he told her somewhat hesitatingly, as though he feared it were a greater company than it befitted him to have at once dependent on him.

THE AUTHOR.

And when Madame, who had been listening to him with the intensest delight, perceived by his manner that he was not at his ease, and was in doubt as to whether he had not engaged for more than he would be able to make good, she said to him, "My friend, I do not think you possibly could have managed better than you have done. And as for the expense, let not that trouble you, for I hope that my Lord, Madame, and my Lords, fair Uncles, especially, will contribute to your assistance. And even if they do not, for the outlay of one year, whatever it may be, your honour shall not be compromised. And, my friend, about your clothes?"

"Madame, I have three suits, all sufficiently the thing. One is crimson damask, richly trimmed with silver braid, and lined with sable martin; and I have another of blue satin, and * * *; and I have a third of black damask, stitched with silver thread all studded with tufts, and set with ostrich feathers,—green, violet, and gray, which are your colours, bordered with white ermine, which is powdered with black tufts. And it is in this latter that I intend to appear on horseback in the lists; that is, if it is your good pleasure. And every one who has seen them says they are magnificent, and a perfect sight to set eyes on. And, besides, I have another, and my coat-of-arms alike, in which I will enter the lists when I come to fight on foot; it is also of crimson satin, all covered with golden tassels, and * * *."

"And, my friend, how do you blazen?"

"Madame, my arms are *de gueulles à une bande d'argent à quatre lambeaulx d'or.*"

"Hey, God," said Madame, "but that should be handsome, too! I should give anything to see them, if it was not for the way people would talk. But I know how I think it can be managed; I will get Madame to ask you to show yourself to her."

"As you will," said Saintré, "I am ready this moment, or as soon as you like; and it seems to me the sooner the better. I dare say Lusignan, the herald, is already there; and if by any chance he has succeeded, I should know of it, and meet him, as was arranged between us."

They then agreed together that he was to set out on the fifteenth day, next following, of July; and having come to this conclusion, they took leave of one another, mid piteous and burning sighs, and tears, and kisses.

CHAPTER XXIV.

How the Lady told the Queen, how sumptuously Saintré was set up in horses and equipage; and how the said Queen desired Saintré to bring his horses into the court, so that she might see them, which he did, and how the King and Queen saw them, and commended them.

The Author.

THE following morning, whilst the Queen was dressing, Madame, who had by no means forgotten all the finery, said to the Queen carelessly, among other chat, "Madame, they say it is something incredible all the fine things Saintré has been getting, but I don't believe a word of it myself. However, Madame, if you chose, we could see them, we women among ourselves, and no more; for I hear, he wants to keep it all close. If you ask him, he will doubtless gratify you with pleasure."

"But are you sure, fair Cousin," said the Queen, "they are so fine?".

"Madame, certainly, as they tell me, for farther I cannot answer." Then said she to the Queen, "If we do not meet with a refusal we will see them, and know from him why he makes all this mystery of them. Desire him to bring his four chargers into the little court below, with all his furniture covered, which he can then unpack, and we can have the door barred to keep everybody out."

"Ha, by my faith," said the Queen, "it is a lucky thought! As soon as we see him again remind me of it."

Presently after the Queen was going to mass, and when in the robing-room Madame saw Saintré, who was there; so, stepping forward, she said gently to the Queen, "Madame, there is Saintré now." Then the Queen desired Guillaume de Lins, her Usher-at-arms, to call Saintré to her. And when he was come, the Queen said, "Saintré, as God is to prosper you, you must yield unto us somewhat; we have much at heart. You must let us see your chargers, with all their trappings on them: they tell us it is a perfect sight."

"And, Madame," said he, "with all due submission to those who told you so, be it said, they are but sorry things, and no better than are becoming a poor companion like myself. I should be distressed, Madame, you should see anything of the sort."

"Even so, fair sir, whatever they are, we beg that you will have them brought by after dinner, into the court below; and we will see that everybody is out of the way, and the door fast, and, if you like, the clothes can come covered, and when you have taken them out and all is ready, let us quietly know, and we will come."

"Madame," said Saintré, "since such is your pleasure, your lightest wish is my commandment."

The Author.

And as soon as the King and Queen had dined, and the tables were removed, Saintré sent for the clothes and the horses; and when the doors were closed and the furniture was opened out, Saintré went to acquaint the Queen, as she had desired him. Then the Queen, not only anxious herself to see them, but edged on by Madame, could not refrain from telling the King that Saintré's horses were in the court below.

"And how," said the King, "are they so worth seeing as all that?"

"My Lord," said she, "you can see them if you choose."

"Then I will," said the King. "Let them bring the parting cup."

"Ah, my Lord," said the Queen, "but let as few as possible be with us."

And after the grace cup the King and Queen arose, and,

from the galleries took a look at the chargers, all covered with their furniture, and which seemed to them to be everything that had been promised. Then all the ladies and gentlemen began to praise Saintré, and to offer up their vows and prayers that God would vouchsafe to be with him, and to bring him back with honour. And when the King was going away he called Saintré to him, and questioned him about sundry matters; and presently leaving him, he went into his dressing-room, and taking out, in three sacks, three thousand écus, he sent them to him by Jehan de Seuffle, his valet-de-chambre, to help towards the expenses of his voyage. And when the Queen heard that the King had given him three thousand écus, she was delighted. So she sent for Madame, and said to her, " Fair Cousin, I am right well pleased; the King has given Saintré three thousand écus; I do not see how I can well offer him less than a thousand; and I do think you might give him two or three hundred yourself."

"Ah, Madame," said Madame to the Queen, "now you are going to be generous with other people's money;" so that the Queen was almost obliged to force her to part with it. And when my Lords of Anjou, of Berry, and Bourgoyne came to know what the King had done, they each gave him a thousand. And so he had seven thousand, over and above the presents that he received from the other Lords. And, in verity, he neither asked nor looked for anything, and for which he was highly commended; every one saying, "Surely we ought to do what we can for a young squire like this, who is little more than a lad, and who, out of sheer spirit, is setting out on such an expedition; surely we ought to back him up, and encourage him."

H

CHAPTER XXV.

How Saintré, as soon as he was ready to set out, came to ask the King for permission to depart, to accomplish his enterprise; which thing the King allowed to, though sorry to see him go.

THE AUTHOR.

AND when the term for his departure was at hand, eight or ten days before, Saintré, accompanied by all his three Knights, his nine Squires, his Kings-at-arms, Heralds, and all the residue of his people; he and they, accoutred in his livery, together with a number of other Lords, Knights, and Squires, his intimates, came; and when they were all on their knees before the King, present my Lords of Anjou, Berry, and Bourgoyne, Saintré said, "Our sovereign Lord, your Grace has been already pleased to allow that I am to wear this bracelet, in accomplishment of the engagements at arms, on horse and on foot, which in writing you have seen. And so I have come, most humbly entreating you, that it will be your farther good pleasure to grant me your permission that, the fifteenth day of July, I, with these gentlemen, my brothers and my friends, here present, and who of their courtesy are to accompany me, may God, our Lady, and my Lord, St. Michael, willing, set out and commence our voyage."

THE AUTHOR.

To this the King, who already had, as has been stated, assented to his leaving, said, "How, Saintré, is it that you are so soon ready?"

"Sir," said he, "Yes."

Then he said to him, "Saintré, you are come of noble blood, of a race of valiant men. God grant to you the grace to be like to them, as I have no doubt but you will, for you are giving us an early earnest. One thing mark;

you must not be too sanguine in what you are going about, for you have, as yet, had no sort of experience in arms, and though you are but in your paces now, questionless, one day, you will arrive to be a master. And another thing bear in your memory; whatever be your fortune, conqueror or conquered, be yourself the same; carry yourself equally, and lose, if lose you must, with a good grace."

Then the King told him he was well content he should go, for which Saintré most humbly thanked him. And when the King had retired, Saintré most respectfully did as much to the other Lords for the presents they had made him.

CHAPTER XXVI.

How Saintré was in the meadow, to take leave of the Lady, who admonished him again of all he was to do.—And how, at last, they parted from one another; not, however, without abundance of tears, as well on the one side as the other.

The Author again.

AND when the tenth, twelvth, and fourteenth days of the month were come, Madame, out of the sad and agonizing regrets which she had at the thoughts of parting, made him, every day, her signal with her pin, and which he acknowledged. And when they were in the meadow together, great were the tears and the sighs at the recollection of in how little a time they were to separate. Then Madame said, "My only friend, friend more than I have words to tell, my Lord the King has given you three thousand écus, Madame a thousand, my Lords, fair Uncles, each a thousand, which makes seven thousand, independently of what you got from the other lords; and as one does not know what may happen, I will give you three thousand, making ten in all; and this, if there is no reckless or unnecessary waste, ought to be ample to meet every legitimate call upon you for a considerable time to come. One thing I have to pray of you, and that is, that every day after mass, and whilst you are still on your knees, as soon as the priest shall have given you the benediction, which our Lord gave, with his own mouth, to Moses, as is written in the Bible, and which I told you of before, farther to confirm it to you, you will bid him add,

Benedicat tibi Dominus, et custodiat te, ostendat faciem suam tibi, et misereatur tui.
Convertat Dominus vultum suum ad te, et det tibi pacem.

And I also entreat of you that, when on the point of setting out to perform your arms, whether on foot or on horseback, you will, having first crossed yourself, repeat, from your heart, the following benediction :—

Benedicat michi Dominus, et custodiat me.
Ostendat michi faciem suam Dominus, et misereatur mei.
Convertat Dominus vultum suum ad me, et det minchi pacem.

And after this, step forth boldly, and do what you have to do manfully. Thus prepared, come what will, victory or defeat, it will alike be to your honour, and trust me, never will they fail you." And as she said this, the very tears of her heart started from her eyes, and as not another word could he or she utter, for a little they were each lost, as in a trance.

THE AUTHOR.

And when Saintré had revolved with himself all the inestimable advantages and kindnesses which Madame had extended to him, so that of all lovers beneath the sun he was the most favoured, and when he had recalled how every day had been witness of some new proof of her attachment, some condescension, some grace, some generous effusion, in the bitterness of his distress he said to her, " Ha, my high and supreme goddess, nonpareille of womankind, you who should be comforting me in all the agony of such a separation from one who is my only thought, my only pleasure, and my sovereign weal; alas, to see your grief, so like my own, has so overwhelmed and unnerved me, that my very heart is like to rend in twain. I am sickened to the death, and I leave you but to die. Madame, God be with you!" and thus saying he turned to leave her.

THE AUTHOR.

Madame, the fountain of whose anguish had well nigh now ceased to flow, hearing the words of Saintré, mingling her own with her tears and her sobbings, said, "Ha, my friend, come back if you will; alas, as you well know, we women have tender hearts, and are compassionate to those we love. Also be under no sort of distress for me; I am now collected, trusting that God will bring you again in double honour and in double joy. So, my very true friend, my ever-present thought, my heaven, my treasure, life of my life, and death of my death, be of good heart. Fret not yourself, for on my honour, for your sake I will pass my time cheerfully and resignedly; and one thing remember, as you value my life, nothing must come to me when you are away; write only to Madame, and let it be full, for through her I will hear everything, without any sort of risk. And now, my friend, let us seal this compact with a kiss." And now were kisses, thick and innumerable, given and taken on either side, all broken with tears and sobs and sighs; and in this agonizing solace, and this melancholy joy, they continued, till midnight, to their horror, struck, and they saw that needs was they must part. And as he was leaving, Madame, kissing him, put a beautiful and precious diamond ring upon his finger, and tearing herself from him, ... said only, "God be with you!"

CHAPTER XXVII.

How Saintré took his farewell of the King, the Queen, and the Ladies, to each of whom he gave a golden wand.—And how the Queen asked, "If there was not one for her?" On which he gave her one, excusing himself, saying, "he had not thought she would condescend to care for such a trifle."

The Author.

THE following morning, being the fifteenth day of July, which was the one fixed for his departure, after mass, and that the priest had given Saintré his benediction, Saintré and all his company, arrayed in his livery, came to take their farewell of the King, who said to him, "Saintré, God be with you; do your work well, and come back to us with honour. One thing I have already entreated of you; I now do it again, and that is, if you lose, it will be done with a good grace; and if you win, it shall be fairly and honourably."

"Sir," said he, "with God's grace you shall never have other report to hear of me."

And when the good King had given him his hand, Saintré took his leave and went to the Queen, who said to him, "Hey, Saintré, since you must go, we pray God the prize of arms may be yours, and we wish you all joy with, and welcome homeward from, your Lady."

"Madame," said he, "as to the prize of arms, since you are pleased to wish me well, I wish it too; but as for the Lady part of the matter, I have no other aspiration than to serve the King, and, Madame, yourself."

With these words he took his leave of her, then hurriedly, the same of Madame, who merely said to him, sighing, "You have already taken your farewell of me, go to the other Ladies and Gentlewomen." This he did, giving to each of them a golden cane, all covered with *Forget-me-nots*; nor was there one dry eye in all the company, so dearly was he loved, and had he been loved of all. And when the Queen heard about the rods, how they were being given away, she sent for Saintré and said to him, laughing, "Ha, fair sir Saintré, are not we, fair Cousin here, and myself as much ladies as the rest, that we are to be passed over in this manner?"

"Ah! Madame," said Saintré, "'fore God, I am not to blame; I had not the presumption to suppose such Ladies would ever condescend to accept so light a gift from me."

"But," said she, "we will from you, though it is what we would not do from all."

Then he gave them the choice of those he had, though, indeed, they were all alike. Then they said to him, "Thank you, Saintré," and with these words Saintré took his leave. And when Madame saw him going, she could not refrain, but the tears would flow; so, to excuse herself, she said to the Queen, "I never remember the scene or the parting yet could wring a tear from me on my own account. The only thing that ever troubles me or sets me off, is to see others affected."

"And in truth, Madame," said the rest, "it needs no apology; where is the breast of woman could forbear from tears to see this lad thus going from us upon so perilous an enterprise; he who has been brought up among us from an infant, and whose company every day has been a source to us of entertainment and delight."

CHAPTER XXVIII.

How, after Saintré had taken his leave of the Barons, and Lords of the Court, he went away to dine with his companions; and how, when at dinner, the Queen sent him a rich cloth of silver; and several Lords subsidies and presents.—And how he had himself escorted, at his outset, by the heralds, trumpets, and musicians; giving them a supper at the burgh of the Queen, where he lodged.

The Author, upon the departure of Saintré.

AND when Saintré had taken his farewell of the ladies at the Court he went to take the like of my said Lords, of each of whom he had a kindly word. And after this he returned, with all his company, to his hotel to dine. And when they were dining, the Queen sent him a magnificent roll of silver cloth; my Lord of Anjou a splendid charger, with all his furniture; my Lord of Berry a cloak, and five hundred martens' skins; and my Lord of Bourgoyne fifty marks of plate; and there was not one of those that brought them to whom he did not give a hundred écus, out of his love and respect toward the Queen and the said Lords. And when they had all dined and the horses were saddled, and everything was packed and trussed, there were got together Knights, and Squires, as well of the King's Court as the Queen's, and of my said Lords, as his friends, and others, well nigh a thousand horsemen, all assembled to see him off. And when it was time to go, he sent first his two couriers, his cooks, and his chaplain, with four trumpets, carrying his banners, with his arms; next, his three heralds; and, after them, his three Knights, and nine Squires, two and two abreast, and all their people after, all in his livery. Next came his five sumpter-horses, covered with cloths, on which were wrought his arms, and led by two footmen. Then came his drummers, and after his four war-horses, richly caparisoned in fine Florence taffeta, gray, and green, and violet, all broidered with his device, in silver letters. And on each of their heads there was a vice of steel, in which were set a bunch of ostrich plumes, and among them silver bells; and on them were four tiny graceful little pages, dressed in his device: from their arms hung silver tassels, and on their heads were caps with feathers, all of his colours. And after the war-horses came the two grooms, and then the smith; after were the drums and the minstrels who came to see him off; and after the minstrels came the bachelors; next, the heralds of the Lords, then that of the King, and then the royal Kings-at-arms. Then came all the trumpets, and clarions; first, those of the Lords, then those of the King. And after the trumpets he came himself, arrayed in his device; and, as his pages, his sleeves all glittering with silver tassels, and on his head a similar cap of feathers; and he was on the noble charger which my Lord of Anjou had sent him. And he came surrounded by four Lords, two before and two behind; then came the other Lords, Knights, and Squires, any way and as they could. And in all this state they conducted him from the Court in Paris, a good league from the town. And when it was time for them to turn, he called to him all the Kings-at-arms, heralds, batchelors, trumpets, minstrels, drummers, and other good fellows, and made them sup with him at the Queen's burgh, where, for that night, he lay, as did they all; and in the morning he gave them fifty écus. And now I will say no more about his departure, but will speak of his journey, and the return of Lusignan, the herald.

CHAPTER XXIX.

How Saintré, being at Avignon, the Anjou King-at-arms brought him the seal, and the reply to his Letter-of-arms; and told him all how he had spoken with Enguerrant, and published the Letter-of-arms, at which he was delighted.

THE AUTHOR.

AND when Saintré had got to Avignon, through the noise of his arrival, the Anjou herald-at-arms got to know that it was Saintré; and so, as he was coming from mass, he presented the said sealed letter to him. And when the little Saintré had fully read it, and considered it, the said Saintré immediately returned, in the face of everybody, to the church, devoutly to thank his God. Then he demanded of the King, before all the company, all the history of his delivery, and who it was that was to release him.

Then said Lusignan, "I first got to Barcelona on the third day of June, late, so for that night I rested myself. In the morning, next day, after mass, I returned to my hotel, and put on your coat-of-arms, as I had a right to do; and I placed the case, in which was your letter-of-arms, in my pocket; then, by a varlet of the place, I had myself conducted to the Court of the King. And, as God's will would have it, as I got to the gate, I met a Knight, an exceedingly comely man, with all his people about him, named Sir Enguerrant de Servillon; whom, in passing, I humbly saluted. And when he saw me clad in your coat-of-arms, all of a sudden, stopping, he called to me, saying, 'Herald, who are you? Whose coat-of-arms is that you have on? What is your name?' 'My Lord,' said I, 'in virtue of my office, I am King-at-arms of Anjou, Lorraine and of Maine.' 'Then' said he, 'King-at-arms, you are welcome. I suppose you are come to our King's court on some affair of arms; if so be, I must entreat of you to tell me the same.' 'My Lord,' said I, 'it is true. I have been sent on the part of a noble and renowned Squire, called Jehan de Saintré, who, on the first day of May past, vowed, in the presence of many high and potent Dames, Gentlewomen; Lords, Knights, Squires, in abundance; and announced his determination to wear, on his left arm, a rich bracelet of gold, set with precious stones; and this, for the space of a year, unless he should have found some Knight, or Squire, of name and reputation, without reproach, to deliver him, on horse and on foot, as this letter will show. And to this end, he is coming, first into this kingdom, to the Court of this most noble King, where he will remain an entire month, in the hope of his release by some Knight, or Squire, of the condition I spoke of. And if he does not find such here, he will then go, in the like search to the Court of the King of Navarre, and next to that of the King of Portugal; and he will remain one month in each, should he not first meet with his despatch, as I have said.' 'King-at-arms,' then said the Knight to me, 'I have to request that you will let me look at these letters; promising you, on the faith of a noble Knight, that if the proposition is above board, and an honourable one; and if it be the good pleasure of God; of my Lord Saint Gregory; and of my sovereign Lord, the King, I will be the man, who, to the best of my power, will satisfy him as to what he wants.' And when I saw his authoritative manner, his commanding appearance, and the train that was with him; and when I thought on the faith he had pledged me, I came to the conclusion, that I had found the party I had been desired to look out for. So I took your letters out of my pocket, and gave them to him, and when he had read them at his leisure, he said to me, 'King-at-arms, come this way.' Then he turned back, and spoke with several Knights and Gentlemen of the Court to whom he showed the letters. After that he said, ' King, come with me.' Then he took me by the hand, and led me towards the King, who was returning from mass. Then he and I, he holding me by the hand, knelt down, as did the rest. Then in his language, he said, ' My Lord, as I was leaving your palace, it so fortuned that I met Anjou King-at-arms, who here is; and seeing him in his coat-of-arms, I presently divined that it could not be without cause, but must be for some affair of arms ; especially it happening in the Court of so mighty a Prince as yourself. So I stopped him, and asked him, Whence he came, and why, in our King's Court, he was wearing his coat-of-arms, seeing you were in peace with all Christian princes? He then answered me in terms which, if it is your pleasure to hear, I shall give you.' "

CHAPTER XXX.

How the Anjou King-at-arms told Saintré, that the King of Arragon had consented that Enguerrant should deliver him from his engagement; and how he had given him a gracious reception; at which Saintré and his companions were beyond expression delighted.

THE KING-AT-ARMS.

" AND when he had done speaking, the King, who had been looking hard at me, said, taking me by the hand, ' You are very welcome.' Then he told me, to let him hear what it was I had said to Sir Enguerrant de Servillon. Then I repeated to him, word for word, what you have already heard. ' And where are the letters?' said the King. ' My Lord,' said Sir Enguerrant, ' here they are.' Then the King had them read. And when they were read, Sir Enguerrant said to him, ' Lord, seeing the right noble pre-eminences which mundane tribute will procure to valiant breasts, by feats of arms, each one will vie, to the best of his capability, and on every opportunity, to purchase for himself reputation, fame, honour; whether in the more courteous combat of the list, or whether in the ruder strife of war; as on all allowable occasions. And farther, seeing that the refusal of this adventure was first submitted to me; and albeit I well know, that there are many in this company, and in your Court, not only as able as, but more able and sufficient than myself; nevertheless, Lord, as it in a manner fell to my part, as humbly as I can, and as I ought, I beg and entreat of you, that, if permission is to be given to any to accept this challenge, it may be to me.'"

The King-at-arms.

"And when the King heard his request, like a wise Prince as he is, before giving him an answer, he withdrew, taking with him certain aged and experienced Lords, and Knights and Squires, then present. And when he had remained with them some little time, he called him before him, before everybody, and said, ' Sir Enguerrant, we have considered your humble and honourable demand, which for the love and honour we bear you, as also out of respect to the engagement of the noble Squire, we grant you; and appoint, for the day, the fifteenth from that of his arrival, if God shall spare you both till then. And in addition to this, we will be gratifying the Ladies.' And for this gracious reply of the King, Sir Enguerrant, and all his friends, most humbly thanked him; as did I also, on your part. Then the King retired, and went to dinner, and Sir Enguerrant took me to his hotel; and he sent for my horses, and had them stabled with his own; then he made me dine with him; and after dinner, he bid me take off my coat-of-arms, and my doublet, and he gave me a rich and beautiful cloak of blue figured velvet, and most richly trimmed in gold, and lined with marten, and which I have here in my trunk. And he made me stay with him that day, and the next, and had longer, would I have consented. And as soon as he had given me his acceptance, the heralds of the King came to treat me, and conduct me about the town. And when the letters were written, he brought me to take my leave of the King, who behaved most nobly to me; and out of the love of our Lord the King, and also of you, he ordered me to have a cape of black figured velvet, lined with marten, and a hundred florins of Arragon. And as I was going away, he said to me most courteously, 'that I was to emember him to you.' And of these promised arms, as I have heard from more than one, the Queen, with the Ladies and Gentlewomen, as also the Knights and Squires, with all the city and roundabout; were in such delight, that the whole country was ringing at the thought; and when I was taking leave of Sir Enguerrant, he said to me, 'You will remember me kindly to my brother, Jehan de Saintré, and tell him, that, God will, I shall be all ready against the day our King has appointed, and you will also commend me to all his people, and God be with you.' And as I was getting on my horse, he sent me forty florins of Arragon."

THE AUTHOR.

And when Saintré and all his company heard his report, and all this good news, and how speedily he was to have his deliverance, their delight was unbounded; and in a little it was spread everywhere, and the King and Queen had come to hear of it; by which means Madame did too, as also the whole Court and country. Then began Ladies and Gentlewomen to fast, to make their vows, and prayers, and to go on pilgrimages; so much was he loved of all. But, on hearing them,

Saintré, like a good Christian, and one who looked to God for all his honour and for all his aid, returned at once to the church, and there, on his knees, with bared head and clasped hands, devoutly offered up his prayers and oblations to God, and our Lady, and after that he went to dinner.

CHAPTER XXXI.

How Saintré, being at Perpignan, the news came to the King of Arragon, who appointed him lodgings at Barcelona.—And after, how Enguerrant came out, a good league, from the town to meet him; and how honourably he received him; and of the civilities and discourse that passed between them.

THE AUTHOR. OF THE ENTRY INTO BARCELONA.

AND while all this was going on, and that Sir Enguerrant was preparing himself, Saintré had arrived at the town of Perpignan. Then was the King apprised of his coming, of his state, and of all the noble company he had with him. Then the King and all the Lords saw, that clearly he must be somebody of consideration: and so he at once ordered an hotel to be got ready for him at Barcelona, and which was made over to his harbingers, two days before he arrived. And as he was making his entry, Sir Enguerrant, who, with a large following, together with many Lords, Knights, and Squires, had gone a league and more to meet him, was strangely taken back at two things; the one, the extreme youthfulness of Saintré; the other, the extraordinary pomp in which he and his people were coming, and which was the same in which they had left Paris. And when Sir Enguerrant saw the boyishness of Saintré, he was aghasted to find that he had engaged himself to combat with a person who might be his own son. And so he kept looking hard at him, and wondering within himself, how so young a man as he was could ever have dreamt of embarking himself in so perilous an affair. And when they had got to the hotel, Sir Enguerrant, ashamed to find with whom it was he had undertaken to fight, said to him apart, "Jehan de Saintré, my brother; you are a young gentleman, a Squire; and I am an old one, and a Knight. If you would consent to release me from my engagement, I have here my own nephew, a young gentleman of your own age, and a Knight besides, as much I am myself, and who would willingly take my place. In this you would oblige me." To this Saintré, deliberate and courteous, like himself, made answer, and said, "Sir Enguerrant, it has been the will of God, and to my great good fortune, that this offer was first accepted at your hands; for which, as best I am able, I do, and will continue most humbly to thank you; for it is no mean obligation, which, as a gentle Knight you have laid me under, by pledging yourself, under your seal, to release me. And although Monsieur your nephew may, doubtless, be equal to, and worthy to deliver the stoutest Knight of France this day alive; nevertheless, since fate would first that I should have affair with yourself, I must still be permitted to look to you, and you alone; and for this, sir, you must pardon me. And if, for any considerations which I am unacquainted with, or may be unable to divine, you shall think proper to withdraw from your engagement, I will then have only to consider myself to be lawfully and honourably discharged from my vow, and to return."

THE AUTHOR.

And when Sir Enguerrant heard, from so young a man, so wary a retort, he was quite astonished, and saw plainly in his own mind, that he had given him to understand he dared not meet him; and so would hold himself acquitted. So, making up his mind to satisfy him, he said, "Saintré, my brother, I have considered your very handsome speech; what I promised you, under my seal, God willing, our Lady, and my Lord Saint George, I will gratify you in, at the day and hour that my Lord the King has appointed us. And the sooner to bring these matters to an end, and as honourably as may be, I think it would be well, when the King has returned from vespers, that I should come and fetch you. You will then be ready, and come and pay your respects to the King and Queen, who will gladly see you. And there, in presence of the King, I will undo your bracelet, and to-morrow you shall have it again, as are the terms of your letter. And I trust, with the favour of my Lord St. George, and of our Lady, all will go well."

And with this Saintré took his leave; nor, for any entreaty would he remain to dine; though, to see more of him, his carriage and his state, Sir Enguerrant would gladly have had him stay.

CHAPTER XXXII.

How Sir Enguerrant presented Saintré to the King, and to the Queen, who gave him a most handsome reception, and solemnly feasted him.

THE AUTHOR AGAIN.

THEN Sir Enguerrant went to the King, to tell him of the extraordinary handsomeness of Saintré, and of his graceful delivery, of which, as the King had already heard the report, he enjoined him urgently to bring him to see him, as did the Queen and all the Ladies of the Court. So, after vespers, Enguerrant, with all his people, with Saintré leaning on his arm, brought him to the King, in the presence of the Queen, and before whom they both and all knelt down. And as soon as the King saw him coming, he advanced two or three paces, and said to him, "Welcome, fair son and youthful Squire." Then he bade them rise. And when they had risen, Sir Enguerrant

I

led him to present him to the Queen, who said to him, "Jehan, we are glad to see you;" then she took his hand and made him rise. Next Sir Enguerrant led him towards the Ladies, and notwithstanding it was not the custom, he made him kiss them all, for so it had been ordered. Then they came back to the King, and when they were both on their knees, Sir Enguerrant said to the King, "Lord, you have heard the letter of my brother, Saintré, wherein is detailed the condition of his arms; and, of your grace, you have appointed me a day and place when and where I am to deliver him. As a preface, Sir, to this, is it your will that I now commence with the preliminary article imposed upon us, which is this, to undo the bracelet that he now has on his left arm?"

Then the King, as a wise Prince, determining to hear from Saintré's own lips, and before all, if he would allow to it, had his letter read openly. Then he said to him, "Jehan de Saintré, is that that you have on, the one referred to in your letter?"

"Yes, Sir," said Saintré.

Then said the king to Sir Enguerrant, "You are at liberty to undo it."

Then Sir Enguerrant took the bracelet off; and all that day he wore it round his neck, hanging from a handsome twine of silk and gold; and in the morning he restored it to him. And when this was over, they went to the Queen and the other Ladies, who received them most courteously, and made them all sorts of good cheer. Then they went to the reception-hall, where they played at all kinds of games till supper-time. Then Saintré took his leave, retiring with Sir Enguerrant, and the other Knights and Squires, who had invited him to supper; and who never once slacked, either that evening or the following days, to entertain one another with the beauty and the gracefulness of Saintré, and of all his company.

And the fourth day, the king desired the Queen to send for and invite Saintré, and all the Gentlemen who were with him, to dinner; and at the dancing and the singing, Saintré, with several of his people, who sung surpassingly, greatly pleased the King, and Queen, and all who heard them. And in this manner, they were fêted every day at the Court. But for the rest, to be short, I will come to the point.

CHAPTER XXXIII.

How Saintré entered magnificently into the lists, surrounded by a noble assemblage of Princes and of Knights; and of the order of the day.

THE AUTHOR, UPON THE ENTRY OF SAINTRÉ TO THE LISTS.

AND when the xv day after his arrival was come, being the one appointed on which they were to fight, they were both armed and in readiness. And on the said day, the King, like a wise and magnificent Prince, to show his respect to the strangers, sent to Saintré, to conduct him, the Count de Cardonne, Don Frederic de Lune, Sir Arnauld de Pareilles, and Sir Francis de Moncade; four great nobles, and Knights of his Court, with all their suites. And this was to do him honour; and they were to ride in ranks. And when he had ordered this, the King set out himself, and got into his box, which was on one side of the lists, and gorgeously hung with tapestry on every side; together with many Princes, Lords, Knights and Squires of his council. And on his left hand, the Queen was in her box, accompanied by many Princesses, Ladies and Gentlewomen of her Court, and of the Kingdom, who had come to the town to see the combat. And when the King and Queen had taken their seats, then, at the King's command, the Kings-at-arms and heralds carried his commands to either party, "that they were to do as they had undertaken." Then Saintré, who was already prepared, as the originator and challenger, got upon his horse, with all his people, and set out in the following order :—

First; left his hotel, the drummers, on horseback, with all the company who came to conduct him, two and two. Next, after the drummers came his three sumpter-horses, carrying his trunks and coffers, all covered with cloths, richly embroidered with his arms; each led by his groom, on foot. And after them came his two armorers, on foot. After the armorers came the bachelors, with their coats-of-arms emblazoned on their sides, two and two. And after the bachelors came Saintré's minstrels. After Saintré's minstrels came the King's minstrels, and the trumpets of Arragon. After the trumpets of Arragon came the heralds of Arragon. After the heralds of Arragon came the French heralds. After the French heralds came the Arragon Kings-at-arms, and those of Anjou; the former wearing the coats-of-arms of their respective Lords; and those of France the arms of Saintré, richly wrought.

After, the Kings-at-arms, his four trumpets, and clarions; and, after them, the Knights and Squires, each bearing on his thigh a ponderous lance; and six of them were armed, *cap-à-pied*, and covered with a cloak of silver cloth, of Saintrè's colour, and lined with marten. The other six were no less magnificently equipped, saving only the armour. After the twelve lances came the said Don Bernard de Cardonne, carrying on his thigh a lance, with its gonfanon, of a delicate crimson velvet, backed with ermine, and trimmed with a rich fringe of gold; and each side was blazoned with the arms of Saintré. After the gonfanon came Don Frederic de Lune, upon a powerful courser, dressed as were the six armed lances, and carrying in his hand the trunk of a lance, on which was his helmet, and on its top a great thistle, with four golden leaves, that covered the whole helmet. And from below the thistle floated a long streamer, richly sown with golden thread, and studded with great pearls; the whole embroidered with golden letters. After the helmet came Saintré, upon a magnificent and plunging charger, which had at its head a gorgeous crest of ostrich feathers, all in Saintré's three colours; he and his horse covered with a rich caparison of crimson satin, all studded with hearts of ermine, * * * * *. On his head was a gay and jaunty cap of feathers; and he was armed simply with his gauntlets, and on his thighs and feet. In his right hand was his banner, on which was our Lady and her child, and with which, at every pace, he crossed himself. After Saintré came Sir Francis de Moncade, and Sir Arnauld de Pareilles, each upon a splendid war-horse, and side by side. And after them came all the body of the other Knights and Squires, who, by the order of the King, had accompanied him. And all this princely procession and array alighted at the door of the great tent, which the King had had spread for him, at the barriers of the lists; and into it entered Saintré with his four counsellors, and those of his own party who had come with him. And besides came, after the said Saintré, and in front of the said Lords, his four Pages, all mounted upon his plunging battle-horses, covered with his caparisons; and the said Pages were also dressed as they had appeared on leaving Paris, as before described.

CHAPTER XXXIV.

How Sir Enguerrant besides entered the lists, in a like triumphant array.

THE AUTHOR, ON THE ENTRY OF SIR ENGUERRANT INTO THE LISTS.

UNWILLING to run the risk of wearying the reader, this Chapter, which, in its general character, is little else than a repetition of the last, is purposely omitted.—*Translator.*

CHAPTER XXXV.

How the King had the lances of the two champions measured.—And how popularly Saintré demeaned himself, in passing before the King and Queen: they in their boxes.

THE AUTHOR, ON THE ARMS.

AND when they had both come, incontinent the King had their lances measured, which ought to be, from rest to point, XIII feet in length. And when they had been measured, and each had been restored his own, the King ordered Saintré to lead the way, which he prepared to do. And as soon as he was mounted on his battle-horse, he called for his banner, and then made the major sign of the cross, repeating all the time to himself his benediction, as Madame had taught him; and then bowing, and crossing himself at every plunge, he proudly made for the lists; and beside him were the four Lords, his counsellors, with a like number of his own people, and others, on horse and foot. And as custom was that the champions should ride backwards and forwards the whole length of the barrier, which was hung with green cloth; when he came to the boxes where the King and Queen were, as profoundly as he was able, he made his reverence before them. And when the King saw the awfulness of Saintré, he said to his people, "Truly this Squire, as well in everything he does, as in everything he says, shows himself a man of a wonderful ascendancy. Truly he has been nourished at the Court and fount of honour." And the like said the Queen, and all the Ladies present: there was not one that was not lost in wonder, and the most part fell to to pray for him. Then stately and measuredly he walked to the head of the lists, from whence, placing his lance upon his thigh, he gallopped to the other end, and then back again. Then the King sent for Sir Enguerrant, who, to be short, did the same as Saintré. And when they had each retreated to their respective ends, the King told them, "that they had now to do what had brought them into that field."

CHAPTER XXXVI.

How Saintré made the sign of the cross three times before he couched his lance: then, how the two champions encountered valiantly.—And how, the first day, the King made Enguerrant retire the first from the lists; saying, that Saintré had won for that day.

THE AUTHOR, ON THE FIRST DAY.

THEN Saintré, who was holding his banner, began again to make the sign of the cross, and three times to say his benediction. Then lowering their lances, as hard as their horses would carry them, they made for one another. At the second course, the point of Sir Enguerrant's lance slipped against the venew of Saintré; and Saintré struck him at the bottom of his vambrace; and, in breaking his lance, swerved a little. And as the lance being broken, trumpets, to deafen one, began to sound. At the third course, Sir Enguerrant, who had too far lowered his lance, broke it on Saintré's saddlebow, and Saintré carried off the golden stag from Sir Enguerrant's helmet. Then the trumpets began again to blow; but because the lance had not been properly broken, the King desired them to stop. At the fourth course, the said Sir Enguerrant took him full in the breast, and admirably broke his lance; and Saintré wounded him on the shoulder, and his lance slipping, entered between the gauntlet and his arm, which became so benumbed, that, for four days, they were unable to renew their arms. At the same time, Saintré broke his lance; but as it was near the head, it was not counted. Then the King ordered the letters to be read, declaring that either was to wait upon the other eight days after. He then gave orders that each of them was to return to his hotel, and that they were to retire armed, saving only the head. But the King wished so far to honour Saintré, that he made Sir Enguerrant retire the first, saying, "that Saintré had remained master of the field."

CHAPTER XXXVII.

How the King sent for the two champions to sup with him.—And how, on the following day, they returned to the lists, performing prodigies, one upon the other.

THE AUTHOR.

AND when they were each unarmed, and had rested themselves, and Sir Enguerrant had had his hand attended to, the King sent for them to sup with him. And he placed Saintré on his right hand, as being a stranger, and Sir Enguerrant on his left, as a subject; the said Sir Enguerrant having his hand bound, and in a sling. And when the tables were removed, the King sent for the Queen and the Ladies. And then the dances began; and the Queen chose Saintré, and the other Ladies and Gentlewomen took the Knights and Squires who had come with him. And Saintré was commended by every body, man and woman, present. Sir Enguerrant, also, on his part, did what he could to honour and to entertain Saintré. And in this manner he was feasted till Sir Enguerrant was recovered. And on the fourth day, to complete their arms, the King ordered that they were to be in their places, all armed, as on the former occasion. And so they came, their heads only bare; and as well they, as their horses, were entirely new caparisoned. And as soon as they were in the lists, the King desired them to do well what they had to do. Then, couching their spears, they spurred their horses one against the other. At this fifth course, Sir Enguerrant took Saintré on the chest, exactly on the shoulder-blade; and Saintré him, full upon his helmet. And they each shivered their lances, so that the splinters flew into the air; and it was as much as the horses could do to keep their legs. Then the trumpets began to sound, and the people to shout, as though they would never stop; for both the lances had been fairly broken. At the sixth course Sir Enguerrant struck him again, exactly in the same place, and Saintré him * * , and each of them broke their lances. Thus each had broken his three lances. At the seventh course, as they were crossing their lances, Sir Enguerrant's horse shied, and so nothing came of it. At the eighth course, when his horse saw Saintré's coming, he wheeled right round; and if Saintré had not instantly raised his lance, he would infallibly have pierced Sir Enguerrant in the back. And for this address the King, and Queen, and all the company loudly praised him. Then Sir Euguerrant returned to his tent to change his horse. And when he came back they first lowered their lances, and then made for one another, without, however, encountering. At this eighth course, through the ardour of his horse, which was fresh, Sir Enguerrant raised his lance a little too high, whilst Saintré struck him, so that the lance, in slipping, unriveted all his breastplate; and with the shock Sir Enguerrant was seen terribly to stagger. And so Saintré had fairly broken his four lances, whilst Sir Enguerrant was obliged to withdraw to change his armour. And when they were again in their places, and each one had his lance upon his thigh, they first spurred their horses, as hard as they could, one upon another, and then passed. At this ninth course, as fortune would have it, they crossed lances; and such was the violence with which they met, for the barrier, which was merely a scarlet curtain, hanging between them, was as nothing, that Sir Enguerrant's horse was thrown on his haunches, and that of Saintré had his shoulder driven in. Then Saintré dismounted, and went to his tent to get another, which was a sorrel coloured, and on which he mounted. But on no account, for any urgence they could employ, would he consent to take off his helmet. And when Sir Enguerrant had risen, and returned to his end of the lists, he there waited for Saintré, who speedily appeared. At the eleventh course Sir Enguerrant lowered, a little, his lance and struck him in the fissure of a plate, and Saintré him, upon the buckler, which he drove right before him. And though Sir Enguerrant was slightly stunned, they each honourably broke their lances. However, Sir Enguerrant had only broken four, but as Saintré had shivered five to splinters, all the trumpets began so to blow, and the people to shout, that it was a long while before they stopped. And as, with this round, the v lances of Saintré had been broken, which was the number fixed on by the terms of Saintré's letter, Sir Enguerrant, who clearly saw that the honour of the day remained with Saintré, asked him, "If he would care to break a lance in honour of the Ladies?" to which Saintré said, "He was well content." And when the King heard that they were about to break a lance in honour of the Ladies, he sent to them, and forbid them, as they had first to perform their arms on foot. And then he ordered them each, exactly as they were, to appear before him. And when they were come, he desired them both to disarm. Then, by his King-at-arms, whom he had made to mount into his box, he had the following proclamation read.

CHAPTER XXXVIII.

How the Herald-at-arms pronounced the decision of the victory; that Saintré had gained it.—Of the prizes and courtesies exchanged between them; and of their leaving the lists.

THE DECISION TOUCHING THE ARMS.

"YOU two noble Lords, here present, and whose names I have not to mention, my Lord the King has been witness to your magnificent assaults, so happily and so vigorously contested, that better could no man living have acquitted himself, and which now I will recall." Then, course by course, and step by step, he read the notes of the whole eleven courses. Then he continued; "But seeing that up to the last course, you had each, alike, broken your four lances, but that in it the most noble Squire, Jehan de Saintré, broke his fifth, the said noble Squire, Jehan de Saintré is declared, by so having done, to have closed the assault by lance; and the Lord, the King, adjudges to him the prize." Then Sir Enguerrant made for Saintré to restore to him the ruby. But when Saintré saw him coming, as quick as he could he turned his courser towards him, and approached to meet him. Then, humbly bowing to him, he took him by the hand; and then embracing him, as well as he could, he said, "My Lord, and my brother, from the bottom of my heart, and with all the earnestness I can, I thank you for the great honour you have done me. Then Sir Enguerrant, like a thoughtful and courteous Knight, replied, "What, my brother, is this you are telling me? It is I who should thank you, for you have right soundly beaten me. And I pray to God, and to my Lord St. George, that you may have the grace, as you have begun, so to continue. And to your lovely Lady, to whose favour you are aspiring, you will humbly recommend me. All this company here present being witness to my words, I now renounce all claim to this ruby, which she has been the means of fairly winning you; begging that she will accept this, my acknowledgment, in good part. Then Saintré, bowing, took the princely ruby, and having kindly thanked him, continued, "No, my Lord, and my brother, it is to you, solely, that I owe my victory, who, through your courtesy, refused to put forth your strength. But, that your ever-to-be desired Lady may not be defrauded of her rights, I have to request, that you will be good enough to recommend me to her, and to take to her, and give her this little diamond." And when Sir Enguerrant saw, at once, the great and lustrous diamond, and Saintré's airy, open, and bewitching manner, he turned to the other Lords near him, and said in his Catelan, "and truly, of young people, this young fellow is the very flower." Then he said to Saintré, "Allow me, Sir, to thank you, as well on her Ladyship's account as on my own, and as gratefully as though I had accepted it and she had had it. But, for this once, you must pardon me, for I will not deprive you of it. More fitting you should bestow it upon her who so richly has deserved it, and is entitled to it." And so urgently did Saintré press him, and so steadily did Sir Enguerrant decline, that, at last, the King took notice of it, and asked, "What it was, was between them." And when he came to know, as did the Queen, it need hardly be inquired what they, the Lords, the Ladies, the Knights, the Gentlewomen, the Squires, as everybody else, thought of Saintré. However, the King, perceiving how much Saintré's heart was set on it, desired Sir Enguerrant to take it, seeing it was out of civility that it was offered to him. Then Sir Enguerrant took it. Then the trumpets and the minstrels began to sound; and the King ordered them to go and disarm. Then was it the wish of each to be permitted the honour of escorting the other, and many entreaties passed between them. But at last Sir Enguerrant prevailed; and, the more amply to show his respect, placing himself by his side, he took him by the right hand. And when they had reached Saintré's hotel, Saintré urged everything he could think of, or was able, to be allowed to reconduct him; and he had certainly done it had not the Lords, as well on the one side as the other, prevented him. Then Saintré pressed the Lords, his counsellors, with others, to sup with him; but for no consideration would they agree to it. So they all left him to repose himself for the night, as did they also Sir Enguerrant. And on the following day they were to perform on foot. But the King, like a thoughtful, wise and gracious Prince, and Lord, determined with himself, that, after such a day they were entitled to one to refresh themselves.

CHAPTER XXXIX.

How Saintré, after he had heard mass, sent by two Heralds-at-arms two axes to Sir Enguerrant, as required by the terms of his challenge.—And after, how the King sent his Herald to signify to Saintré the hour he was to be at the lists.

THE AUTHOR.

ON the second day after, being the one fixed for their arms on foot, Saintré, before proceeding to do anything else, heard a mass of the Holy Spirit, and called for his benediction. Then, by two heralds and a varlet, he sent two axes to Sir Enguerrant, covered up, to take his choice, as were the terms of his engagement. And when he had chosen one and returned the other, the heralds met the Arragon King-at-arms, who was going first to Saintré, from the King, to tell him that, at two o'clock in the afternoon, he was to be at the lists to perform the arms on foot. And when he had most humbly thanked the

King, through the herald, he gave the said herald a costly mantle of crimson damask, trimmed with silver and lined with martin, for the great and joyous news he brought him. Then the herald went and made his report to the King.

THE AUTHOR.

And when one in the afternoon had struck, the King, with the Queen, to be in readiness, were mounted in their boxes. Then he sent to the two parties, that they should appear. Then Saintré, foremost, as the challenger, appellant, and not appellee, got upon his horse, and taking his banner in his hand, and making with it the greater sign of the cross, and repeating to himself his benediction, and the rest, entered the lists in the following manner.

CHAPTER XL.
How the two champions entered, for the third time, solemnly into the lists.

THE AUTHOR AGAIN.

As with some few and immaterial variations, as to dress and armour, the substance of the opening of this Chapter has already appeared in Chapters XXXIII. and XXXIV.; it is omitted.—*Translator.*

* * * * *

* * * * . Then the King commanded the King-at-arms to call the parties. Then Saintré, accompanied by his Lords and counsellors, came to the entrance of the lists, all on foot. And there was the King's Seneschal, who demanded of him, "Who he was, and what he came there to do?" To whom, smiling, he humbly rejoined. "My Lord Mareschal, I am Jehan de Saintré, and I have come at the day and time appointed by the most mighty Prince, the King, now present, as sole arbitor and judge between my Lord, my brother, Sir Enguerrant de Servillon and myself, in the combat, which, by his appointment, we are about to wage; and as, by my letters, I demanded." And when the Mareschal heard his reply, he went to the King to make his report. Then the King ordered the gate to the lists to be thrown open, so that he might proceed to his tent. And when the gate was opened, he passed, and, taking his banner in his hand, having first made with it the greater sign of the cross, and kissed it, he entered his tent. And, to be short, Sir Enguerrant made his entrance in the like manner. But they had scarcely got to their tents before the Mareschal, followed by four guards, one after the other, appeared. And beginning with Saintré, when they had armed him with all his arms, they took and presented him, surrounded by his assigned counsellors, to the King, who was in his box. And as he was going, he had to pass before the one where the Queen was, and all the other Ladies. Then Saintré, bowing himself, humbled himself on his knees before them. Then might you have seen them wildly clasp their hands, and crying to God to shield him and protect him. And presently after, Sir Enguerrant appeared. Then Saintré, lowly saluting him, which, however, was not the custom, said to him, " My Lord, my brother, without wishing any prejudice to any, I pray God he send you success and honour.' " And as much to you, my brother," said Sir Enguerrant. Then they both went on their knees before the King. Then the King ordered the Seneschal to make them take the customary oaths. Then the Mareschal made them swear, upon the holy Evangelists, "that, as they believed, in a God, on their lives, and on their honours, they neither had put about them, nor did they believe to be about them, either charm, herb, incantation, enchantment, conjuration, or any other sort of sorcery, or devilish invention, either for their own preservation, or the detriment of their antagonist—that there was no ground of jealousy, or quarrel between them; but that all was done to purchase to themselves honour and renown, and the ever-to-be-desired grace of their ever-lovely Ladies." These oaths taken, they each got up, and made for their tents. But when Saintré rose, before going away, he made again his reverence, first to the King, and then to the Queen and the Ladies, as he had already done. Then they each went to their tents to have their beavers closed.

CHAPTER XLI.
How they issued from their tents to perform their Arms.

WHEN they were each ready, and, to be short, the usual proclamations and defences had been made, the King commanded that they were to be told to come forth from their tents; but in leaving, Saintré, having opened his vizor, kissed his banner, repeating, the while, the benediction that Madame had taught him. Then, making with it the greater sign of the cross, he kissed it a second time, and then handed it to one of his counsellors. Then he lowered his vizor, and began, in all his harness, to wield his arms, stoop, skip, rise, fall, turn, back, bound, and all as readily as if he had been in his shirt, holding all the time his axe in his hand. And when they were both out of their tents, and their tents out of the lists, then, by ordinance of the King, the Mareschal, in the middle of the lists, began to cry, with a loud voice, "Let them go!"

CHAPTER XLII.
How they marched one against the other; each doing valiantly.

AND when the Mareschal had given them leave to go, as they advanced one upon the other, you had thought they had been two lions unchained. But there was this difference; as Saintré was making for him, he cried aloud, so that all might hear him, "Hah, my ever-gentle dame, and whose I am!" and then they began to fall upon one another. Then Sir Enguerrant, who was a most valiant Knight, strong and powerful, and larger built than Saintré, raised his axe, and dealt him such a blow upon the shoulder that he made him reel, while Saintré, in return, struck him with the handle of his axe upon the bars of his vizor, driving him several paces back. Then Sir Enguerrant elevated his axe to strike a second time; but Saintré, making for him, gave him such a cut over the hand with the sharp of his axe, that neither guard nor anything else could avail, so that all his fingers were smashed and benumbed. Sir Enguerrant, who was now hot, nor knew anything of what had happened to his fingers, thought again to lift his axe, and it was only then he began to feel the pain, and that he could no longer wield it. So, as a wary and a dauntless Knight, holding his axe in his left hand, he opened his arms to seize Saintré by the waist. But when Saintré perceived his aim, * * * * * * * * he continued to strike, nor ever once let him approach. And when he saw his moment, all on a sudden he gave him such a blow on the hand in which he was holding the axe, that he sent it flying in the air; and when Sir Enguerrant saw that his axe was gone, in sheer desperation he rushed upon Saintré, to close with him, catching him by one arm. But when the King saw the axe of Sir Enguerrant upon the ground, and the two together by the middle, as Prince and Judge sovereign, he at once threw down his wardour, and said, "Ho, ho!" Then were the two champions separated by the guards. Then the King, by the Mareschal, called the two champions before him, and then had said to them, "You, Sir Enguerrant, and you, Jehan de Saintré, the King desires you should know, that you have each so nobly and so valiantly acquitted yourselves that it would have been impossible to have done better; but, according to the articles, the Lord, the King, who here is, has recognized that the combat was to end either when one or other of you were borne to the ground, or either had lost his axe from both his hands. So, by the terms, Jehan de Saintré, the Lord, the King, adjudges to you the prize."

Then the King commanded them both, they being on their knees, to rise, and to take off their helmets. And when Saintré understood the decision and sentence of the King, as humbly as he could he thanked him, saying, "Ha, most excellent and puissant Prince, for the honour you have done me by your sentence, as humbly as I can find words to thank you, I do; but as to the prize, which you have said is to be mine, as humbly as I can, I crave that you will a little reconsider your award, and recall the manner in which my Lord, my brother, who here is, belaboured me with his axe. And as for any little advantage that I may have had over him, Sir, you must have clearly seen that it came only by the merest accident."

At such a speech from Saintré every one who heard him was amazed, and all tongues were loosed in his praise; each one striving who most could extol him.[6] And however much they might naturally lean to Sir Enguerrant as their countryman, they could not help admitting that Saintré was the *Mountjoy* and the very nonpareil of all honour, condescension, and of humility; and the King in his box, and all those who were with him, were quite astonished, as were the Queen, Madame Elinor de Cardonne, wife to the said Sir Enguerrant, and all the other Princesses, Countesses, Baronesses, Ladies, and Gentlewomen that were in the Queen's box; and they all began to praise him unmeasuredly. And Sir Enguerrant himself, to those who were about him, could not refrain from saying, "Just listen to him; is it not royal the way he talks? Who is there alive but him, or who was there ever lived that would thus waive so high an honour, or recede but from the slightest of his right, out of mere delicacy toward an antagonist?"

All this time the King, who was in a sort of reverie, lost in admiration with all this praise of Saintré, quite forgot that he had left him on his knees, which, at last observing, he hurriedly bade him rise, and then said, " Jehan de Saintré, as to what you have desired me to reconsider, I have reconsidered; and that all the world may know the grace and the honour that God has done you, I cannot depart or retreat from anything."

Then the King desired Sir Enguerrant to deliver up his axe; and, when he was disarmed, to fulfil the remaining part of their engagement. Then Sir Enguerrant called for his axe, and, taking it in his maimed hand, as well as he could, with the assistance of the other, he courteously handed it to Saintré, saying, "My brother, I here give you your axe, and for the rest it shall be all discharged, conformably as in your letter of arms is contained; praying to God, and to my Lord St. George that, more and more, may you increase in honour."

And when Saintré had heard the orders of the King, and the handsome words of Sir Enguerrant, he called for his bracelet, which one of his people was holding; then, having taken the axe, and bowing to Sir Enguerrant, he said, " My Lord, my brother, seeing such is the good pleasure of the King, I submit to it; but, personally, towards yourself, who have so richly merited otherwise, I must be allowed to hold myself discharged and nonconsentant. I must give you this bracelet, entreating you most sincerely that you will kindly accept of it."

On hearing this, Sir Enguerrant and all the rest were even more astonished than they had been, and Sir Enguerrant said to him, " Ha, my brother, Jehan de Saintré, is there never to be an end of your condescensions! As for the bracelet, for the honour which you do me, I thank you from my heart, but accept it I cannot. It must assuredly be restored to your lovely Lady."

And seeing them in words, the King called to know what it was they were protesting about. Then the Mareschal said, "Sir, it is Jehan de Saintré here, who will absolutely insist on Sir Enguerrant's having the bracelet, exactly as if he had won or gained the prize!"

"The bracelet!" returned the King; then he turned towards the Princes and other Lords that were with him, and said, "What do you say to the courteousness and the valiancy of this, so young a Squire? I, for one, never saw the like."

"Nor did we either," said they. "And it is easy to be seen that he is come of a generous stock, and that he has had his wits about him, and turned all that was going on to account in the noble Court where he was born and bred, and as much for that matter may be said of all those that are with him."

Then the King desired him to keep his bracelet to himself. And when Saintré heard the King, he said to him, on his knees, "At the least, Sir, grant that I may otherwise dispose of it."

"Any where else," said the King, "readily. The bracelet is your own, do what you like with it. But we would not have it thought or said that it was through us, or by our orders, that it was given."

"Sir," said Saintré, "I am obliged to you."

Then he called to him the Arragon and Touraine Kings-at-arms, and Lusignan the herald, who had come with him; and to the King-at-arms he gave the bracelet, and then sent the three to Madame de Cardonne, wife to Sir Enguerrant, who was in the box with the Queen, desiring them to tell her "that he most humbly commended himself to her, and that as it was she, as he could not but know, who, the most righteously was entitled to the bracelet, he had to beg and pray of her, on the part of his ever-to-be-redoubted Lady, who had given it to him, that she would be pleased, out of an esteem and regard for her, to accept it; excusing her that it was neither so rich nor so matchless as it were befitting to such an one to be tendered."

If the Queen, Madame Elinor, and the other Princesses and Ladies who were with her, and the King, who was in his box on her right, and all the Lords with him were amazed, I leave you to think; no words could picture their astonishment. Then Madame Elinor, to the Kings-at-arms and heralds, replied, "Kings-at-arms and you others, heralds, my friends: the most generous and valiant Squire de Saintré, I thank; but, with his permission, it is not I who have either won or merited this bracelet for him, as he alleges; but it is another who has purchased for him the honours and distinctions of this day, and for this reason you are to take it back to him, and tell him that he must pardon me."

And when the Queen, as a wise and thoughtful Lady, heard her excuse, she said to her, "Really, fair Cousin, this is not the kind of thing to refuse, and from so accomplished a gentleman as this is. I request and insist on your taking it."

Then Madame Elinor bowed to the decision of the Queen, and the Queen herself undertook to fasten it on her left arm. And when the bracelet was on her arm, she took from her necklace a handsome locket which was hanging from it (it was a large pearl of five carats, bordered with three large and beautiful diamonds, and three great rubies), and giving it to the King-at-arms, said to him, "You, and you, heralds, here present: this little trifle, which I now give to you, you are to present to this most gentle and generous Squire, Jehan de Saintré, on my part, recommending me in all kindness to him. And you will tell him that, although by rights the bracelet should rather pertain to his most fair and gracious Lady than to myself; nevertheless, to satisfy him, it shall be kept, and that I doubt not but so worthy and so good a Lady will requite to him all the honour which, this day, he has acquired. And this little trinket you will present to him, requesting him, with my regards, to be good enough to give it to her."

These words exchanged, and jewels offered and accepted, the King, when he came to hear of it, was well pleased. Then he ordered that they both should be disarmed. Then each one returned to his own tent to mount his horse, and when Saintré was in his saddle, he presently made for Sir Enguerrant, who, through the pain that he was suffering, was obliged to be attended. And when he saw Saintré coming, he said to him, "Ho, ho, brother, brother! and is it thus your Lady then requires you to lay on with those who game with you?"

And when they were both mounted, then were there great prayers between them, as to which of them was to be allowed the honour of following the other. But the King, who knew well that the precedence was due to Saintré, instantly desired that they were to retire side by side; but that Saintré, as he had gained the prize, was to be on the right. Then they departed for their hotels exactly as they had arrived; but, in separating, there were again great prayers, for each insisted on seeing his companion home. And when the King saw the prayers, he immediately sent to them to say that they were to have no more of those ceremonies, but each one to take his own road. Then they took leave of one another, and went each to his hotel, to disarm and repose himself for the rest of the day, till supper-time, when the Queen sent for them, when, to be brief, were excellent wines, victuals, dishes, and side dishes, and all on the grandest scale. Then were they with singing, dancing, *à la Moresque*, and after other fashions, right royally entertained. And now I will forbear to speak of the great honours, of the dinners and the suppers which the King, the Queen, and other Lords and Ladies gave to Saintré, and Saintré to them, and will turn to the farewell that he took, and the presents which were made on the one part and on the other.

CHAPTER XLIII.
How Saintré took leave of the King and Queen, and of all those of the Court; and of the presents that were made.

AND when Saintré had fulfilled his arms, in the manner you have heard, he remained two days at Barcelona, feasting and making merry. And on the fourth day he took his leave of the King, the Queen, the Lords, the Ladies and Gentlewomen of the Court, as also of the other Princes, Princesses, Ladies of the provinces, who had come to see his arms, which were then thought much more of than they are at present. And it was the pleasure of the King and Queen, that, for this once, the custom of the country should be departed from in favour of Saintré, and the Knights and Squires of his party; that is, that they should all be kissed by the Ladies. And the Queen herself determined to set the example, for she kissed Saintré first, then all the Knights and Squires of his company. Then all the other Ladies did the like; which, till then, had never been done, and never has been done since, excepting only in especial cases, as those of alliance. And at this farewell, on either side, was many a sorry *Alas!* for, already in the gentle breast of many a Lady and of Knight were kindled and were struck those tender sparks, which quited love alone can cover or can quench. And however much they might try to laugh it off, and smile amid their tears, they could not so command themselves but they came trickling down their cheeks. And when it was all over, and his baggage trussed, he sent to the King the finest and the most powerful of his four war-horses, covered with the richest housings that he had, and on him was a beautiful and dapper little page, his own proper nephew * * * *

The remainder of this Chapter is omitted, as it consists of a mere dry detail of the presents exchanged between the Court and Saintré. —*Translator.*

CHAPTER XLIV.

How Saintré, accompanied by all the Lords, departed from Barcelona, on his way for France.

This Chapter, possessing no sort of new interest, is passed over.— *Translator.*

CHAPTER XLV.

How Saintré and his companions came; and of the good reception which they met with from the King, the Queen, Madame, and the rest.

AND when Saintré had got to his first night's lodging, on the evening of the day he had left Barcelona ; as he was turning over how he might, the most becomingly, apprise Madame of all he had done, and how matters had gone, and he was coming back ; he thought that it would hardly do to send one of the heralds, for people would say that he had done it through vanity, and so he might bring himself into envy and trouble. And so he determined to consult with Sir Guillaume de Prouilly, as one whom he could trust, which Prouilly told him, that certainly, it would be better taste that such news should be announced by some other than the herald, even although it was legitimately his business; and that he would not any more advise him to write, himself, to King, or Queen, or anybody else.

"But," said he, "if you like, I will send my cousin, Guillaume; or, what will be better, I will write in my own name to the King, the Queen, and all the Ladies of honour, all that has happened; and Guillaume, who has been with us all through, can enlarge on everything, and confirm to them its truth."

And so they did. And when the King, the Queen, and all the other Ladies, and especially Madame, knew it, there was jubilee everywhere; nor, for several days, was there almost anything else spoken of. Every one was longing for his return. And Madame, from the day of his departure, had hardly ever a moment, day or night, relaxed from her prayers and orisons; nor ever once from following her promised vow, never to wear next her naked flesh any linen, either on the Friday or Saturday, till such time as she had been assured of his safety. And when she had first heard the news, how, at the Court of Arragon, he was to be delivered by a Knight, with the consent of the King; over and above her vow, she engaged herself to have masses said every Wednesday, and to give in alms to the value of ten écus; and besides, to go quietly on pilgrimages about the town;[7] and in this discipline she never failed to exercise herself, especially about the time when the news of the battle might be expected to arrive. And at the very moment when Guillaume de Prouilly, sent by his Uncle, arrived, she was on her knees. And when Madame heard these long-wished-for news, which Isabelle came running to tell her, and had made her repeat it to her, incontinent raising her eyes to heaven, she thanked her Saviour. Then hurrying to her chamber, she threw herself on her naked knees, and, with clasped hands, devoutly thanked God. What need I say more?

Such was her delight, and her ecstacy, that, on the one hand, it was as much as ever she could do to keep, for a moment, quiet: and, on the other, so passionately did she long to see him, that neither day nor night could she be still; so that all her rapture was well nigh turned to pain. And now, for the present, I will give over to speak of how all her great delight was changed into anguish, out of her ardent desire to see him; and will tell you of his arrival at the Court, and of the great honour and good cheer that awaited him.

CHAPTER XLVI.

How Saintré, by dint of journeying, made his appearance before the King, and of the honours and good cheer which were made him; and how Madame's heart was cured.

AND when Saintré and his company had arrived, by their stages, at about two leagues from Paris, they there found many a good Knight, Squire, Citizen, with others of the Court and of the city, who had come to meet him, to honour him, and escort him into the town; so much was he loved of all. Then was there such congratulation, on either side, that it was a perfect pleasure to look on. And when he had made his reverence to the King, and to the Queen, who were delighted to see him back, he then went to Madame, who, from the state she was in could hardly keep herself within bounds. However, like a wary Lady as she was, her agonies she stifled as best she could. Then he went to the rest, who all gave him the kindest reception; and kissed him every one. Then, in honour of his return, the Queen called for dancing. And when the Ladies were all dancing, Madame, who was with the Queen, said to her, "Hey, Madame, surely Saintré has had enough of dancing in Arragon; and, besides, he must be tired; for God's sake call him here, and make him sit down quietly among ourselves, and ask him about the manners and appearance of the Ladies of Arragon."

"Faith, fair Cousin," said the Queen, "you are right."

Then the Queen sent for Saintré, and besides, called three other Ladies to her. Then she said to Saintré, "Saintré, good friend, you must rest yourself;" then to the other three Ladies, "Now sit you all down, and the most good-natured must be our spokesman."

Madame, for one, that she might be the better able to feast her eyes upon him, made up her mind, that she, whoever else might, was not to be the most good-natured; and so she conveniently contrived not to hear. Then the Queen, herself, began to interrogate Saintré, as to everything about his arrival at the Court of Arragon, and of the reception he had met with from the King, the Queen, and all the Lords, and especially of that of the Ladies. Then she asked him all about his arms, as well on horse as on foot; and after that, of the beauty, customs, and the dresses of the Ladies; in all which Saintré satisfied her; negligently passing, however, as became him, whatever regarded himself or his arms. And the little he did say of them, was rather to the credit of Sir Enguerrant than of himself. For the other matters, he extolled the Ladies to the skies, from whatever point of view he considered them; as did he also the King, and all the Court: in fact, more was impossible.

And now, for the present, I will give over to speak of the ceremonies, the honours, and the triumphs whereof he was cross-questioned by the Queen and the Ladies, and I will tell you of the transcendant joy of Madame, and of the good cheer she made him; and of how she fed her eyes upon him, from time to time; that is, as often as she could.

THE AUTHOR.

Madame, when all this examination was going on, as if her thoughts were elsewhere, or she was thinking of nothing, first of all looking one way, then another; then this direction, then that, all of a sudden darted her piteous glance upon him; then, whipping her bodkin from her breast, she began to pick her teeth, for that was their signal. And when Saintré saw Madame's signal, incontinent, he replied by rubbing his right eye. And thus, in this ecstatic agony, passed these two true lovers' hearts this never ending and most tedious day long, even till the shades of night set in, and the hour appointed between them had come, when they met in the garden. Then they commenced to congratulate, and each to entertain the other; and many were the kisses given, and many were the kisses taken. And there were all their joys. There was every thought of their heart exchanged, and there was every trouble healed. And in all this felicity they remained from eleven of the clock till the second hour after midnight, when, needs was, they must part. And at present I will forbear to further speak of their perfect delight, and I will turn to the advancement of Saintré, and to acquaintance which he made with Bouciqualt the first of the name.

———•◦•———

CHAPTER XLVII.
Here tells how Saintré became Chamberlain to the King, and of the alliances between him, and Myngre, otherwise Bouciqualt.

AND so much, and in so little a time, did he increase in honour, that the King, who so dearly loved Saintré, as you have heard, had him first to sleep in his chamber, and next to be his chief chamberlain. And Saintré, who had perfectly retained in his memory the inculcations of Madame, when, in his infancy she had instilled into him the seeds of virtue and of good manners, had never forgotten the saying of Albertus:—

> Non tua claudatur ad vocem pauperis auris;

nor yet the inimitable verses of Aristotle, who says likewise:—

> Vir bonè qui curas res viles res perituras.
> Nil profuturas, dampno quandoque futuras.
> Nemo diu mansit in crimine sed cito transit.
> Et brevis atque levis in mundo gloria quevis;

nor any other of the pithy sentences touching those who had risen to a prominent position. So that, despite all this countenance that he had from the King, never once was his heart lifted up, nor were his manners changed; but, to every one, he continued urbane and gracious, as he had ever been. And about this time there was in the Court a certain young Squire, of the Duchy of Touraine, exceedingly comely, and who, in sport, was called Bouciqualt; grandfather of the Bouciqualts now living: a young person, for his years, exceeding subtle, bold, resolute, and standing high in the good opinion of the King. And this Bouciqualt, seeing Saintré to be also so, and more regarded of him than any of the others, determined to be acquainted with him. Whilst Saintré, who, besides, that he was young, seeing him to be a man as resolved as himself, as well as of his own country, readily met his advances; and in a short time, they became so intimate, and so fond of one another, that had they been brothers they could not have been more so. And the King, who had always liked Bouciqualt, was so well pleased to see their familiarity, that he was content to allow him to sleep in the same bed with Saintré; that is to say, when he did not lie with the Queen. What need I say more? These two Squires so took to one another, that never did two brothers love more; and they were, each to the other, so loyal and so true, that misunderstanding or mistrust never once arose between them. And whenever either of them was abroad, whether upon business or for their engagements, or affairs of arms, the other would take his place, so that no one should step in. And though Bouciqualt was a right hardy Knight, and more subtle and experienced than was Saintré; nevertheless, in the field, Saintré was reputed the more daring of the two. And speaking of them, the Heralds and the King-at-arms had a common way of saying, that, *For an assault, Saintré is better worth than Bouciqualt; but when it comes to a parley, Bouciqualt is better worth than Saintré.* That is to say, one was made for arms, the other for counsel. And so it came, that so long as they lived, so long lasted, unbroken, their understanding and attachment.

And now I will say no more of these two, but will turn to the other new arms which were performed between Saintré and the Lord de Loiselench, a Polish Baron, whose arms were * *; which combat took place, at Paris, before the King, the Queen, Madame, and other Lords and and Ladies, innumerable.

CHAPTER XLVIII.
How Madame desired Saintré to deliver the Polish Baron from the enterprise he had undertaken.

The first portion of this chapter is omitted, as, in its general character, the engagement of the Pole was the counterpart of that already given, of Saintré, at Barcelona.—*Translator.*

THE AUTHOR.

*   *   *   *   *

AND when Madame had read the challenge, as it was announced; without so much as losing a moment, she sent for Saintré. And then as quietly, and as shortly as she could, she said to him, " My friend, at length the day has come, which God and fortune have been preparing for you; to bring you unto honour, and that you may be exalted. This Polish Knight has come, and has published his Arms; and so I have to beg of you, with all the earnestness I can, that you will be the first with my Lord, the King, with the request to be allowed to deliver him. And as for the expense, let not that trouble your head, for God and we will provide withal. And in this you will oblige me, as my very dearest friend, my all in all to me. And though I, who entreat you thus, am the one, above all others, who should the rather seek to turn you from it; the most affray you of such mortal perils; nevertheless, so much have I your reputation and your fame at heart, that I would wish you to show yourself on every occasion, as well the most courageous, as the most ready; trusting that God will bring you off with honour."

And when Saintré saw the earnestness of Madame, and how passionately her soul was set on it, he immediately fell on his knees, and humbly thanked her, and said, "Ever-to-be-redoubted Lady; on the love I bear, and on the fealty I owe you, your thoughts were my thoughts, for I was already contriving how we could meet about it."

"Then away with you, this instant," said she, "so that none be before you."

Then, in all haste, he went after the King; and when he was on his knees, he made his prayer in such a manner as was becoming. Hearing him, the King, who liked him greatly, looked at him, half incredulous and amazed, to see so young a man, and of so slight a build, proposing to measure himself with this Polish Knight. And presently he said to him, "And Saintré, are you quite sure you are aware of what it is you are about?"

"Sir," said he, "yes; and from the first moment that I saw him, I have had no other thought."

And while they were speaking, in came the Viscount de Beaumont, making the same request to the King. And while the words were in his mouth, in followed the Lord de Craon, on the same errand ; and on the back of him, the Lord de Vergy ; then the Viscount de Quesnes, the Lord de Harcour, the Lord de Hangest, with several of the others ; all upon the same business.

Then the King said to them, " My Lords and friends ; first come have the first claim. You see here Saintré, before you all, and still on his knees. And though, unquestionably he is not of your years, our Lord is the God alike of the strong and of the weak, of the old and of the young. And as much as He is for the strong, so much is He for the weak ; and as much as He is for the young, so much is He for the old. And for this reason, it seems to us, that it would be offering him an injustice to deny him, seeing how much his heart is set on it."

Then they all rose, allowing to the reasonableness of his will and pleasure ; and better satisfied to find Saintré chosen than they had been to see one of themselves. Then Saintré, as humbly as he could, thanked the King And, for the following day, the King requested the company of the Lord de Loyselench, the other four Barons, and Knights and Squires who were with them. And all sorts of honours were paid them. And after dinner, and that they had danced with the Ladies, the Queen, who was present, most condescendingly entertained them ; inquiring of them, through interpreters, about the Ladies, and the manners of their country ; and telling them, how vexed she was to be unable to understand them. And when the dances were over, and before the dessert, and the stirrup-cup had been handed round, the French Mountjoy King-at-arms, by order of the King, read the letter-of-arms ; present the Queen, Lords, Ladies in plenty. And when the letter was read, Mountjoy demanded of the said Knight, " Were he the party who had written that letter, and did he allow to it ?"

And when what was asked had been explained to the said Knight, he answered, "That that was his seal; and that all which was in it, he had come to make good."

Then Saintré went on his knees before the King, and made him confirm his licence. Then he rose and said to the Knight, "My Lord, you are very welcome; and, with the grace of God, our Lady; and of my Lord, Saint Michael;[8] I will release you from your vow, and from the hoops and the chains in which you are fettered."

And then he advanced to remove the hoops. And when the Knight saw Saintré, so young and slight-looking, taking himself to be trifled with, he stepped back, saying to his people, in his Polish, "And is this the way I am to be delivered; surely there must be another sort of man in such a Court as this?"

Then it was explained to him, who he was, and how high he stood in the graces of the King; and how he had already fought in Arragon, as well on horse as on foot; and how, on both occasions, he had come off with honour. Then looking at him again, closely, he presently said, "If such is the case, I have no right to take exception: since he wishes it, let it stand: such men are often more formidable than those of twice their appearance."

Then it was told to Saintré, that he had deliberated to go through with it; and that he was to do as the letter required; and that the Knight thanked him with all his heart. Then Saintré removed the fetters and chains; and this done, the King appointed the thirtieth day from that for the combat on horseback; and then he withdrew to his chamber. Then Saintré, carrying the two fetters of gold; the one before, and the other behind, with the chain around his neck; together with the rest of the company, conducted the said Knight to his hotel.

And now I will give over to speak of the great honours, and of the good cheer which were made him, as long as

L

he was there, and I will tell you of all the piteous sorrows of Madame's heart, and of all the touching things she said to Saintré.

CHAPTER XLIX.
How Madame bemoaned herself to Saintré, and of the tender things she said to him.

MADAME, who, till the time the hoops were taken off, had never seen the Knight, when she came to find him so tall and big of bone, was so terribly frightened, and so repented her of what she had been spiriting on poor Saintré to, that all her peace of mind was gone. But seeing the length to which matters had proceeded, and that there was no way of getting out of it, she found that there was nothing left for her, day nor night, but to bewail and to bemoan herself. And as she wept, she cried, "Alas, wretched I, and what hast thou done; what were you thinking of when you thus put it in his head, and deliberately goaded on to all these extremities, the man, of all men, whom you loved the best; you, too, who should have been the first to dissuade him from all such foolery. Alas, he is pitted with a man, such an adept, so large, so powerful, that the stoutest might well think twice. What is to become of me? for, either let him fall, be wounded in his person, or his honour, which, heaven defend—broken, embittered, lost, never again shall this poor heart know peace. And what is worse than all this, peradventure he will detest you; and, conscience tells you, not without a cause. Though true it is, that I never prayed for anything more than to see him famous among the paladins, the great, the good, the virtuous of the land. And to the truth of this, O my God, I call thee to witness, as also thy blessed Mother, to whom I dedicate him, [9] armed with all his armour, on his war-horse, the whole weighing three thousand pounds; here on my knees, and with clasped hands, imploring of you, O Virgin, that, in safety and in honour, he may be brought back to me." And when Madame had ended her prayers, she came to where the Queen was; and, in a little, she perceived Saintré. Then she made her signal; and Saintré, who, on his side, was no less anxious to speak with her, as instantly replied to her. And when the night was come, and the hour besides, and they were together, Madame, finding him all radiant, all at once altered her way of thinking, and all her great fear was turned into as great confidence. So she said to him, "Now, my friend, what you have to do, you must do stoutly and commendably, winner or loser. And a fig for the kind of man he is; don't you be alarming yourself because he looks, and is so much bigger and stronger than you are. What, and if he is a giant? remember that there is a God above us all, and that he will be on the side of those, his friends, who are in extremity, and who seek to him with their whole heart. And you have no cause to be under apprehension; for the strong despise the weak, and combat in their pride: whilst the feeble, they look to God for aid, and he gives it, and is for them, be they man, or be they woman. There is no battle was ever gained of other than of God. And if the battle be of those who are, in prowess, or in numbers, equal; and who all, with like heart, seek their aid of God, then will God look well who is in the right; for God is the true judge, and will render unto each one his desert. So, my friend, let come what God will, however much or little it may be; and though, alongside of you, he may topple, a very giant, in no case can any disgrace come of your failure; for I have heard it said, by those who understand these matters, that the gentleman who gratuitously engages himself, that is, without malice or quarrel, even though he gets the worst of it, is for all that more to be considered than he was before ; for, albeit men fight, it is God who gives the victory, and to whom he will. And as for the expense and your clothes, his entertainment, all that is my affair. Here is a purse with six thousand écus; let them be employed as they should be, and God be with you."

THE AUTHOR.

Saintré, who saw the love of Madame towards him, to increase from day to day, as handsomely as he could, thanked her. To be short, he then took leave of her; and such was his delight, with this new prospect before him, that he never slept a wink that night. And as soon as it was day, and he had heard mass, and had said his prayers, he got to work, and never halted till, with the help of God, of the King, and Madame, he had got him his horses, his clothes, his armour, and everything in order. To tell you, in a word, how he was equipped; it was as a royal Baron. And now I will speak no more of all these things, and of all the noise there was of the coming arms, and of all the prayers that were offered up for him, by reason he was so young, and small, in comparison of this Polish Knight, any one of whose blows one would imagine to be enough to demolish him ; and I will turn to the combat, as was appointed.

CHAPTER L.

How the Lord de Loiselench and Saintré came into the lists, to perform their arms on horseback: present, the King, the Queen, and many Lords and Ladies.

The opening portion of this Chapter is omitted ; offering no sort of entertainment to a modern reader.—*Translator.*

* * * * *

* * *. And after him came Saintré; on his right hand the Duke of Anjou and of Touraine, wishing to show him every honour. And after them followed a crowd of Knights and Squires, who had made up their minds to be with him. And when he came to the entry of the lists, like a good Christian, he made the sign of the cross with his banner, repeating his benediction, as Madame had instructed him. And when Madame saw him, he appeared to her, if possible, even more lovely than he had ever done. And incontinent all her great affection was stirred up again within her, and all her agony and remorse, for all the peril she had been the means of bringing him into, and of which she now repented her; so that, do what she would, she could not so command herself, but that, in a little time, she fainted and she fell. And when the Queen and the other Ladies saw her swoon, as one dead, having no idea of her real malady, so as not to disturb the King, or the rest of the company, they set to to rub her temples and her palms with vinegar, and to apply the usual remedies. And so effectually did they rub her, and attend to her, that, at last, she came round. Then, by degrees, she began to open her eyes, then to look this way, then that; now on one side, now another; then to speak, but only to say, " Ha, support me, O ever blessed Lady!" Then they comforted her as well as they could; but not for anything that the Queen could say or do would she be induced to turn her eyes again toward the lists.

THE AUTHOR.

Saintré now entered the lists, and, smiling to himself, looked up into the King's box, and then into that of the Ladies. And in passing, he removed his cap, and saluted them as lowly as he was able; and when he missed Madame, he was at first taken back. However, he quickly recovered himself, concluding how it was; that Madame simply had not had the heart to see it out, as she had already assured him she never would. * * *

A considerable portion is suppressed here. The usual stereotype amount of compliment, extravagance, courtesy, and blows, is to be found in this account, as in that of every other combat of the times. —*Translator.*

* * * * *

* * * . And when the Queen and the other Ladies saw the Lord de Loisclench to be thus disarmed, they all ran together to Madame, who was lying stretched on some cushions, making her prayers to God, and to our Lady of Leisse, to whom, as has been said, in her passion she had dedicated him. And the Queen said to her, "Really, fair Cousin, you must get up: you have no conception what is going on. Here is fair son, Saintré, has disarmed this Pole; and my Lord has stopped the whole thing, and ordered them both up."

Madame, who, on hearing this, felt as if an incredible load was off her mind, nevertheless pretended not so much as to catch a word. Then the Queen said to her, "By my faith, fair Cousin, you have made it plain enough this day how little it matters to you, had this game young fellow lost or won. However, unfortunately for ourselves, my Lord and I cannot take these things quite so coolly; you would be better in the air than here." Then the Queen took her by one hand, and another Lady by another, and led her to the front of the box.

Presently Madame, who was now beginning to be herself again, availing herself of the reproach the Queen had cast in her teeth, said to her, "Ho, Madame; but how came this giant of a Pole to be disarmed?" Then the Queen told her how it all went, and how Saintré had broken the first lance, and how he had struck the Knight's silver ox, and turned it with the tail forwards, and how he had disarmed him. And when all this was telling, Madame, out of her ecstacy, never once could take her eyes off Saintré. And Saintré kept looking for her in every direction; and at last, on a sudden, his eyes met hers. Then Madame made him her signal, to which, right graciously, he responded. * * *

There is another omission, purposely, at this place.—*Translator.*

The Author.

And in the evening, after they had made their signals, they met in the meadow. Then were kisses scattered and devoured by thousands. Is it not enough? none would believe felicity could be more. Then Madame said to him, "Alas, my joy, my sovereign, and my only weal, at the time I never thought again to see you alive. And when you first came into the lists I was in such a terror to think of you, and my heart so sunk within me, that I fell down as one dead; and I verily do believe, if they had not come to me I should have died upon the spot. But as soon as I heard the famous news, on the instant I was brought to life again: for Madame, with the other Ladies, who came to help me, brought me them." And when Saintré heard her, he said, "Alas, my noble dame, what is this you are telling me? God, had I known this, where had been, in such an hour, this wretched arm of mine! I had rather have died than have failed to acquit myself with honour. But God be praised and be thanked, I knew nothing of all this. When first I entered the lists I saw you with the Queen, among the other Ladies; and afterwards, when I came armed, and missed you, I merely thought that your courage had failed you at the last, as you had told me you were sure it would do, and so I troubled myself no more about it. So, my most redoubted dame, praise be to God, and to our Lady, for the honour which, this day, you have won me; wishing you ever, Madame, more and more felicity. So I beg of you to keep up your spirits, for the God who was with me when I fought on horse will be also for me when I fight on foot." And with these words they took, one of the other, a solemn adieu. And now I will cease to speak of their affairs, and tell you of the other combat, and how it passed.

CHAPTER LI.

How the Lord de Loiselench and Saintré entered the lists, to perform their arms on foot.

The account of this combat is omitted. It is hardly necessary to say, that the address and activity of Saintré prove to be more than a match for the prowess of the Pole.—*Translator*.

*   *   *   *   *

* * * . And now I will say no more of how the prizes were given, and will turn to the incredible joy of the Queen, of Madame, the other Ladies and Gentlewomen, and how Madame took to her devotions.

Then the Queen, and Madame, with the other Ladies and Gentlewomen, never for a moment ceased to laugh and to make themselves merry; so gratified were they, for the sake of Saintré, who had come off the better. And when Madame, who never once could remove her eyes from Saintré, recollected how unmistakeably all this had come through the manifest interposition of our Lord, who had permitted it at the request of our Lady, she thought it but right she should thank him; so, feigning that her head ached, she told the Queen, "that she must pardon her, for she could sit up no longer." To which the Queen replied, "Fair Cousin, by all means, go." And when Madame had lain down in the retreat at the back of the box, she sent away all her women. Then she rose, and on bared knees, and with joined hands, she lifted up her eyes to heaven, and devoutly tendered her thanks to God and to our Lady, for all the favour they had already shown to Saintré, entreating them to be pleased to continue the same. And as soon as her devotions were ended, finding herself completely restored, she returned, all gracious, to the Queen. Whilst Saintré, who, from time to time, and often, had been looking towards the Ladies, when he missed her, began to fear that it was again with her as it had been. So that, when he saw her come back, his heart danced within him an hundred thousand times lighter than before. And now I will say no more of these matters, and will tell of how the prizes were given.

CHAPTER LII.
The manner the King ordered the prizes to be distributed.

THEN the King, who held in his hand eight great jewels, which were the prizes, four on one side, and four on the other, to give at his good pleasure, desired the said French Mountjoy, King-at-arms, to pronounce his decision as follows. Then the herald, having enjoined silence, with a loud voice, on the part of the King, read, so that all might hear, " My Lord de Loiselench, and you, Jehan de Saintré, the King, our sovereign Lord, here present, has empowered and ordered me to tell you that, in both encounters, you have each done well and valiantly ; but seeing that you, my Lord de Loiselench, found yourself, in each case, unable to go through with them under the conditions which, by your own letter, were stipulated, he, as sole arbitor and judge, desires you to dispose of your four prizes as you engaged ; and which prizes, with his consent, approbation, and orders, I now hand to you." And when the Lord de Loiselench saw that Mountjoy had finished, he asked, " What it was that he had said ?" And when it was explained to him, and he understood the sentence of the King, for it was no more than he expected, on his knees, he humbly thanked the King, and told him, " how bitterly he regretted the ill luck that had prevented him from finishing his arms, as well on horse as on foot, thus depriving the Ladies of so long an expected entertainment. But seeing that such was his fate, he was willing to submit to it, as he required him; and that, as reason was, he was prepared to obey him." And when he had said this, Mountjoy descended, handing him the four jewels, so that he might dispense them. And when he had received them, he went toward Saintré, to give them to him; but when he reached him, his heart was so full, that, so much as a word, he was unable to utter. Then the four Polish Barons who were with him, and who well knew the cause of all his distress, as well as they were able, what was to be said for him, said. Then Saintré, whom Monsieur d'Anjou was escorting, advanced, and bowing himself, and taking the four jewels, said, " My Lord, my brother, for the honour you are pleased to do me, I thank you as heartily as I have words to do." Then the trumpets and the clarions began to blow in such a manner that one would almost fancy they could never stop. * * *

The remainder of this Chapter is omitted.—*Translator.*

CHAPTER LIII.

How the Lord de Loiselench supped with the King.

This Chapter is omitted.—*Translator.*

CHAPTER LIV.

How the Lord de Loiselench took his leave.

About a twelvemonth after the departure of the Pole, Madame, as usual, solicitous for the honour of her protegé, began to think it were time to get him again to work. And satisfied, probably, with his previous performances, she now determines to measure him with "foemen worthy of his steel"—the English; and so, a grand tournament is brought about upon the Calais marches. Though there is much that is curious, in a mere antiquarian point of view, in this Chapter, touching truces, passports, arms, temporary barracks, tents, furniture, &c., I have passed it all over; unwilling to weary the more general reader.—*Translator.*

THE COMMENCEMENT OF THE PASSAGE OF ARMS.

AND the Sunday, the first day of the month, and the opening of the tournament, arrived the said lord, the Earl of Buckingham; and it was after mass, and a great company was with him; and he fixed on the pinnacle of his barrack, his banner, quartered with that of England, with a border of silver; and his cry was "England! Saint George!"

THE AUTHOR.

And when the hour was come when the tournament was to open, the judges, the Kings-at-arms of Champaigne, and Garter, accompanied by their heralds, mounted into their boxes, that they might the better see. Then the tilting commenced, which was terrible, fierce, and honourable alike to each party. And although the Earl in the last course was a little hurt, nevertheless, as his lance was better broken, he won the diamond.

The second day came the Earl Marischal, who also had his banner, splendidly waving, on the top of his hut; and his cry was "England! St. George!" He also did famously, but as Saintré broke his lances better, he got the diamond.

The details of the remaining courses are purposely omitted.—*Translator.*

THE AUTHOR.

* * * * *

* * * . And of this course the judges were unable to decide, for the lances had been so evenly broken that they could not determine which had the better. So, at last, they had almost agreed that each was to keep his own prize. However, it was finally arranged that neither was to be considered either to have lost or to have won; and they were ordered each to pay the other, and the Earl to begin, for Saintré had broken the first. And so Saintré lost three diamonds and won eight, which make eleven; and the twelfth was exchanged.

THE AUTHOR AGAIN.

Here follows a tedious narrative of all the courtesies and presents interchanged between Saintré and the English Lords, Heralds, &c.; and which is consequently omitted.—*Translator*.

CHAPTER LV.

How Sir Nicolles de Malle-Teste, and Gallias of Mantua, Squire, came to the Court to perform their arms.

THE fifth day after Saintré had returned, there arrived at Paris two young noblemen of that part of Italy which we call Lombardy, the one a Knight, the other a Squire, and with them was a great company. And they were returning, having fought before the Emperor, with the Lord de Unal Lembergue, whose arms were *d'ermines à ung escusson de guelles*; and the Lord de Stambourg, whose arms were *trois tourteaulx de guelles*, in vindication of the enterprise the Lombards had undertaken, but which was still in abeyance; as the Emperor, who had seen the battle, as well on horse as on foot, to be fierce and hard, for the honour of either party, had ordered it to be stopped; and so it came, that though the one side was satisfied, the other was just where it was, and had as much to be released as ever.

THE AUTHOR.

And when they had got to Paris, and had put up at the Hôtel de l'Ours, by the Baudois barrier, they were recognized by a herald of the King, who had seen one of them before. And when he had got to know what brought them, he immediately went and told the King: present, the Queen and Madame. Then Madame sent, in all haste, for Saintré, and, at the same time forbade the herald to say a word to any one about their arrival. And when Saintré had come, she told him as quick as she could, all about these Lombards; how they had come, in such state, to carry through their arms. And when she had told him, she put it to him, " If he thought he had the heart to be one of the two to deliver them?"

"Heart!" said he, " Alas, Madame, and what have you ever perceived in me to lead you to suppose I now should shrink from what I never shrunk before?"

"Then," said she, "to lose no more time, before the news spreads, off with you to Bouciqualt, your brother, and, above all others, let him be your second."

And when Saintré heard of Madame these famous tidings, he thanked her as humbly as he could, without however, making any outward demonstration. Then he made for Bouciqualt, and when he found him, he said, " Brother, God and our Lady for ever, I bring you glorious news! An hour ago there alighted, at the Hôtel de l'Ours, by the barrier Baudois, two gentlemen of Lombardy, with no end of state, and they have come on some affair of honour, and are looking for one, or rather two, to deliver them. What say you, shall we do their business for them?"

"Deliver them!" said Bouciqualt. " Brother, welcome you and your news; and, as heartily as I can, I beg and pray of you that, so as to be the first, we set off this instant to find the King."

Which they did; but it was not without much disputing, and great prayers that he would listen to them. However, at last, he consented; but he determined, first, to know more about them, and what was the nature of their engagement. Then they sent the Guyenne King-at-arms, an old stager and an experienced herald, to ascertain exactly how the matter was; which herald brought them back word that there were two; the one a Knight, called Sir Nicolles de Malle-Teste, an highly considered, a noble and puissant Baron of the Ancona Marches; and the other a Lombard Squire, of a great house, and named Gallias of Mantua. And that each of them were wearing on the elbows of their left arms a great hoop of gold, all set in precious stones; and that they were under an engagement to visit the courts of the six Christian Kings, for among the Saracens they dared not trust themselves, till such time as they should meet with two Knights or Squires of fame and name, without reproach, as were they themselves, who would fight with them, with battle-axes simply, and broadswords, till one or other party was borne to the ground, or had been deprived of their weapons. This Gallias, of Mantua, was, I believe, that famous Knight who fought in mortal combat with Sir Jehan le Maingre, Mareschal of France, in the presence of the last Prince of Padua. It was a little while before the Venetians, by persisting in the siege, had become master of his person. The same was afterwards cast in prison and strangled, which was an irreparable loss to many; for, all through Italy, he had been reputed as a father and hospitaller to the straggling and the travelling Knights and Nobles.

CHAPTER LVI.

How Saintré and Bouciqualt went in search of the two champions, to bring them to the King of France; and of how they fought with them.

The Author.

BUT to return to the matter in hand. When Saintré and Bouciqualt heard the glorious news, they, as becoming Knights, at once amorous and valiant, hurried away to the King, telling him the whole affair at length, and asking permission to satisfy them. And when the news had spread abroad how the Lombards had come, and how the King had already named Saintré and Bouciqualt, of course every one saw that it was useless to make any more entreaty. Then the two brothers, with a large retinue, and seemingly simply to make their acquaintance, and to do them honour, learned from their own mouths the nature of their undertaking, as you have heard. And when the time was come, the King wanted to see them. Then Saintré and Bouciqualt, and a number with them, went to conduct them; and by the King, the Queen, and all the Lords they were given a very hearty welcome. Why should I be tedious? Saintré detached the one hoop from the arm of Sir Nicolles, and Bouciqualt the other, from that of Gallias. And then the king appointed the day. And when the day was come, and the King, the Queen, and the Lords, and Madame, and all the rest, were in their boxes, and the champions in their pavilions; all the honours and the triumphs, to be brief, I will omit. The King who, before his other battles, had always sent for Saintré, and begged to be allowed to Knight him, did the like on this occasion. But he had always excused himself, and did so still, protesting "that he never would be made one, unless it was under the banner of the Saracens, and against them."

And when they had been to their pavilions, and had taken their oaths, and had again left their tents, and the Mareschal had drawn up his edict, then all four, who had been sitting upon stools opposite to one another, rose, and, like lions unloosed, rushed upon each other. Then was the battle stern and terrible; nor, for a long time, could any one say which side had the better, till, at last, as ill-luck would have it, Saintré had his axe sent flying by Sir Nicolles, and at this if Madame and all his party were aghasted, I leave you to think: but he, as an undaunted Squire, without so much as yielding an inch of ground, incontinent drew his sword, and taking it in both his hands, each time that Sir Nicolles raised his axe, with his swoops prevented him from approaching. So he kept him at his distance; but at length Sir Nicolles, by reason of the great advantage that his axe gave him, made a rush, and succeeded in driving, by a left-handed blow, the edge into one of the openings in Saintré's vizor, completely stunning him, * * *   so that Saintré, slipping aside by his own proper weight, Sir Nicolles fell upon all fours. Then, on the instant, Saintré lifted his sword to strike him on the side, so as to knock him over; but, recollecting himself, out of a sense of honour, he let it fall. Then he ran to the assistance of his brother, who had already won more than a lance's length on Gallias. And while Saintré was running to him, Sir Nicolles had got up, having still his axe in his hand, and was making for Saintré; but the King, when he saw it, ordered him to be stopped. Then Gallias, who was now fighting with two, being quickly borne to the ground, handsomely confessed the day was lost * * *.

The remainder of this Chapter, presenting no sort of interest, is omitted.—*Translator.*

CHAPTER LVII.

How Saintré tilted against the Baron de Tresto, and they were adjudged equal.

The opening portion of this Chapter is passed over. Suffice to say, that the prowess of the English Baron is allowed to, with all the wonted liberality of these old, inveterate, chivalrous and traditional rivals and foemen of our race; as well in letters as in arms—the French.—*Translator.*

THE AUTHOR.

AND thus increased Saintré in the good graces of the King, the Lords, Madame, and everybody else. In a word, he was the most loved and honoured of all the Squires of France, and this on account of his great gentleness and humility, as also of his generosity, which helps much. And neither for all the account that the King made of him, nor for all the court was paid to him on every hand, was one spark of pride ever once detected in him. And a little after, or about this time, news came to him that his father was dead, and by this means he became the Lord de Saintré.

CHAPTER LVIII.

How the Lady asked Saintré to set out for Prussia, against the Saracens, and he promised to go; and how the King made him the head of five hundred lances.

The opening portion of this Chapter is passed over. The reader should know that this crusade was against the Pagans, here confounded with the Saracens.—*Translator.*

* * *. And to accompany his banner he ordered that from the twelve marches of his empire should be chosen fifty. And when the news spread abroad about the kingdom, Lords and nobles came flocking up in such numbers that the King was compelled to grant his licence to one hundred and sixty banners, whom he put under the orders of Saintré. And when Saintré, whose excuses the King would not admit of, had thanked the King, he called all the Lords together, and said to them, laughing, "My Lords, you have seen how the King, out of his grace, and in spite of everything I could say to the contrary, has determined to put all this honour upon me, and give me all this great charge, sufficient in itself for a Prince of the blood. Faith, methinks, my Lords, I am pitched upon on the principle of the youngster of a monk the story tells of.

There was once a Lord who, with all his trappings and his folk about him, went to an abbey not far from his house, to hear mass. And when the mass was said, out there came running five or six little rascals, monklings of the place, who began unbuckling his spurs. And when he found all the young rogues tugging away at his heels, he asked, "What on earth it was they were at?" Then his people told him, laughing, that it was the custom in all churches to redeem one's spurs, which, otherwise, were forfeited to the choir. So, giving them an écus, he called the youngest and simplest looking of the pack of them to him, and said to him, "Which, of the lot of you, has the oldest head?" to which the child, without any sort of hesitation, replied, "Whichever Damp Abbot pleases." And the reply was thought worth remembering, and, methinks, the cap fits here too. For, albeit, I am the simplest of you all here present; nevertheless, since the King has been pleased to say I am the wisest, I suppose there is nothing for it but that it must be so."

And then they all began to laugh, and they told him, "That the King knew well what he was about, and that they would be well satisfied and delighted to serve under him."

And now I will speak no more of these matters, and

will tell you of the Lords, Barons, and banners that went, and whose arms follow.

THE AUTHOR.

Here follow the names of the Princes and Lords who went to Prussia against the Saracens: and first, of those of the Marches of the Isle of France.

The remainder of this Chapter, though invaluable in an heraldic point of view, is, in other respects, of no sort of interest; and, accordingly, it is passed over. The hundred and sixty heroes, it is hardly necessary to say, are entirely composed of the Montmorencys, Chabots, Clermonts, Rohans, with the like great feudal and historic names.—*Translator*.

CHAPTER LIX.

How, when the time was come, that they were to set out for Prussia, the King gave his standard to Saintré, constituting him his Lieutenant.—And after, how the said Saintré and the other Lords took their leave of the King, the Queen, and the Ladies; and of the great mourning there was at their departure; especially on the part of Madame.

AND when, at length, the time to set out was come, and all the company were ready, and they had got their harness and their baggage together, and their baggage carts, and all their people, wearing red jackets, with the white cross in front, then Saintré, and also all the nobles, who were dressed in the same manner, having heard mass, which the Archbishop sung at Nôtre Dame, at Paris, as soon as they had confessed themselves, received the Papal benediction and absolution. Then, in the presence of the King, the royal banner was blessed; then, the others were. Then they returned with the King, and all went to dinner. And when it came to two of the clock they all went in a body to the King, who was in the great hall: present the Queen, Lords, and Ladies. And when they had told him how they were all come to bid him farewell, and they had all got on their knees, the King said to

Saintré, "Saintré, I put this expedition into your hands, as also the charge of this banner, which represents my person; with the Lords and other noble gentlemen here present, and who are to be with you." Then, turning to, and looking on the others, he said, "My friends, you are all noble, and come of noble houses; houses that have been ever fertile of valiant men, and whose representatives you have ofttimes proved yourselves to be. And seeing that you are this day about to embark yourselves in the service of the true God, Jesus Christ, and in which is to be purchased the eternal salvation of your souls, I commend unto you all this, my banner of the true Cross, with the care, besides, of your own honours. Mortals fight, but God gives the victory to those who are his. And it is not to be doubted, but that if you and the other Christian Lords and Princes, with the remainder who will have to fight, are so well in the sight of God that he will be well with you; let the power of the Saracens be what it may, or their numbers as the sands upon the sea-shore, they will be brought to nought before you. And as for myself, I swear to you on my faith, that were it not for the weighty affairs at home on hand, I had been one of your company; but it is not to be thought of. And there is one thing I do pray of you, from the greatest to the least, and that is, that you will be to one another friends and brothers, without bearing any sort of envy, grudge, noise, or quarrel; for through such bickering, it oftentimes comes that companies are broken and put to the worse." And then he took his banner, and handed it to the Lord de Château-Froumont, to carry. Then he said to them all, "Now, my friends, as your King and as your chief, I am about to give you all my blessing." Then, lifting his hands, he made the sign of the cross, and said, "In the name of God the Father, our Creator; in the name of God the Son, our Redeemer; and in the name of God the Holy

Spirit, the God Illuminator: one God in three names and in three persons, may you all go. Those of you who are never to return he will take to himself, and those of you who are, it will be to the redemption of your souls in the world to come, and to your eternal fames in this. And this I need hardly entreat of you, whatever befals you, whether you be the victors, or whether you be the vanquished, let all be done in honour; and if with any of you it otherwise is, I pray you, spare these eyes to see him more!" And having delivered these words, the tears running down his eyes, and his voice half choked, he said, taking them all by the hand, "My friends, God be with you!"

Then might you have seen many a gentle breast was like to rend, and eyes to pour their last; nor was there man or woman present could so much as speak a word.

Then they went to the Queen, who, with the other Ladies, had been obliged to leave to hide her tears. Then Saintré began to speak in the name of all, and said, "Sovereign Lady, are there any commands you would deign to put upon us?"

Then the Queen turned to them, and without saying so much as a word, touched them each one by the hand.

Then they went to my three Lords, the King's brothers, and made the same demand. Then said my Lord of Anjou, "Saintré and the rest, my fair cousins and my good friends, you have heard what my Lord the King has said to you; go with a good heart, begin as you should do, and, for the end, there need be no fear."

Then they went to Madame. Of her I need hardly speak; for although she stifled, with all her might, the agony of her soul in seeing Saintré, do what she would, she could not keep her limbs, and had certainly fallen if her Ladies had not supported her.

Then they went to the other Ladies and Gentlewomen, who, all with one voice, broke out into such a lamentation and a wailing, that had all their friends and relatives been dead, they could not have wept more bitterly. And as they wept, they cried, "Alas! alas! for never again shall we look alive on all this joyous company!" And all the officers of the Court were in tears, and seeking, in vain, to comfort one another, crying, each one to his fellow, "Alas! alas! for he is leaving us; he who in all our troubles comforted us; in all our little matters advised us; and in all our wants befriended us; and God only knows if ever again we are to see him!" And so, on all hands, was seen nor heard no other thing save weeping and mourning, and such as you would think had never ceased. And then they all went, for that night, to repose themselves.

THE AUTHOR.

And when the morning was come, the trumpets began to tell them all, 'twas time to saddle and to boot. Then every man of them went to the minster. And after mass, they all got on their horses, and under way. Then the Lords of Anjou, Berry, and Bourgoyne, with all their people, met them, out of honour toward the King's banner. And, besides them, were such a crowd of other Knights, Squires, Burgesses and Merchants of the town, that hardly a soul was left behind.

THE ORDER OF THE BANNERS.

Some dry details are here passed over.—*Translator.*

* * *. And as they traversed the length of the town, every balcony, window, door, entrance, cranny, was covered, or choked with Ladies, Gentlewomen; Citizens, and their wives, and people of all sorts and conditions, assembled to see these noble heroes pass. And, on every side, were tears, and groans, and sighs; nor when they came in sight, was there man or woman could so restrain themselves, but that, convulsively, they would wring their hands; all crying together after him, as far as he could hear, "Ah, Saintré, Saintré, gentle Squire; God, may God go with you; and may you be brought again to us, and all your company, in safety and in honour!" And with this they vowed to God, masses, pilgrimages, and alms.

And when they had got a little way out of Paris, they insisted that my Lords, and all the company should come no further. Then they all took leave of one another. And now I will dwell no more on their partings and their tears, or the great regrets of the King, the Queen, the Lords, the Ladies, and Gentlewomen, or on all they did; and principally Madame, who never ceased to be on pilgrimages, to have masses said; and in solitude, to weep, to mourn and to pray; and, instead, I will tell you of Saintré, and of all his company, who, to their great joy, all arrived safe and sound, at the town of Torn, in Prussia.

THE AUTHOR.

Thus, by their stages, Saintré, and all his men-at-arms, so made their way, that, at last, they got to the town of Torn, in Prussia, where all were to meet. And there they found the Prelates, Princes, and Lords that follow; the most part of whom were well pleased to hear of their coming, and went to meet them, out of respect to the King's banner. And when they saw Saintré, they were delighted to find with him so many nobles and their followers, so well equipped; for, five or six thousand hardier men, one could nowhere find.

THE AUTHOR.

Concerning the King of England; by reason of matters he had in hand, he neither would go himself, nor yet send. And it was not without great difficulty that he consented to allow the Lords, here named, to go.

Here follow, in the original, the names and arms of eight Lords; but omitted in this place.—*Translator.*

* *; which Lords took with them, one hundred lances, and three hundred archers.

And to divide, and weaken the overwhelming power and assemblage of the Saracens, the four Kings of Spain; that is to say, of Castile, of Arragon, of Portugal and Navarre, had allied themselves together, to war upon, by sea and by land, the Kings of Granada, of Maroc, and of Belmarine; the nearest Saracens to them. But for all that, it did not prevent their numbers being something incredible, as you will after hear.

The Prelates, and Princes, and other Lords, who were there. And first:—

Here follows a roll now omitted.—*Translator.*

The Assebennoys of the county of Alost, who were there.

* * * * *

The Reysters of the Duchies of Lembourg, of Luxembourg, and Blancquebourg, who were there.

* * * * *

The Bavarian Germans, who were there.

* * * * *

The German Reysters of Brabant, who were there.

* * * * *

The Holland and Zeland Reysters, who were there.

* * * * *

* * *. (10) In which assembly were from one hundred to one hundred and twenty horsemen; from thirty to forty thousand Knights and Squires, completely armed; besides bowmen and others, about one hundred and forty, or fifty thousand able men.

CHAPTER LX.

How the Saracens were in a greater number of Turks and infidels than had ever been seen together since the time of Mahomet.

The Author.

AND on the part of the Saracens was the battle more great than was ever seen since Mahomet gave the law. For all the Soldans, Kings, and Lords of the four regions were there: that is to say, of Asia Major, with its six provinces, namely, Judea, Persia, Syria, Egypt, Assyria, Arabia. That of Judea is bounded, on the south, by the sea, commonly called The Black Sea, but others call it The Stormy Sea, on account of the horrible turmoil in which it is continually kept, by reason of the seven thousand five hundred and forty-eight islands that are in it; one of which is very large, having ten cities in it. The principal is called Gelbona; and in its chief city is an incredible amount of gold, and precious stones; and elephants multiply more there than in any other quarter of the world. And this country was originally converted by Saint Thomas, the Apostle. However, the greater part of them are now recreants.

The Author.

And those of the second region of the Saracens who were there, were those of Persia, and of Turkey, and of their different provinces; that is to say, Auffric, Media, Persia, Mesopotamia, where is the great city of Nineveh, which is three days' journey in length, and now called Babylon; and where are the foundations of the monstrous tower of Babylon, which are four thousand paces wide. And with them, came from the Provinces of Chaldea, of Arabia, of Sabaath, and Tarsus. And in this country is the mount of Sinai, where the Angels bore the body of

Madame, Saint Catherine, which now lies in the church of Saint Marie de Ruer, near the said Mount.

THE AUTHOR.

And those of the third region who were there, were of the country of Syria, in which are the provinces of Damascus, of Antioch, of Phinicia. In them were Tyre and Sidon; and there is Mount Lebanon, out of which comes the River Jordan. And in it are the cities of Palestine, of Judea, of Jerusalem, of Samaria, of Gabeste, of Galilee, of Nazareth. And in this land were the two cities of Sodom and Gomorrah, which, for their abominable wickedness, were swallowed up in the abyss. And from these three regions came so many Kings, Lords, and such multitudes of every sort, that the whole country was covered with them; thinking, in their hearts, as you have heard, to conquer all the rest. And of which Lords of the Saracens I will afterwards name a few.

THE AUTHOR.

And when the day appointed for the battle was come, and all the Christians were in the field, then they heard their high and solemn mass, which was chanted by the Archbishop of Cologne; and being all, as became good Christians, in a state of grace, absolution was given to them by the Cardinal d'Aste, who was Legate from the Pope. And when every man had asked pardon of his neighbour, then those who wanted to breakfast, breakfasted. Then they mounted their horses, and made, each one, for his battle; whilst Saintré, getting on his, went in search of the King of Bohemia. And when he was before him, he drew his sword; and in the name of God, our Lady, and of my Lord, Saint Denis, he required him to confer on him the rank and order of Knighthood. Then the good King, who loved the good Jehan, and all the

French, dubbed him, with the greatest readiness, and gave him the order; praying God to give him all the honour and the success he could wish for. And from this time he was only known as the Lord de Saintré. Then all who wished to be Knights stepped forward.[11] And many banners were unfurled, and the points of many a pennon cut. And when all this was over, each one returned to his place; and when they had made the sign of the cross, they all began to move.

The order of the Battles.

This order is here omitted.—*Translator*.

The order and disposition of the battles of the Saracens.

This order is here omitted.—*Translator*.

CHAPTER LXI.

How, in the battle of the Saracens, Saintré, at the very first onslaught, slew the Grand Turk, and did so well his work, that all the infidels made way for him.—And then, of how the Emperor of Carthage, the two Soldans of Babylon, and Mabaleth, the Grand Turk, were killed; with many others, as well on the one part as the other.

This more than half apocryphal account of this great battle, offering no kind of interest to a modern reader, is here suppressed.—*Translator*.

CHAPTER LXII.

How the news were blown about everywhere, but especially into France, how Saintré had performed prodigies; and of how, in particular, among other things, he had killed the Great Turk, and trampled on his banner; at which the King was greatly delighted, and thanked God, and all the Saints, in great solemnity.

THE AUTHOR.

* * * * *

AND of this most holy victory, the news soon spread abroad, on every hand, as did that of Perseus, by his Pegasus, the flying horse. For every one was writing of it into his own country, and how it had passed, and of all the valiant feats that had been performed. But above all else, of how a young, and new-made Knight of France, called the Lord de Saintré, was the theme of every tongue; and how in the very first charge, he had killed the Grand Turk; and after, performed such prodigies of valour, that he had made his way to the standard, taken it, and trampled it under his horse's hoofs; with so many other incredible feats, that to describe them would be too long.

THE AUTHOR.

And as soon as these most precious news were everywhere confirmed, incontinent, all true Christians, of whatever country they were, rushed to the churches; the bells being everywhere peeling out, to thank their Creator. And among the other Christian Princes, the King of France at once got on his horse, and went to the great church, to thank, first, God and our Lady, and then Saint Denis. And a little after, it came, that the Anjou King-at-arms arrived, who had been at the battle; and he came to the King, and told him, by word of mouth, how the whole had been; and how splendidly his nobles had behaved;

those who survived, as well as those who fell; but especially, the Lord de Saintré, of whom, he said, all his letters were full. And when the King was certified of the truth of the matter, he presently exclaimed, "Ha, great God, thine be the glory: have Thou mercy on those who this day, in Thy cause, have fallen!" And for these glorious tidings, he gave to the said King-at-arms the robe from his back, and three hundred écus. Then was there such joy as one can well imagine, throughout the Court, the city, and the kingdom; excepting only among such Ladies, Gentlewomen, and others, as had lost their lovers or their friends. And now I will say no more of them, or their matters; but will return to the Lord de Saintré.

CHAPTER LXIII.

How Saintré and all his noble host of French Christians, after the overthrow of the infidels, returned to Paris, where they were joyfully received of the King, the Queen, and all the realm.

AND when the Lord de Saintré and all his chivalry had got to the church of Saint Denis, and had paid their devotions there; as they were entering into Paris, they were met by the three before-named Lord-dukes, and such an host of others, that hardly one remained behind. And in the same order and state that they had departed, they returned; and descended in the court-yard of the Hôtel Saint Pol; saving only the banners of such as had fallen, and those of the Lord du Chastel-Froumont, and the others, who had been left behind, wounded. And in his place, the Lord de Maulevrier bore the King's banner, by the election of all. And when they came before the King, the Queen, Madame, and all the company, who were in the great hall, and they had made their obeisance to the King; the King, who was seated, to do them honour, and out of the great delight he was in, got on his feet, and went several paces forward to meet them. Then, to show them all how glad he was to see them, he took them each one by the hand. And when he had shaken hands with them round, the Lord de Saintré and the others went to make their reverence to the Queen, to Madame, and all the rest of the Ladies present, who were in the greatest spirits possible, to have them back; excepting only those that had lost their friends or relatives. And when they had paid the Ladies their respects, and kissed and embraced them all, the King, sitting down again in his chair, spoke as follows:—"My friends, God be praised, and his blessed Mother, in honour and in triumph you have this day come back to us. Those of you who have fallen, I trust God will have mercy on their souls, as, according to our holy faith, we are all bound to believe, and that they are saved. But in order that our Lord may the sooner deliver their souls from the pains of purgatory, and take them to repose, and to his ever-glorious kingdom of Paradise, we will and ordain, that, at dusk, you will all be at Nôtre Dame; and there we will have vespers said, and vigils for the dead; and to-morrow we will have the commendatory, and solemn masses, which the bishop shall chant. And in all the other churches shall masses for the dead be said, and anywhere else that priests may happen to be; so I have to beg that all of you will be forthcoming. And these services, we will and order to be continued for thirty successive days."

Now, for the present, I will say no more of these matters, but will tell you how Madame, being impatient to speak with the said Lord de Saintré, made him her signal; and how, by his, he replied to her.

THE AUTHOR.

And after all these matters were over; in the evening, when the King, the Queen, and all the Lords and Ladies were vieing who most could do honour to the returned Lords, especially the Lord de Saintré, Madame, who for all she pretended to care but little for what was going on, could not so far control the hurry of her heart, but that, before them all, she came up to him, and said, "My Lord de Saintré, at least when you shall have received the respects of all the other Ladies, may I, in my turn, be allowed the privilege of seeing you? Time was, I know well, you both passed for, and were an unpretending Squire; mayhap now, a Knight, and my Lord to boot, access may not be quite so much a matter of course."

And when she had done speaking, she took her pin, and made her signal, to which, instantly, the Lord de Saintré replied; and, smiling, said, "Madame, whatever man I now am, or may have become, since last we met, believe me I am still the same I ever was."

Then he fell into conversation with the others present. And when, after supper, the tables were removed, some of the younger sort began to hint about dancing. But when it came to the King's and Queen's ears, they said, "that out of a regard to the dead, it would ill become them to be showing themselves merry; and that they would neither have dancing nor singing."

And inasmuch as they were to be early next morning at the church, he called for the dessert and the parting cup.

CHAPTER LXIV.

This Chapter, it were perhaps as well that the reader should read to him or herself.—Translator.

How Saintré told the King that, to show that he was really glad to see him back, he should let him sleep with the Queen; which the King promised him.—And how the Queen, quite tickled, asked him, "What, on earth, had put such a piece of assurance into his head?"—And after, how, at midnight, he went to speak with the Lady alone; who gave him the kindest reception in the world; not, however, without many kisses and embracings.

THE AUTHOR.

AND when the King was in his chamber, the Lord de Saintré said to him, laughing, "Sir, to show that you are really in earnest in saying you are glad to see us back, I think you might for once stretch a point, and let me sleep to-night with the Queen."

Then the King, no less a gallant than himself, and loving him heartily, besides, quite tickled at the idea, said, "Ever the same; ever for the ladies! faith, Saintré, then you shall."

Then Saintré, laughing as hard as he could, made after the Queen, and when he found her, he said to her, "Ah, Madame, I have a boon at heart; promise me I shall have it."

And when the Queen saw him smiling, she said, "And what, Saintré, is this great boon to be?"

"Madame, grant it," said he, "and you shall hear after."

"Hey, but you must tell me first," said she. "I see well you want to make a fool of me."

"Madame, it is a thing in which the King, yourself, and I, will all find our pleasure. Will you not believe me on my honour?"

"On your honour, I will," said she, "and, since such is the case, you shall have it with much pleasure."

Then the Lord de Saintré said to her, "Then, Madame, be of good heart; for, please the fates, this night, if the King has not been beforehand with me, I hope to make you the mother of a fine boy. The King, out of the good humour he is in to see me back, has promised me that I am to sleep with you."

"Hey," said the Queen, "and is this your boon? You are a pretty fellow too. It is not two days since I slept with the King. But tell me, what was it put it into your head to make such a request to my Lord?"

"Madame," said he, "I will tell you. You know that when any Lord or Lady comes into the schoolroom when the scholars are at their lessons, at their demand the little people are dismissed and sent to play."

"Ha," said she, "Saintré, that is not what really set you on. I charge you, by love and by arms, to tell me the truth." Then she caught him by the sleeve, and said to him, at least as far as I know, "You are not going to get off that way."

Then the Lord de Saintré called to Madame, and said to her, "Help! help! here is the Queen wanting to force me!" And then he told her all about his prayer to the King, and how he had made it to the Queen.

Then said Madame to the Queen, "Hey, Madame, let him go; he has told you the truth."

"No," said she, "he has other game in hand; for my Lord told me but yesterday, that he was wanting badly to see him, to speak with him about some matters; and he has contrived all this in order to get away."

Madame, who began to fear that this might be the case, alarmed lest their signals might be detected, the better to cover her manner, said to the Lord de Saintré, "Hey, sir, sir, if Madame follows my advice, she will get it out of you before she lets you go."

Then he said to them, "Ladies, will you give me your honours that, if I tell you the truth, afterwards you will let me go?"

"Yes, we will," said the Queen.

"And you also, Madame?" said Saintré.

"Yes," said she, "on my honour."

Then he said, "Madame, the fact of it is, for the last month or six weeks we have hardly a moment been off our legs, and, seeing the King wanted to have all we had been doing over, whilst I, on the contrary, was wanting to go home and get to my bed, I hit upon this way of making my escape."

"Ha," said the Queen, "at length we have got the truth from him."

Then said Madame, now venturing on her signal, "You are right, Madame; now you may let him go."

The Author.

And at length the long longed-for hour was come, when Madame and her friend were to be with one another alone. What need I tell you more? There were kisses given and snatched, as quick as ever they could follow; a thousand interrogations put and satisfied, which love alone could respond to, or could prompt. And on this delightful footing they remained, meeting as often as fortune would indulge them, which was only when the Queen slept with the King; for, othertimes, they were always in waiting about him. And all this felicity and infelicity continued fifteen months. And now I will say no more of their loves, which were so loyal, and so secret, that never, in this world, were loves more warily, more truly, or happily conducted.

CHAPTER LXV.

How Saintré deliberated with himself to wear a golden vizor for the space of three years; and how the King consented to it, though much against his will.

THE AUTHOR.

AND it happened, about fifteen months after his return from Prussia, that a new idea got into his head, and he was always saying to himself, "Alas, poor thoughtless that you are; where is your invention? Is there any one enterprise or thing you ever yet did, till you were put up to it by your ever gentle and your guardian goddess? Faith, I am determined that, for her sake, something shall be done which the world shall ring with."

(12)Then he made up his mind to select five Knights, of which himself was to be one; and five Squires, the stoutest and most famous to be found in France, and who were to be all together companions and brothers, and to wear vails covered with batchelors' buttons—of gold for the Knights, and of silver for the Squires—and a rich diamond was to be in the centre of each. And they were to wear them till they found a like number of Knights and Squires who would contest with them, in mortal combat, each of the said diamonds and as many of the like vails. And no one was to hear of it till the last day of April, when he was to put his scheme to the Knights and Squires whom he would elect. And when he had so far completed his plan, he sent to Florence a pattern of the vails, which were to be of white satin, richly figured; and the robes of the Knights, and the caparisons of their horses were to be of the same. And, unknown to every one, he got together white horses, the most beautiful and spirited that money could procure, and had them stabled away in a secret place. And, besides, he had ten of the newest and handsomest caps made, all broidered, and of one cut, with ostrich feathers, set in a clamp of gold for the Knights, and of silver for the Squires. And when the said cloth of satin had arrived from Florence, and the said horses were found, he then had the said satin cut into ten dresses, upon the measure of parties of the same height and build as those whom he had pitched on, and all was sown with gold and silver thread. But of these preparations no one knew. And when the following day, the first of April, was come, he invited to sup with him the Lord de Pressigny, the Lord de Beuil, the Lord de Mailly, Sir Hue de Craon; with himself, making five Knights; and, besides, the Lord de Jaully, the Lord de May, the Lord d'Erby, the Lord des Barres, and the Lord de Clermont, Squires; to whom he gave a famous entertainment at his hotel. And when the cloths were removed, and before the tables, and they had all given thanks to God, he called for the varlet, who had the charge of his chamber, and made him bring him a little box. Then, when he had sent every one out of the room to supper, he said, smiling, to the company, "My Lords and brothers, should there appear to you anything presumptuous in what I am about to break to you, I beg you to pardon me; for, on my honour, I am content to be the least of you. And what I have been about, and am now going to disclose to you, you must not be angry with me for; for it is only purposed to redound to our honours, which, to generous spirits, cannot, I trust, but be agreeable, and, for this end, I have selected you, above all others in this kingdom, to be brothers and companions together in an affair of arms, for the love and honour of our Ladies. Now my Lords and brothers, what do you say to all this?"

Then they all began, delighted at the idea, to glance from one to the other; each one, out of deference to Saintré, shifting it upon his neighbour to answer for all, saying, "You speak for us all," or "You." At length, the Lord de Jaully spoke first, and said, "My Lord de Saintré, better each one to speak for himself. But, to be privileged to be one of such a company, or party to such an enterprise, methinks, requires but little hesitation. For my own part, I, for one, with the grace of God and of our Lady, consent, thanking you for the honour you have done me in originally thinking of me, and offering me the refusal."

Then it was, who readiest could thank him, and promise to accede. Nor was there one of them, however highly he might think of himself, who, for a moment, presumed to measure himself with Saintré; for such was his valour, as you have heard, his largess, his gentleness, his courtesy, which passed all bounds, and all one ever sees, or hears of, that there was not one who had not staked his life for his. And, besides, as the King loved him above all his Court, every one naturally took a pleasure in obliging him. Then, thanking them all most kindly, he opened the box, and gave to each one his mask, all being alike as to make, and the diamonds. Then he said to them, "Now, my Lords and my brothers, in the name of God the Father, the Son, and the Holy Spirit, also of the blessed Virgin Mary, his Daughter and Mother, I give them to you; and you are to take them on this condition, that each of you is to wear them on his left shoulder for the space of three years, if within the same we do not meet with a like number of Knights and Squires of name and renown, without reproach, who, with lances, battle-axes, broadswords and daggers, shall have fought with us, and we with them, till either side may have won at every point, or borne the other to the ground. And whichever party God sends the worst, shall forfeit; if our, the vails and the diamonds; if their, the like to the other. And to secure our deliverance, we will send to the Court of the

King of the Romans, and into England, or wherever else we think necessary. But I am willing to take all this on myself; and, besides, I will see the King about it, and make him do something for us toward the expense."

And when they had all told him, how much they were obliged to him, he continued, " And that all may be done *en régle*, and we may be encouraged the more in our enterprise, I think we should each one see his Lady, and get her to pin it on lightly with the hand, without fastening it, till the morning, on our left shoulders. And, in order that we may take every one by surprise, I have to ask that you will all be ready by four o'clock in the morning, at latest, when we will go and wake up the King and Queen, who sleep together to-night; and, please the fates, we will give them a good morrow."

And to this they all consented, being as satisfied as they could well be with anything. However, the Lord de May said, " Alas! but what is the unhappy wretch to do whose Lady will not let him go?"

To which the Lord de Saintré answered, " Ah, my brother, such a thing is not to be supposed; for, if she be not the cruelest of the cruel, in no conscience could she oppose herself to any such prayer."

And then they all took leave of one another, and went, each one his way. And now I will say no more of these Lords, or of their Lady loves, but will tell you how it fared with Saintré, touching the matter of his dame.

CHAPTER LXVI.

How Saintré went to speak with his Lady in the meadow, and how he told her of his enterprise; at which she was horribly vexed and displeased.—But how, being passionately entreated by Saintré, at last, she gave him her consent, placing his ensign on his shoulder.

AND in the evening, being the eve of the first of May, after the King had taken his dessert, and the parting cup, the Lord de Saintré approached the Queen, and calling Madame to them, said before her, laughing, to the Queen, "And what, Madame, will you give me if I so manage that you shall sleep with the King to-night?"

"Faith," said she, laughing in her turn, "I will give you, for your impudence, just nothing at all."

And while all this was going on, he managed to make his signal to Madame, and Madame, who well knew by his manner when he had called her, that he had wanted to apprise her how the Queen was to sleep that night with the King, proved herself, and that too without so much as opening her lips, to be neither deaf nor dumb; for, immediately, she replied by her signal. And when the King and Queen were in bed, and the Lord de Saintré, as custom was to Princes and Princesses, great Lords and Ladies, had, as Chamberlain, sprinkled them with the holy water (but which many, now-a-days, are ashamed to have done to them, and think there is no necessity for, so little fear have they of the enemy), and when he had closed the curtains, and wished them both a good night, he returned to his chamber, and there he remained till the long-wished-for hour when Madame and he were to be together. Then was there kissing and rekissing, and all the toying, the fondling, and the sport which love alone can ever prompt his minions to conceive. And when they had thus a good while entertained one another, the Lord de Saintré, falling on his knees, said to Madame, "Ah, my high and sovereign goddess, nonpareille of women, as humbly as I can find words to entreat—a boon, grace, pardon, mercy, I crave at your hands!"

"And what, my friend, is your boon?" said Madame.

"Madame," said Saintré, "since the day when first I knew you, I became your most humble slave and faithful and devoted servant, never once did I evince the spirit to be in me, to undertake anything in advancement of your honour, of my own accord; but everything I may have achieved, or wherever I may have gone, it was all at your suggestion. Everything was done by your orders, and upon your advice and encouragement; and, seeing that by such thoughtlessness and negligence I have shamefully sinned, and been wanting to you, and that it is better to do well late than never; for this reason, Madame, I have, as respectfully as I can find words, to entreat of you that you will be pleased to attach this ensign now, for the first time, to my shoulder. Nine other companions, with myself, in honour of their Ladies, have undertaken as much. They are So and So, and So and So," and then he named them. And when he had said thus far, he drew his ensign from his pocket, where he had it wrapped up in a handkerchief, and, handing it to her, thought to kiss her.

Madame, who all the time had been listening to him in silent astonishment, and by this had wrought herself into a towering rage, drawing herself up, thus obligingly condescended to his whim: "And have you then actually allowed things to go this length, and do you really fancy you are to go here, and there, and everywhere, and without my knowledge or consent? Never, while I live, shall you be again to me what you have been!"

Who was taken back at this if it was not Saintré?" Then he began to look closely at her, and when he saw her a little calmer, he said, "Alas! Madame, this is a sorry reception, when, thinking to do all I could to gain you honour, instead of thanks I meet with blame; I who have so long and so faithfully served you, and not only whose heart, whose days, whose honour, but whose life and limb have been imperilled for your sake, and in obedience to your commands. Thinking, from my soul, to do you honour and a kindness, can it be that I am to lose the woman, above all women, to whom I am so deeply bounden? Hah, ever-to-be-redoubted Lady, look with pity on your poor supplicant, and, for this once, let him be pardoned. If a second time I wander, then let mercy be denied me!"

But Madame only replied, "Go, tell your companions that the thing is at end; that is all you have to do."

"Alas, Madame!" said Saintré, "how can I do that? matters have gone too far to be now broken, and as there is nothing, Madame, in this world, in which I am not obliged to obey you, even to the very laying down of my life, were you to require it of me; for this reason, on my knees, with uplifted hands, as humbly as I can, I beseech you that, of your own accord, and in all unfeignedness, you will forgive me, and pin my ensign here. And for the rest, do not be alarming yourself; for, with the grace of God and of our Lady, all will be for the best."

And when he had done, Madame, sulking however, took the ensign, and placed it on his shoulder, and then, half "Yes," half "No," she permitted him to kiss her. By this, the night being far spent, he respectfully took his leave, and departed. And now I will say no more of Madame, and will tell you of how the nine companions came to Saintré, and of the magnificent appearance they made at his hotel.

CHAPTER LXVII.

How the ten companions came, in the morning, to see the King.

THE AUTHOR.

AND in the morning, which was the first day of May, the nine companions, as soon as it was light, were all with Saintré, at his hotel. To be short, as soon as they had heard mass there, the Lord de Saintré brought them all into his chamber. Then he handed to each of them a robe of silk, with the vails of gold, and of silver, all embroidered as you have heard. Then he gave them each one a cap, as handsome and becoming as anything could be; then, such belts of gold and of silver to strap their waists, that they could not help staring at the sight of them, one at another. Then he took back the vails, and, with his own hands, placed them on the shoulders of each; at the same time laughing, and asking them, "What their respective Ladies thought of all this?"

Alas, he told them not of his; nor of all the misery, and the sickness of his heart. And when they had all descended into the court, there they found the ten prancing chargers, all of them snow white, and which he had had secretly procured. And they were all covered with cloths of the same material that the robes were; and in all the corners, they were sown with vizors, of gold for the Knights, and of silver for the Squires. And then he handed them all dice, and said; "Now, my Lords, we will all throw, and the one who has the highest points, will choose first."

Then they all thanked him, almost overpowered; saying one to the other, "Was there ever the like of this?"

And as they were mounting, spurs, all gilded, were

presented to the Knights, and of silver to the Squires; and their reins were plaited with silken cord, as was then the custom on occasions of ceremony. And as they left the gate, it was a perfect sight to see the horses; what with the capering, dancing, plunging, snorting, neighing, kicking; so that every one was either scampering to get out of their way, or hurrying to get a sight of them; for the like of it was never seen. And in this manner they proceeded to the great court yard of the Hôtel Saint Pol. And by the time they had got there, they were all in the highest spirits, for they knew well that the King would be awake. And when the King heard all this abominable clatter, and hullaballoo, he desired the Gentlewomen who were sleeping in the chamber, "to get up and see what it was was the matter."

Then they went to the grating; and when they had looked, they all began to cry, together, "O, Sir, Sir, do but come here! If here is not the most extraordinary thing that ever happened!"

On hearing this, the Queen, who was awake, wondering what on earth it could be, said to the King, "Let us go see what it is."

Then the Gentlewomen came back, so astonished, that they had well nigh lost the use of their speech.[13] Then the King and the Queen called for their clothes; and then the King, in his nightcap and his shirt, and the Queen the same, went, the King to the great window, and the Queen to the trellis. And when the ten companions, who were singing, and shouting, and hallooing, saw the King, they all made for him. And when the Queen showed herself, they all began to cry, at the top of their voices, "Sir, Sir, and Lady, a merry, merry May to you both!"

Then the King said to them, "Good morning to you, companions; good morning to you."

Then the King and Queen withdrew to dress themselves; and the ten companions alighted, and came into the King's closet, where they found him surrounded by his valets-de-chambre, who were dressing him. Then, when all were on their knees, the Lord de Saintré began first, and said, " Our sovereign Prince : My Lords, my brothers, who here are, and with them myself, have, each of us, this day, vowed, that is, saving your good will and licence, to wear this ensign, which you see upon our left shoulders, for the space of three years. The particulars are such as you may see, if you will deign to look on it, in the Letter-of-arms which we have had indited; beseeching you, that it may be your good pleasure to allow us to go through with it."

And when the King heard this new project, and saw upon their shoulders, the ensigns, he was not too well satisfied; so he said to them, " My friends, it seems to me, you have done as the man did who married his cousin first, and asked for dispensation after. You had no right, either to contrive or to execute anything of the sort, without the consent of your Lord and Master, who has the charge and authority over you; and whose business it had been rigorously to examine what advantage was like to come of it. And the one who proceeds without it merits to be severely punished."

And when he had done speaking, he took their Letter, and began to read it; telling them, " He would think about it. And as for you, Saintré," he continued, " you have not a thought in your head but challenges and voyages. Methinks you ought to have had enough, by this, of that sort of work."

" Ah, Sir," said Saintré, " it is not so much any gratification to myself, as a sense of honour, and in which you have your part, that spurs me on." By this the King was ready, and went to mass.

In a few minutes after, in came my Lords, the King's

brothers, who saw the ten companions, thus dressed, and with their new devices on. And when the companions had paid them their reverences, they presently asked them for their good offices. But they told them, "that as to their enterprise, they had very ill laid their measures: that the King was in the right, and they had had no business to go the lengths they had without his knowledge; and that if he had acted otherwise than he did, he had done foolishly. However," they added, "we will see him presently, and try what can be done for you."

And after the King and the Lords, in a little while, came in the Queen, who was delighted to see them. And after her came Madame, who received them coldly enough. Then all went to hear grand mass. And all the time, you might see Ladies, Gentlewomen, Knights and Squires, staring, with all their might, at the new companions. And when the King was in his chamber, he sent for my Lords, his brothers, and showed them the Letters, and then asked them for their advice. To cut the matter short, the conclusion was, that, for this once, he would give his consent; it being understood, that if anything of the sort was ever attempted again, either by them or any other of the kingdom, without his previous consent, it would be to bring down on the party his severest indignation, and they should be punished. Then they all began most humbly to thank him, &c.

The remainder of this Chapter, as tedious, is omitted.—*Translator.*

CHAPTER LXVIII.

How the King spoke with Saintré; and of the presents that he made to him, and his companions.

THE AUTHOR.

AND while the clothes were being made, which I have told you of, the King, who greatly loved Saintré, said to him, " Saintré, who was it put it into your head to undertake this new enterprise without my consent? What suretyship has fortune ever given to you, that, often as she has been on your side, she may not, at the length, be wearied of you? And if that is not enough; make you little of the anger of our Lord, who defends as all such idle vanities? And if he has in so many manners and times stood your good friend, by so much the more are you bounden to him, as you are a true Christian; the more mindful should you be not to provoke him. However, since the affair has gone so far that it cannot now in decency be stopped, for this once you may proceed. But I forbid you ever again to attempt anything of the kind."

"Ah, Sir," said Saintré, " forgive me!"

" From my heart, Saintré, I do," said the King, &c.

A portion of this Chapter, which, in its general character, has, upon a previous occasion, been presented to the reader, is here suppressed.—*Translator*.

Of the great grief of Madame, and of how she left the Court.

Madame, now left thus solitary, deprived of her friend, could neither find in tilt, nor tournament, nor yet dancing, nor the chase, nor any other pastime, delight to entertain her heart, or wherewithal to fill the aching void. And ever as she looked on the lovers, side by side, as they toyed the live-long day away, would break out afresh the misery that consumed her. Till, at length, so settled became her melancholy, that, instead of eating and drinking, she fell to fasting; and, for all her sleeping, came waking. So that, little by little, all her ruddiness forsook her; and on that cheek where late was seen to bloom the rose, now lurked the lily pale: so that every one began to wonder. And among the rest the Queen, who clearly saw her to to be unwell, so wan and pensive, would often ask her, "What was it was the matter with her?"

To which Madame would only reply. "It is nothing, Madame; you know well, we Ladies, when we have a mind, are often ill."

"Nay, but, fair Cousin, seriously, tell me, I entreat you, what it is is wrong, and what part of you it is that ails; for you must know how much we have at heart to see you yourself again."

"Ah, my good Lady," sighed Madame, "you are too kind."

And at this time they said no more; but the Queen, who liked her greatly, did not, for that, forbear to send for her physician, Hue de Fisol, a philosopher, and a man of much skill; desiring him to go to Madame, on her part, and to inform himself of what it was was the matter; and then to let her see him again in the morning, so that she might know what it could be. And so by the next morning, our said Hue had made himself master of Madame's case. And he ascertained her body, and all her members to be sound, and capable of all their sundry functions; nor could he discover either headaches, or fevers, or chills, or disorder, saving only that he fancied he detected something unusual, like a fulness, in the lower regions of the breast, which if not quickly disburdened, would infallibly bring her to her grave. Besides, all her spirits were gone, being retreated to the heart, which he found was like to burst. However, as well as he could, he comforted her, and then he said, "Madame, as regards your person, I find all right and working; but as for your mind, there is certainly something preying upon it, which, if not speedily discharged, will render it beyond my power, or any man's power, to save you. And, for this reason, Madame, it must, some way, be got rid of: anything farther which may be necessary toward your restoration, it will be my affair to attend to."

What Madame said to Master Hue, and how he comforted her.

And when Madame had thus heard Master Hue's opinion of her case, she said to him, "Alas, Master Hue, it is true, I have a grief at heart, but it is one which a word from you would go far to remove. And, I give you my honour, if you will but help me toward it, that the obligation shall never be forgotten; and, besides, you shall have the richest scarlet mantle that money can procure."

And when Master Hue heard talk of the scarlet mantle, the notion pleased him well, so he said to her, "Madame, I am in all things your obedient servant. Lay the obligation you will upon me, and it shall be a pleasure to me to obey you."

"Now, for that, Master Hue," said Madame, "we thank you. Physicians, you know, must be confessors too, at times. And although what I am about to admit to you, is neither anything that I need be ashamed to confess, or you afraid to hear; nevertheless, I have to request that you will keep it a secret. So I will tell you, Master Hue, that what is vexing me is this: how to contrive to get away, for two or three months, to revisit our property, which we ought to have done long ago; for it is now more than sixteen years since we were there. And, for this, our affairs, Master Hue, have fared none the better; and we know well, that Madame will never consent to our going."

"Ho, Madame," said Master Hue, on hearing this, "if there is nothing more serious than this amiss with you, I'll manage matters for you. So make your mind easy, for you shall go. I know how to settle all such jobs. Just you keep your room for three or four days, and for the rest, leave it to me."

Then went straight Master Hue to the Queen, and said to her, "Madame, I have just seen your cousin."

And "Alas," said the Queen, "and how did you leave her?"

"Ah, Madame," said he, "poorly, very poorly: I see only one hope for her."

"Alas," said the Queen, "and is it so serious? what is it you would have her do?"

"'Fore God, Madame," said he, "I see nothing for it but that she should throw away all care; and refresh herself, for two or three months, in her native air."

"Alas, and you think that that would bring her round?" said the Queen.

"Madame, with God's assistance," said Master Hue, "I think it will. Something, too, may be done in the way of electuaries and of diet."

Then the Queen went to see Madame, whom she found, as you have heard, in bed. Then she comforted her as well as she could, dwelling more particularly on how speedily she would be cured if once again in her native air, and how Master Hue had told her so; and bidding her to keep up her spirits, and to set out at once; for, the sooner the better, when health was at stake. Madame, who was not in want of any other remedy than to be spared the anguish of her heart, at seeing the other lovers dancing, singing, and making merry; whispering, each one, the other in the ear; when all such delights were to be proscribed to her, till the return of the joy of her heart, was marvellously recovered at this permission

o

to be off. Brief, as soon as was possible, she had taken her farewell of the King and Queen. And it was for two months that the Queen gave her leave to be absent; she promising, that if, by that time, she found herself restored, she would at once return. And after this, she went.

CHAPTER LXIX.

How Madame arrived at her country-house; and of how she was received.

THE AUTHOR.

NOW, it is not in our power to give the name either of the country, property, or hotel where the Lady descended; and for the simple reason, that history makes no mention of them; and this, from considerations which will presently appear. So we can only inform our reader, that her principal seat was at a league from a principal city, and that at another league from the said seat was an Abbey, which the Lady's ancestors had founded—the said Abbey being at a like distance from the city: so that the said city, Madame's hotel, and the Abbey may be said to have lain in a triangle.

Of the arrival of Madame; and of the joy it caused in the country, and the reception she met with.

THE AUTHOR.

And when the news had spread, that Madame was in the country, incontinent, all the Lords and Ladies, Squires and Gentlemen, citizens and their wives, of the vicinity, came to pay her their respects. So that, already, her grief began to assuage.

[14]And now I will refrain a moment, to speak of Madame and her country-house, and I will tell you of the Abbey, and of Damp Abbot.

Here tells of Damp Abbot, and of his Abbey.

THE AUTHOR.

This Abbey, which is nameless, was, as you have heard, founded by the ancestors of Madame, who had so bountifully endowed it, that, at this day, it is accounted one of the ten richest in France; and Damp Abbot, of it, for the time being, was the son of a rich burgess of the town, who, in consideration of a timely word in the ear of the King, and from his friends at the Court of Rome, so judiciously placed his money to account, that said son at length was made Abbot. And now, at the age of twenty-five, our Abbot was big and brawny; and whether to wrestle, jump, vault, throw, pitch the sledge, or put the stone; at tennis, or what you will, there was not a monk, knight, squire or citizen alive, who, when Damp Abbot had chosen to do his best, had ever proved his match; and if on the one hand he kept himself in condition with all sorts of exercises and sports; on the other, he spent his money with so good a grace, so handsomely, that he was exceedingly beloved and praised of all. And when Damp Abbot heard of the arrival of Madame, he was wonderfully pleased; and he immediately ordered one of his carts to be filled with haunches of venison, boars' heads, hares, conies, pheasants, partridges, fat capons, pullets, pigeons, &c.; and all this he sent to Madame, together with a pipe of wine *de Beaulne;* praying of her to be good enough to accept it, as it was meant, at his hands. And when Madame saw all this fine present, you need hardly ask if she was flattered! So she ordered the party who brought it to be well provided for, sending back her compliments to Damp Abbot.

And the time when all this happened was not far from Lent; and in the Abbey, the greater pardons were to be had on the Mondays, Tuesdays, Wednesdays, and Fridays of

Lent. Now Madame, in a spirit of deep devotion, as became that holy season, determined to be there. But in order to allow the press of the common sort to be over, she refrained for some fifteen days. Then she sent word to Damp Abbot, that the next day she would attend at high mass; and after, procure her pardons. On hearing this, Damp Abbot, who had never seen her, was delighted. So he gave orders to have all the holy reliques laid out on the grand altar, in the oratory of the chapel, where all her ancestors lay interred. And, in addition to this, he sent a requisition to the good town for whatever was to be found in the way of lampreys, salmon, or other fresh or salt water fish. Then he had stabling provided for all her equipage, and viands got together of every sort; and besides, he had fires lighted in all the rooms, for the season was such as required them. And when at length Madame was come, and had alighted at the door of the monastry, she was there met by all the officers, and the noblest churchmen of the same, who, on their knees, with Damp Abbot at their head, presented to her the keys, with all the choicest of their ornaments, as also the tender of their humble duties; for all which Madame thanked them greatly. And when she had made her offering at the great altar, she was conducted to her chapel to hear mass. Then, as she was leaving, after prayers, she was met by Damp Abbot and all his convent, on their knees; the said Damp Abbot saying to her, " Ever, and our most redoubted Lady, deign to accept your welcome from your own hall; and truly joyful and thankful are we, God has vouchsafed to us the grace to see, and to receive you in it. Into your hands, Lady, as at once our patron and our founder, we resign and offer up the Abbey with all that is in it, our bodies as our goods." Then said Madame to him, " Abbot, from our heart we thank you; and if there is anything we can either do for you or for your convent, you may count upon us." Then, Madame asked, "if she could see the holy reliques?" On this, Damp Abbot, who was on his knees, got up, and diving his great fist into the chest, brought up arms and bones by the dozen, which were in it, of holy Saints deceased. And then he harangued Madame as follows, telling her,—" Madame, yonder lies the body of that most valiant Prince, your ancestor, our first founder, who, on his return from the Holy Land, brought back with him this skull, this hand, and other bone of Such and Such a blessed saint, martyr, or holy woman. My Lord, his brother, who lies near him, it was, who gave us these thumbs, with the under jaw, and the toe-nail. They once belonged to So and So, and So and So; blessed virgins and sufferers, now with God. And, not to weary you; one or other of your progenitors have presented us with, I may say, all these reliques, and made this church, and much of all you see attached to it, what they are. The remainder has been the work of my predecessors, the Abbots, and the divers Lords and Ladies of the country, whose monuments you see around."

And when Madame had kissed these most precious reliques, she offered a cope, and two tunics, with a covering for the great altar, of rich crimson velvet, all wrought with gold. And when Madame thought to return, and her people were baiting the horses, or hurrying on their bridles, Damp Abbot led her into his room, to warm herself; which said room was all neat, and trim and carpeted, and it had glass windows in it; brief, was such as became a good fellow, like himself, and one who knew how to take his ease. Then he said to all, "Let us retire, and leave Madame alone, that she may warm and refresh herself."

And so they did. And when Madame, and the Ladies and Gentlewomen who were with her, had warmed and rested themselves, Madame sent word to know, "if the chariots were ready?"

Then Damp Abbot, who had already told his maître-d'hôtel that Madame was to dine with him, when everything was ready, came and said to her—"That if she must go, he hoped she would accept his arm." And so saying, Damp Abbot stepped up to Madame, and taking her by the hand, led her into his dining-room, for all the world like an audience-hall, so nicely was it hung, carpeted, and glazed. And he had had a good fire put in it. And in the hall were three tables, each covered with the whitest of linen; and on the cupboards was show plate of every sort. And when Madame saw the tables laid, she said to Damp Abbot, "And is this your dinner-hour?"

"And is it not time?" said he: "it must be twelve by this."

But he had had the clock put on; and as he spoke it struck. And when Madame heard it strike, she was for hurrying away. And when Damp Abbot saw that she was determined to go, he said to her, "Madame, by the fealty I owe you, you are not going to leave us till you have had your dinner!"

"Dinner!" said Madame, "it is not to be thought of. I have too much to do elsewhere."

Then said Damp Abbot, "Ha, maître-d'hôtel; and you, my Ladies, will you stand by, and see me denied in this manner?"

Then the maître-d'hôtel, and the Ladies and Gentlewomen, who were all fasting, and as hungry as could be, thinking, besides, that they would get a better dinner by dining with Damp Abbot than they might at home, began to nudge one another for each to appeal to Madame. And at last, on their telling her, that it was the first prayer Damp Abbot had ever made her, she consented.

Then Damp Abbot, all bowing, smiles, and gracious, fell on his knees, and humbly thanked Madame, and the other Ladies and Gentlewomen. Then the horses were sent back to the stables, and all were restored to good humour.

Then said Damp Abbot to Madame, "Madame, we are now in the holy season of penitence, so you are not to be surprised with the miserable fare before you. Besides, it was only late last evening that I heard of your intention to visit our Abbey."

"Abbot," said Madame, "we are sure we shall want for nothing."

Then Damp Abbot called for water, that they might wash their hands. And when it came, it was rose-water, with the chill off; an attention which pleased Madame and the other Ladies greatly. Then Madame required Damp Abbot, as Prelate, to wash after: which he would on no account do: so, to let the chaplains of Madame proceed, he withdrew to the sideboard, as if to see to something. And when the table was all ready, Madame desired Damp Abbot "To be seated."

Then said Damp Abbot to her, "Madame, you are the Lady, and the Abbess of this house: it is for you to sit, leave me to take care of myself."

And at the foot of the table, where Madame presided, sat Madame Jehanne, Madame Katharine, and the Lord de Gency, who had come with her. And at the second table were the Prior of the convent, Isabelle, and the other Gentlewomen, and two or three Squires; and Sir Geoffrey de Sainct-Amant was opposite the said Isabelle. Then Damp Abbot, with his napkin before him, went to the cupboard, where was the wine, and brought to Madame a sop of white ypocras; then handing it about to the other tables. Then he carried round the Lenten fruits, then the sweatmeats. Madame, all this time, was begging him to be seated; but he would only answer, "Madame, you must allow me this once to keep the company of maître-d'hôtel; and show him how his Lady should be served."

But when the first dishes were on the table, and she still found Damp Abbot standing before them, Madame said to Damp Abbot, " Really, Abbot, if you will persist this way in standing, we will get up too."

" Sooner than that, Madame," said Damp Abbot, " I will obey you."

Madame was then going to bid some of them rise, to make way for him. But Damp Abbot said, " Let everybody sit still: God forbid that any should be disturbed for such as I."

Then he got a stool, and sat himself down, opposite Madame, only a little lower down. Then he had white wine, *de Beaulne,* handed round; and after it red, of three or four kinds; and all had of them. What need I tell you of all their good cheer, or of how they all encouraged one another to eat and to drink? To be short, for many a long day Madame had never found herself so well entertained. So that soon it came, that the eyes, those archers of the heart, as well on the part of Madame as of Damp Abbot, began to launch their fiery darts: those of Madame at Damp Abbot; and those of Damp Abbot at Madame. Brief, so quickly came they to an understanding, that under cover of the cloth and napkins, which were long and trailing, first, from as if unintentionally touching one another with their feet, they got, at length, to treading on each other's toes. So that, so passionately were they absorbed with this new, below-board pastime, that, what was upon it, was quickly forgotten. However, Damp Abbot, who, on this new insight into the virtues of Dame Abbess and Foundress, was the more joyous of the two; though he might not eat, never once ceased drinking, now to one, now to another. What need I say more? Never, in his life, had Damp Abbot been in better spirits. One moment he was up, and had his stool placed before the Ladies; and when he had sat a little with them, he would be off to the Gentlewomen, telling them, "they had lost their appetites," or "that they were in love;" and "that they must eat away heartily and be merry." Then he would make for Madame's women, and when he had had a jolly good laugh with them, return to Madame, and gloriously plant himself down by her side. Then would begin the archers to shoot again, more hard than ever; and those tender interpreters, the toes, to press the mutual ardour of their flames. And of all the sorts of wines, the viands, the lampreys; the fish, as well fresh as salt: in a word, how they were regaled and entertained, I will, at present, say nothing more; turning rather to the sequel of our tale, which, in all conscience, is rich enough.

CHAPTER LXX.

How Madame and Damp Abbot fell into discourse, and of how she thanked him.

THE AUTHOR.

AND when the tables were removed; and the mâitre-d'hôtel and all the rest had gone to dine, Madame thanked Damp Abbot for the kindly entertainment she had met with; and so, talking, or walking about the hall, they amused themselves as best they could, whilst their people were dining. And Madame had given order, that by the time maître-d'hôtel had done, the horses and carriages were to be at the door. But Damp Abbot, so that Madame might repose herself, had had his own best bed new made with fair fresh linen. So he said to her, "How, Madame, surely you are not going to make so little of the good old customs of the place?"

"And what, Abbot," inquired Madame, "are the good old customs?"

"Madame," said he, "they are, that whenever any

Ladies of condition, or Gentlewomen, have dined at the Abbey, they and their attendants should accept of a bed, either to sleep or rest themselves, as they please; and this as well in winter as in summer; and that they stay supper. So, Madame, for this afternoon, I make over to you my own room, and will sleep, myself, somewhere else. It is a usage has never yet been departed from in our Abbey; so I hope, Madame, you are not going to break in upon it."

At length, such were the prayers of Damp Abbot and the Ladies, that Madame became gracious, and said, "She would keep up the good old customs."

Then Madame withdrew to her apartment; and there she found wine and dessert on the cupboard. Then the door was closed, and Madame was left by herself, with her Ladies, to repose till the time of vespers.

CHAPTER LXXI.

How Damp Abbot was extolled.

AND when the Ladies and Gentlewomen were all left to themselves, first Isabelle began to open, and said, "And how, Madame, have you nothing to say, nor the rest of you, sots, of Damp Abbot's good cheer, and the reception he has given us? Certainly, I never saw such a table; more on one, or drunk better wine."

"Certainly," said Madame, "the man seems a respectable one enough."

"And is that all you have to say for him!" said Madame Jehanne. "A more engaging man I never came across."

"And yet you, Madame," said Katharine, "were not for staying, if we had not made you!"

"Ha!" said Isabelle, "I knew from the first he would carry his point: he was in earnest about it."

Then they all fell to together, as women will do, when alone, to praise the magnificence, the jolliness, and the fine proportions of Damp Abbot, and all with such a relish and a gusto, one would fancy they would never cease. However, Madame, whose great griefs were now beginning to abate, and who, besides, was more taken with Damp Abbot than she cared them to see, allowing them to jabber, simply confined herself to saying, at intervals, "the man seems a respectable one enough."

And while they were all still busy belauding Damp Abbot, the bell rung for vespers, so that they were forced to rise, without having so much as closed an eye.

And as soon as vespers were over, and when Madame was thinking to mount, Damp Abbot took her by the hand, on which Madame said to him, "Hey, Abbot, where next?"

Then said Damp Abbot, "Permit me, Madame, to lead you to a slight collation, for it is high time."

And as he said this, he placed Madame's arm under his, and gently pressing her hand, he led her into a lower hall, which was well hung, and where was a great fire, and the tables were spread. And on them were salads and vinegar, and lampreys, roasted and in pies, and sauces; and roaches, and barbels, and salmon, cut in stakes, griddled and boiled; and fat carp, and great dishes of craw-fish, and huge river eels, swimming in their fat; and, besides these, there were dishes and plates of various devices, covered with dessert; jellies, white, carnation, and of gold; tarts *à la bourbonnoise*, cheese-cakes, flawns, sugar-plums, white almonds, rose-water crackers; together with figs from Melique, Allegarde, and Marseilles, raisins, from Corinth, with abundance of other things, all laid out in the order of a banquet.

CHAPTER LXXII.

How Madame found herself compelled to take part in the Collation.

MADAME who, though hungry, had no idea of taking anything save a cup of wine or a biscuit, found the tables, however, groaning with all these good things. For the traitor, God of love, had so furiously assailed her with his arms during all the time of dinner, that, either to eat or to drink she had had no heed. But as nature seldom fails, sooner or later, to make her wants to be attended to, Madame's appetite was now so much restored, that, to stay, she required but little pressing. And when the rest of the company saw Madame seated, and Damp Abbot at the middle of the table opposite to her, with very little prayers on the part of Damp Abbot, they consented to fall into their places. And, by Madame's orders, and to be better company to one another, it was enjoined them all to sit as well on each side, as at the ends of the table. And that nothing should be wanting, and all might pass more pleasantly, four or five monks of the more jovial of the fraternity were sent for and introduced. And thus the table was full,

What need I tell you more? The mirth and jollity was such, that among the like number of persons, greater was never seen. However, at length, the hour arrived when Madame and Damp Abbot, to their great regret and sorrow, were obliged to part. And as she was stepping into her chariot, there were Damp Abbot and Prior, most humbly thanking Madame for the great honour that she had done them, and recommending to her the church and convent. Then Madame said to them, "We shall often see you, for we hope, from henceforth, more frequently to be sharers of your pardons than hitherto we have been able." On hearing which they were well pleased. Presently she continued, " But as for you, Abbot, we have to request that there may be a truce to all this prodigality; for, assuredly, to-day's feasting has been altogether out of all conscience, and it is not our wish to see the like repeated."

"At least, Madame," said Damp Abbot, "you will not decline or forbid me to offer you, after mass, a morsel, *à la poudre de duc*, with either white wine, or ypocras, or grenasche, or malmsey, or Greek wine, as you would prefer?"

"But I will," said Madame: "at such a season as this it is our business to fast."

"To fast!" said Damp Abbot; "it is not to be thought of. I can always give you absolution."

And after, Damp Abbot mounted on his horse, and conducted Madame a good way, and then took his leave.

CHAPTER LXXIII.

How Madame and her Women praised Damp Abbot, the one to the other.

The Author.

AND as soon as Damp Abbot had left them, and gone back to his Abbey, then commenced his praises, and it was who loudest could extol him. And Isabelle, who was the most rattling, began to say, "Ha, Madame, Madame, you are much to blame to refuse a good thing when it falls in your way."

Then Madame Jehanne said to her, "Isabelle, you are mistaken; Madame often intends to go, and she will dine each time she does."

To this said Madame Katharine, "You are both in the

wrong. There is no occasion whatsoever that Madame should dine every time she goes to the convent; but I certainly think she is perfectly warranted in accepting, once in a way, the civilities of Damp Abbot; for, as far as one can judge, they are offered out of real good nature, and without any afterthoughts. He can well afford it, or it would be another thing. What say you, Madame; am I not in the right?"

Then Madame, when she had heard them all round, said, "Of his mutton we will be content with the wool. So we will confine ourselves to his snatch, *à la poudre de duc*, white wine, ypocras, grenasche, malmsey, or other rich or rarer sort; that will be quite sufficient. But, seriously, it is our intention to acquire for ourselves all these pardons, or, at any rate, most of them; for we hardly know when again we may be in these parts, or able to procure them."

And by this they had gotten to their hotel. Madame, into whose breast this new flame had now wormed its way, was unable, all this night, to sleep, doing nothing but sigh and mourn, and toss and turn; planning with herself how, soonest, she could get again to see Damp Abbot, and open herself to him more fully; whilst Damp Abbot, on his side, tormented with the like imaginations, and who had not yet forgotten all the pleasant earnest had been interchanged between them, either above or below the board, had not another thought, "But when will Madame be coming for her pardons?"

And when the long-wished-for day was come, Madame said to her women, "That, in order the better to prepare herself to receive, fitly and worthily, the pardons, she had resolved to confess herself unfeignedly to Damp Abbot, who was a prelate, and, so far as she could judge of him, a man of a deep devotion."

Then said Madame Jehanne to Madame, "Madame,

you will do very rightly; I was with him yesterday myself."

Then Madame bid the little Perrin, of her bedchamber, to get on a horse, and go and tell Damp Abbot, "that Madame would be glad to see him presently."

On hearing this, Damp Abbot lost no time, as he was anxious to show his great respect for Madame. Then Madame, after he had made his reverence, present all her Ladies, openly said to him,—"Abbot, the more worthily to be constituted partakers of your pardons, we have determined to confess ourselves."

"Ah, Madame," said Damp Abbot, "how stand you with God? And, Madame, who purpose you to be your confessor, so that I may give him dispensation, if unhappily unprovided?"

"Then, said Madame, "There is none here more able or sufficient than yourself."

To which Damp Abbot replied, "Ah, Madame, if there is any good or efficacy in me, it is in virtue of my staff; deprive me of it, and I am no more worthy than is another."

With these words, Madame retired into her dressing-room, in which there was a good fire, Damp Abbot devoutly following her. And when the door was closed, for two hours she poured out before him, in all humbleness and penitence of spirit, all the little kindnesses, and the amorous mercies, in which, from her youth up, she had indulged herself; in all honour, however, and without any sort of villany, and, for all which, Damp Abbot gave her absolution, as tenderly as he could. And before they separated, Madame went to her coffer, and took from it a very large and splendid ruby ring, all set in gold, and putting it on his middle finger, said to him, "Sweetheart, my only thought, my soul's desire, this day I elect you as my only friend, and with this ring I wed you."

Then Damp Abbot, as humbly as he could find words, thanked her, all the while muttering to himself the good old saw, which says,

> He who a chance refuses,
> Deserves when he loses.

Then he gave Madame absolution, and kissing her as softly as he could, with the holy kiss of charity, he took his leave. And as he was returning through the hall, he said, feelingly, to the Ladies and Gentlewomen present, "Till she calls let none of you, my sisters and my friends, disturb her. May God be with you; Madame, I leave to your care."

Whilst Madame, to recover a little the colour which her mortification had withdrawn from her cheeks, remained so long behind, that, at last, her Ladies and her people heard the clock announce the hour for prayers, on which Madame, who heard it too, called for Jehanne, and when she had put on some of the plainest things she had, and, the better to cover her face, a handkerchief over her head; in this simple and unpretending manner, her eyes and her face toward the ground, she went, in deep contrition, to hear mass; and after that to dinner, and so the day passed. And the one following, Wednesday, pardons being again to be dispensed, Madame having signified her intention to be present, Damp Abbot, in the greatest spirits, had all sorts of good things prepared; ypocras, and other foreign wines, of various kinds, decanted; white and red herrings and more substantial victuals for the companions, besides good stabling and provender for the horses. And when Madame had heard mass, Damp Abbot took Madame under his arm, and led her into his apartment, where there was a good fire, and breakfast laid out. And when Madame had plentifully breakfasted, Damp Abbot took her by the hand, saying, "Madame, while all your people are finishing and regaling themselves, allow me to show you our new buildings."

Then they both left the room, and had quickly wandered so far out of one chamber and into another, that her Ladies lost all trace of her. And before they came out of the secret closet, Damp Abbot gave Madame a piece of fine black velvet, which afterwards she quietly sent for. Then Madame returned into the dining-hall, where the company were, and when her Ladies came in from looking for her, Madame, as if in a rage, was down upon them, saying, "I told you to come after me, and I thought, all the time, you were; but you would rather sit here, the lot of you, cramming yourselves with Abbot's good things, and roasting your toes at the fire, than have a thought or care for your mistress!"

"Ah, Madame," said they, "though we went almost immediately after you, do what we would we could not find you!"

On this, Damp Abbot put in a word, saying, "Ah, Madame, do for this once let them be forgiven."

Then Madame, relenting, began to praise Damp Abbot's fine buildings, which she said she had been through. Then she made for her chariot, on which Damp Abbot took his leave of her. What need I say more? Hardly a week of Lent went over in which she did not succeed, with a no less assiduous attendance, in gaining for herself the pardons, &c., as often as not remaining, along with one or two others, banqueting, dining, and supping. And after she got up, it was frequently to hunt, with Damp Abbot, stags, foxes, pheasants, and the like game. And in this manner the season of Lent slipped heedlessly and joyously away.

CHAPTER LXXIV.

How the Queen wrote, the first time, to Madame.

THE AUTHOR.

AND when the two months had passed away, which she had engaged for to the Queen, and not a word was heard of her, either by letter or yet message, the Queen, who knew not well what to make of it, wrote to her as follows:—

TO OUR VERY DEAR AND MUCH-LOVED COUSIN.

VERY dear and much-loved Cousin, seeing that the two months, at the expiration of which you promised us to return, have now elapsed, with half another, and even more; and that since the day you left us, so much as a line, on your part, we have never been honoured with, we cannot altogether suppress our wonder at the same; so, we have to require of you, as soon as this shall have reached your hand, to return to us, so much are we desirous to see you. And if there is any matter in which we can gratify you, it shall be attended to, with all our heart, as our trusty secretary, Julien de Bray, will tell you, and whom you are to listen to in this matter, as you would to ourself. Dear friend and Cousin, God have you in his safe keeping. Written from our town of Paris, this eighth day of April.

BONNE.

CHAPTER LXXV.

How Madame, without waiting for any further explanations, made her answer to the Queen.

THE AUTHOR.

AND one day it came, when Madame was at the Abbey, in search of pardons, that there happened to arrive the said Master Julien de Bray, Secretary to the Queen; the said Secretary finding her seated at table, and at her dinner. And so at once, as one of her old friends, and fresh from Court, presuming, naturally, Madame would be no less pleased to see him than he was to see her, he eagerly handed her the letters; but Madame, who was exceedingly offended he should have found her there above all places, with very little ceremony took the letters from him, and with as little, read them. And then, that she might be the sooner rid of him and his letters, she hurried through with her dinner, and then home, so that she might write her answer. And before she went, she said to Master Julien, "Get your dinner, and then let me see you."

Then Damp Abbot, who, of his own nature, was naturally kind, bade Master Secretary "to be welcome;" and, that he might the more readily chat with him, he sat down opposite to him. And while all this was going on, one of Damp Abbot's keepers came in, and told him, "how he had just put up a splendid buck, and that there were ten or twelve hinds with him, and if they would but come they were certain of a famous run."

Then said Damp Abbot, "It is too late for to-day, keeper. Madame is gone; but, without fail, she will be here to-morrow."

"And how," said Master Julien, "does Madame hunt then, of her own accord?"

"Of her own accord!" said Damp Abbot, without even once thinking; "I rather fancy so. Two or three times a week; sometimes on horseback, sometimes on foot, just as the fit takes her."

"And, sir," said Master Julien, "have you then dogs and hounds?"

"Ay, have I!" said he, "and hawks too, and as fine as any prelate in France."

"Holy Mary," said Master Julien, "and you have reason to be proud of the same!"

And as he was spying Damp Abbot, he saw on his finger the big ruby ring which he at once remembered to have belonged, on a time, to Madame, and though he did not care to have it seen he saw it, he did not the less omit to book it. And when he had had his dinner, and got out of Damp Abbot as much as he had a mind to, he took his leave, most humbly and plentifully thanking him for all his kindness. Then he got upon his horse, and went to Madame, to whom he enlarged himself, as by the Queen's letter Madame had been told he was to do. Then Madame, who had no other thought than how quickest to be rid of him, gave him her answer to the Queen, which ran as follows:—

To MY EVER DREAD AND SOVEREIGN LADY THE QUEEN.

EVER dread and sovereign Lady, to your very good grace, as humbly as I can find words, I recommend myself by Master Julien de Bray, your Secretary. I have received your letter, and, too well, Madame, am sensible of its contents; so, as humbly as I am able, I have to crave that you will pardon, in that, even in appearance I should have failed toward you. Matters of the last importance alone are now delaying me here; for although

already, thank God, I am beginning to find myself in some degree stronger, one or two little affairs still remain unsettled, which none save myself can attend to; these transacted, I shall at once return, in obedience, Madame, to your commands. And in this, as in any other matter, require of me what you will, and, with the grace of the Holy Spirit, it shall be a privilege to me to comply. My ever dread and Sovereign Lady, may all felicity be yours. Written with my hand, this sixteenth day of April.
Your most humble and obedient.

CHAPTER LXXVI.

How Madame handed her letters to Master Julien, and gave him his instructions.

AND when Madame, out of her great haste to get rid of Master Julien, had written her letters, she at once gave them to him, charging him hurriedly with a few words to the same effect, and which he was to carry to the Queen. And for that matter she treated him civilly enough, offering him only, however, a glass of wine, without anything more. And although, at the Court, he had been one of her most intimate friends and obedient servants, and he had been sent direct from the Queen, nevertheless, so impatient was she to see him off that she never even once asked for King, Queen, Lord, or Lady of her acquaintance, merely wishing him " Good-bye."

Master Julien, who had seen enough of the carryings on of Madame and of Damp Abbot, and of all their sporting, whatever he may have thought of it all, judged it, however, advisable to keep his observations to himself. So, hoping she might speedily be more completely restored, he took his leave, and got as far that day as the place where he was to lie for the night. And so continued

Master Julien by his posts that at last he got again to the presence of the Queen, who, as soon as ever she saw him, and before he could get up to her, called out to him, "Fair Cousin, comes she, Master Julien?"

"Madame," said he, coldly, "to your grace she most humbly commends herself, and I was to tell you, you are soon to see her."

Then he delivered his letter, and told her anything farther she might have charged him with; but, like a sagacious man as he was, for the present he said no more.

Then the Queen, who was no better satisfied with Madame's letter than with her message, said to Master Julien, "But how was she; did she look well?"

"Look well!" said Master Julien, "I never in my life saw her looking better."

"And how does she pass her time?" said the Queen; "what is she about?"

"By my faith," said Master Julien, "and that, Madame, is more than I can tell you, for I was hardly an hour with her altogether; in such a hurry was she to give me my despatches, and to pack me off, that I neither had time to speak with Lady nor Gentlewoman; neither Madame Jehanne, nor Madame Katharine, nor Madame Isabelle, nor man nor woman belonging to her, farther than to say, 'How are you, my friend?' as I went in, and 'God be with you, old fellow,' as I went out."

Then the Queen said to him, "Had you any means of judging whether she has any friends, or who they are?"

Then he told her how he had found her at an abbey, where she had gone to procure pardons; and how she had been at table with the Abbot, the two sitting opposite to one another, and hardly anybody else present; and how, when she had heard his errand, and read the letters, she had seemed a good deal put about, and had sent for her horses and gone home. Then he told her about the hunting; how the keeper had come in, and brought Damp Abbot word of the great stag, and the number of hinds which Madame was to hunt the following day. But the affair of the ruby that he saw upon Damp Abbot's finger, like a wary man, he kept to himself. The Queen, when she had heard thus much, probably thinking it to be sufficient, asked him no more questions, simply forbidding him to mention the matter to any one; at the same time, out of a respect for the reputation of Madame, adding, " We will all have our own ideas of happiness; one this, another that: Madame has hers." And with these words the Queen retired, a good deal thoughtful, half unwilling to believe that Madame would have ever so far forgotten herself, or laid herself open to so injurious a construction. And so she made up her mind to let another five or six weeks pass over before she would again either write or send. And when the five or six weeks had elapsed, and still no Madame appeared, nor yet tidings of her, the Queen began to be a little nettled; so she had fresh letters subscribed of the same tenor with the last. And she had them given to her own especial courier, with orders to make all the diligence he could, as well in going as on the way back. And when Master Courier arrived, he found Madame in the fields along with Damp Abbot, with whom she was afterwards to sup. And when Madame had seen and read the letter, there and then, without even so much as returning, she indited her answer, which was brief, and to this effect, *That she would soon be back.* And this she gave to the courier, without so much as offering him a morsel to eat, or a drop to drink, or once inquiring for King, or Queen, or any man or woman alive. And when the Queen had got Madame's answer, and read it, and heard how he had met her in the fields with Damp Abbot, she was a good deal annoyed, and quickly came to her own conclusions on the matter. And so she determined to write no more to her, and that she might come or stay away, exactly as it pleased herself.

On the other hand, Madame, who had been in a mortal fright at the thoughts of having to leave her ghostly father, comforted him in every way she could, telling him, "Good friend, trust me for it, as long as it is possible to find an excuse, or to put off the horrible hour, you and your company I will never forsake."

Is it not enough? In hunting, hawking, fowling, and all sorts of jollity, the greater part of the summer passed away. And now I will say no more of all their matters, or of all the comfort they were to one another, but I will return to the Lord de Saintré and his companions.

CHAPTER LXXVII.

How the Lord de Saintré and his companions came to the Court of the Emperor; and how, to their great honour, they were delivered by the Lords, hereinafter named; being all noblemen, and men of fame and reputation.

The substance of this Chapter having, in its general character, already appeared, it is here omitted.—*Translator*.

CHAPTER LXXVIII.

How the French arrived, and of the honours were paid them.

This Chapter is suppressed, out of the same consideration that the last one was.—*Translator*.

CHAPTER LXXIX.

How the battle went, and of the ordnance of the Emperor.

The account of this battle is omitted. It is sufficient to say that, both sides doing valiantly, the Germans, of course, getting the worst of it; the Emperor, to save the honour of his own people, interposes. —*Translator.*

CHAPTER LXXX.

How the Imperial King-at-arms distributed the prizes, and what he said to the champions.

This Chapter, offering no new interest to the modern reader, is passed over.—*Translator.*

CHAPTER LXXXI.

How the Lord de Saintré and his companions returned to Paris, and came to see the King.

THEN the Lord de Saintré, and the rest, his companions, came by Lusarches to Saint-Cosme, and passing by the shrine of Saint Damien, they got, in the evening, to Saint Denis. And as soon as the news of their long-wished-for return was blown abroad, then were King, Queen, Lords, and Ladies, and indeed, everybody else in the highest spirits. And by the King's orders, my Lords, the Dukes of Berry, and of Bourgoyne, the King's brothers, went out to meet him; and at their return they placed him between them. And with them went the Counts de la Marche, de Flandres, de Clermont, de Retel, de Brienne, de la Perche, de Beaumont, d'Armignac, the Count-dolphin d'Auvergne, all ordered, equally, to do him honour. And when they had got to the King, he gave them a most hearty reception, as did the Queen, as did the other Lords, Ladies, Gentlewomen, and, in fact, everybody connected with the Court. And, not to be tedious, as soon as they had all made their reverences, and the first congratulations were over, and the excitement, on seeing them, had begun a little to subside, the Lord de Saintré, amazed beyond all conception that he could no where see Madame, whom above all the world he was longing most to have a word with, at once concluded, that something surely must have happened to her. So, making for Madame de Sancte-More, his cousin; and first having chatted of one thing, then another, he presently said to her, carelessly, and as if he was thinking of something else, " But, Goody, what has become of Madame? I see most of the old faces; is she about, or is she ill?"

"Faith," said she, "ill or not ill, she is ill enough in the graces of the Queen. For about three weeks after you left, something unaccountable came over her: so that, visibly, she was wasting away. And from what the Queen's physician said, she would certainly be very shortly either dead or in a consumption, supposing her native air to fail to bring her round. So, of course, the Queen told her, by all means, to go; but to come back in two months. But, as at the end of the two months, and a half to the back of it, no Madame was making her appearance, the Queen wrote to her by Master Julien de Bray, reminding her, that her time was up; and since, she sent to her again. But all the answer she could ever get was, 'Coming, Madame; coming;' but with all her coming, she has never come."

And when the Lord de Saintré heard tell how Madame was ill, incontinent flashed upon him all she had ever told him, "How she never would know peace of mind again till she had seen him returned in safety." And surely, said he to himself, It was to hide herself, since her sorrow she could not, that she went. But, presently, comforting himself, he recollected, that if it was sorrow for his departure had driven her away, the tidings of his return, as assuredly, would bring her back. However, on reflection, he came to the conclusion, that, considering everything, he could not do better than be, himself, the herald of his own rightglorious self. And continuing, some ten or twelve days, in the same opinion, he then said to the King, "Sir, if it would be your good pleasure to allow me to absent myself for some few days, I should feel myself very greatly indebted to you. My Lady-Mother is solicitous to see me."

To which the King replied, "How, Saintré; off again? But if your mother really does wish to see you, by all means go, and you may remain for a month."

And when the Lord de Saintré had thanked him, he set to work, and never stopped, day or night, till he had got himself, and all his people, and his horses, and everything about him in the sprucest order, the better to delight Madame, and take her by surprise. And when he had taken his leave of the King, the Queen, and my Lords, he got on his horse, nor ever once halted, but to rest, till he had got to the good town, at one league from the hotel where Madame stayed, and there he dined. And then he dressed and refreshed himself. And when he had put on a doublet of satin, trimmed with gold; with scarlet stockings, all worked in the device and colours of Madame; with a natty little cap upon his head, as was the fashion of those times, with a brooch in it; thus arrayed, accompanied by two Knights and seven Squires; all in a no less costly attire; with the like robes and devices; he set out for the hotel of Madame. And when they had got to the door, and had knocked, the porter inquired of them, "What it was they wanted?"

To which the Lord de Saintré replied, "that he was anxious to see Madame, and that he might say, the Lord Saintré was there."

"She is out, then," said the porter; "she went this

morning to the Abbey to hear mass; and she was to stay dinner."

So, from that he went to the Abbey. And when he got there, he found that they had already dined; and that, after dinner and bed, Madame and Damp Abbot had gone out hawking. Then, having first inquired, " in what direction he was most likely to fall in with them?" he told four or five of his people to put their spurs to their horses, one this way, one that; and that, as soon as they should see any ladies in the fields, they were to come back at once, and tell him. And so they all dispersed about; and, in a very few minutes, one of them came riding in post haste to tell him, " that he had seen a party of at least twenty, on horseback; and that seven or eight of them appeared Ladies, and evidently persons of condition."

Then this faithful Knight, who, till the instant after, never so much as suspected or dreamt of the falseness of his Lady, clapping spurs to his horse, made, as fast as its legs would carry him, for the presence of her whom above all the world he longed the most to feast his eyes upon. And as soon as he saw her, his heart began to bound within him; half conscious to himself of the pretty and the noble fellow he looked. And with this, he rode right up to her. But before he had reached her, one of the monks of Damp Abbot, who had been observing Saintré and his party, coming up to Damp Abbot, who was alongside of Madame, told him " to look, for he strongly suspected there must be strangers about, or something wrong." And when Damp Abbot looked closer, and saw the strange faces, and horsemen all galloping about the country, he was not too much at his ease, for he thought with himself, surely these are Madame's brothers and people, who have heard all about our carryings on, and they have now come down to make mince-meat of poor Damp Abbot. Then, on the instant, he wheeled his mule round, leaving Madame to her fate, and made off; his hawk upon his fist, and his three monks after him, their big-bellied bottles, and their prog-baskets dangling to the wind. However, Madame, her hawk upon her wrist, and seated on her good stout cob, and who was not so easily to be frightened out of her presence of mind, quietly stood her ground, to see who in the world it could be. And as soon as her people perceived it to be the Lord de Saintré, and had told her so; turning on them, she said in a fury, "May the devil seize the lot of you! And is that any reason why, for one man, you should all scamper off like that?"

And as she was yet speaking, the Lord de Saintré, now breathless with emotion, was alighting from his horse. And when Madame saw him on the ground, she said, aloud to him, so that all might hear, "Sir, Sir, a more unwelcome guest may it never be my part to entertain!"

This, however, so little reached the ears of Saintré, that, in an instant, he was down upon his knee; and, taking her by the hand, had already begun, "Ha, and how are you, my ever-to-be-redoubted Lady; and what are you doing?"

"How am I?" said she; "and cannot you look for yourself? Doing? do you not see that I have my hawk on my hand, and that I am sitting in my saddle?"

And without more ado, she turned her horse's head, and calling to her people, told them "to lead on, for that there was no occasion for their stopping;" letting them plainly see how little account she made of Saintré.

Saintré, who, this time, heard Madame clear enough, did not exactly know either what to think of it or what to do. However, as the Ladies and Gentlewomen came up, he shook them by the hand, and kissed them, and embraced them. Then he mounted again on his horse, and went after Madame. And when he got alongside of her, in a distressed tone he said to her, "Hey, Madame; can you possibly have meant it, when you spoke to me the way you did; or was it only done to try me? How had you the heart to speak so cruelly to one who has loved you so long, and never yet, in his life, disobeyed you? Hey, Madame, some one has been imposing upon you. If it be so, depend upon it, time and I will clear all up."

To this, Madame, who all the while was wishing him far enough, only replied, "Is there no other string but that you have to harp upon? if not, you may just as well give over at once."

And by the time all this had passed, Damp Abbot had begun to be a little recovered of his fright; so calling to him one of his monks, he bade him ask the maître-d'hôtel "Who this strange Lord was?" And when Damp Abbot heard that it was the Lord de Saintré; now reassured, he came to him at once, and paid him his respects, saying, "Most honoured Lord, be you the very welcome; you, and all your honourable company; for, I can assure you, there is not a noble in the land I have longer wished to lay my eyes on than yourself."

The Lord de Saintré comprehending, on hearing this, and seeing him, that he was an Abbot, and his people were monks; said to him, "Damp Abbot, you are welcome, as are all with you."

"Sir," said Damp Abbot, who was now himself again, "and what think you of the condescension of this noble Lady; thus deigning to honour with her presence the parlour of her poor confessor; to hunt with an unfortunate monk like myself?"

"Madame," said the Lord de Saintré, "is a Lady of all honour, and none of more discernment. There is no pleasanter pastime; and Madame has been ever a friend to the church."

These compliments interchanged, Damp Abbot gradually fell back, leaving Madame and the Lord de Saintré together. And as the vesper bell was now heard, and they were approaching the convent, Damp Abbot sent one of his monks to the maître-d'hôtel, bidding him to sound Madame, as to whether she would wish the Lord de Saintré to be invited to remain for supper. Then the maître-d'hôtel came to Madame, and asked her, " If she would wish the Lord de Saintré to sup with her ?"

To which, Madame, who had not distinctly heard him, only rejoined, by ordering him, " to speak up, that she could hear."

So he asked her the same thing again, and, this time, loud enough for Saintré to overhear.

And when Madame understood what he wanted, after a moment's reflection, she replied, " Ask him, if you have a mind ; but if he wants to go, he need not be under any ceremony on my account."

On hearing this, which he did clearly enough, the Lord de Saintré thought he had better decline at once, without exposing himself to any sort of pressing. Whilst Madame, now sick of him and his prayers, kept telling every one, "that she was tired, and to get home as quick as they could."

Now, Damp Abbot, who knew well what became a gentleman, had already gone on before, so as to have all things in readiness. And when they were come, the Lord de Saintré got off his horse, offering his assistance to Madame to do the same. But she called for one of her own people. And when they had both alighted, the Lord de Saintré was about to take his leave of Madame. And as she was holding out her hand to him, Damp Abbot, to show him his respect, said to Madame, " Madame, and is he then to go ? it remains with you."

" With him," said Madame.

Then Damp Abbot said to him, " Ha, my Lord de

Saintré; bear a little with Madame. Be entreated to stay."

Then the Lord de Saintré said to Damp Abbot, "Ha, Damp Abbot; your first request it would be uncivil and ill-natured to decline."

Then the Lord de Saintré kept with him two Squires, a varlet, and a page only, sending the remainder of his people to the good town to get their supper; and telling the maître-d'hôtel that they were all to come back to him, after, to Madame's. And by this time, the tables were laid, and supper all ready. Then Madame washed her hands first; and next, Damp Abbot and the Lord de Saintré. And then on account of his position and his dignity, Damp Abbot was placed at the middle of the table, with his face turned toward Madame, who was at the other side, and with her back to the wall. And, after Madame came the Lord de Saintré, then Madame Jehanne, and Madame Katharine next. Then salad was first handed round; of which Madame and Damp Abbot ate freely. Then came the larger dishes, all full of young rabbits, partridges, pigeons, of which they all ate, and then washed well down with the best of wines; Beaulne, de Tournon, Saint-Poursain. And when all their bellies began to be pretty well filled, it was not long after till their tongues commenced to wag; and, incontinent, Damp Abbot began to be facetious. And anon he said, "Ho! my Lord de Saintré; ho! wake up, sir, wake up; I see well by your manner, and your half-lined guts, that you are either half asleep or dreaming!"

Then the Lord de Saintré said to him, "Far from it, my Lord Abbot; really, all these good things of yours, and these excellent wines I find before me, are keeping me so busy, that, to tell you the truth, I have room to think of little else."

Then said Damp Abbot, "My Lord de Saintré, do you

know, it has often occurred to me, in a quiet way, that, occasionally, it may have happened among you others, Noblemen, Knights, and Squires, to be capable of putting tricks on us, poor stick-at-homes; telling us how you were the conquerors at this or that tilt or tournament, when, God knows, things went a very other way." Then turning himself to Madame, he appealed to her, demanding of her, " If it was not so ?"

" Faith, Abbot," said Madame, " it is no more than the truth, and likely enough. Good sir, say on, for you seem to me perfectly to understand the matter."

" Madame," said he, " if I do, remember, it must be by your orders, and with your consent; for, possibly, my Lord de Saintré may not be equally disposed to take it all in like good part; but since you have put it on me, Madame, my opinion is this :—There is a certain sort of Knight and Squire, for the most part to be found, as well in the King's Court, as the Queen's, and those of great Lords and Princes, generally, who give themselves out to the world, to be the devoted champions of the Ladies. And to work themselves the better into your good graces, if not in them already, they will ever have tears at their command, and so sigh and mourn, and rave, and come the disconsolate; that out of sheer commiseration, you, poor Ladies, whose hearts are naturally but too tender and compassionate, inch by inch, are encompassed in their toils; so that, at last, they have their pleasure of you. And then they go to a second, and then a third. And they will take for their badge, a garter, or a bracelet, a smock, a turnip, or a pig, or, God only knows what trumpery; and then they will tell some dozen of them, sighing, one after the other,—' Ah, Madame, it is for your sake I am wearing this token !' So, goodness only knows how the unfortunate wretches are gammoned of their lovers; one, one way; one, another. As for sincerity,

Q

it is a word their mothers never taught them. And then, as if it was not enough to gull their Ladies; for their further recreation, they must worm themselves into the good graces of King, Queen, and all the world and his wife; at whose expense they fig themselves out. What say you, Madame; is it not the case?"

Madame, to whom all this lecture suited most wonderfully, smiling, said to him, " Abbot, how came you to have learned all this? Methinks, however, you are not far from the mark." And as she spoke, she put her foot on Damp Abbot's toes.

"And farther than this, Madame," said Damp Abbot, "you may not be aware, that when these famous Paladins, Knights and Squires, are about to set out on some wonderful exploit or other, and they have taken their leave of the King, no matter for where; let it but happen to be cold, and they take the way of Germany; there to pass the winter; chaffing with the girls over good hot stoves. But if it happens to be summer, they will be off to the delicious realms of Sicily, or of Arragon; there, amid the fragrant groves, by purling fountains, the orange and the lime, to bask the hours away, surrounded by the lovely houris of the land. And glad enough are the gentry of the same to see them; and the best of wine, and fruit, and cheer is theirs. And then, when they think they have been long enough away, they get some Trumpet or other, or a Herald, with a sign-board on his back, and sticking one of their old cloaks upon his shoulders, they give him an écus to shout about the country, '*My Lord, as the most valiant, has gained the prize of Arms!*' Poor Ladies how easily are you imposed upon! and, from my soul, I pity you."

Madame, who, on hearing this, was so delighted, that, more she could not be, turning her head a little round, said to the Lord de Saintré, who was exceedingly displeased to hear so injurious an affront thus laid to the door of his order, "My Lord de Saintré, what have you to reply to this?"

But before he could speak, Damp Abbot went on to say, "Madame you have all your life lived among them; if it is not as much, you must know it."

Then said Madame, "We must certainly allow we have met with some who were capable of better things, but we are far from being able to answer for all. However, as a general principle, we think, Damp Abbot, you are not far off the truth."

And as she said it, she kept winking and nodding to Damp Abbot, and then she would touch him with her foot. On seeing this the Lord de Saintré said, "Ha, Madame, you are saying this on purpose; however, I pray God you may yet return to another mind, and be better informed."

"And how would you have Madame better informed?" said Damp Abbot, "she cannot know better than she does already."

"As to knowing," said the Lord de Saintré, "I have nothing to say; Madame is at liberty to express the opinions she thinks proper; but as to yourself, and the licence you have permitted your tongue, in declaring your notions of Knights and noble men, I have to tell you, that if you were a party to whom it would become me to reply, you should not long be wanting for an answer. But mindful as well of my own dignity, as of who and what you, Damp Abbot, are, I am now silent. It may so hap, however, that on some other and more fitting occasion, the subject will prove such as I shall return upon."

Damp Abbot, now head and tail alike on fire, as if determined to affront the Lord de Saintré, appealing to Madame, said, "Madame, you have been the means of having me insulted in your own house!"

And as he said it, the war of toes went on more hard than ever. And when he saw Madame continue to nod, and wink, and smile, and encourage him, he well knew the sport was to her mind; so he said, "Ho, my Lord de Saintré! ho, my Lord de Saintré! I am no man of war, or man of blood; I am but a poor simple beadsman, with my all upon my back. For the love of God, Sir, is it for the like of me to fight with you? But should there be any one, and I care not one fico for the Who, who will undertake to contradict me in this quarrel, and to wrestle me upon it, I'm his man!"

"Would you, then," said Madame, "would you really?"

"Madame," said he, "at the worst, I can but be thrown; but please God, who will be on my side, and the truth and justice of my cause, I will get the better of him, be he the biggest butcher of the lot of them."

All this while the Lord de Saintré, who could not but see at whom all these outrages were aimed, hearing such encouragement on the part of Madame, was feeling as if his very heart would split, and was wishing himself a thousand times dead. Madame, who saw all this well, without appearing, however, to take any sort of notice of it, said to him, "Ha, my Lord de Saintré, you, the conqueror, as they tell us, of so many a hard-fought field, fear you to wrestle with Damp Abbot? Certainly, if you do not, I shall be forced to think as he does of the matter."

"Ah, Madame," said he, "you know well that I never was taught to wrestle, and that these Lords of churchmen are adepts at the art, as at tennis, hurl-bat, pitch-bar, and every pastime of the sort. They are their only recreations when among themselves, and, for this reason, I know well, Madame, that I would not have a chance with him."

"At least try," said she, "you can do your best; and you have my word for it, that if you do not, you shall be posted in every place I go, for a false and craven-hearted Knight."

"God, Madame!" said he, starting up, "and this to me! One would think I had done enough to satisfy any woman; but since such is your pleasure, you shall be obeyed."

"What's that he says?" said Damp Abbot.

"He says, Abbot," said Madame, "that he will accept your challenge, for that he has been in greater scrapes in his time, yet come out of them triumphant."

"He has, then, has he?" said Damp Abbot, "we'll see for that, presently."

Then, without waiting another second, or till a single thing was removed, Damp Abbot jumped up in an ecstacy, and next Madame rose, and then the Lord de Saintré, to the amazement of all the rest of the company. And the sun was now about setting.[15] Then Damp Abbot took Madame by the arm, and led her into a fair smooth green, and placing her under a spreading pine, bade her "be seated, and to be their judge."

Then Madame sat down, more joyous than she had ever been before in all her life, calling to her women to sit down by her. But they, to see all this, however much they might dissimulate, for Madame's sake, their feelings, at heart were not over-well pleased. Then went Damp Abbot through a ceremony, which neither Saint Benoist, Saint Richard, Saint Augustin, Saint Bernard, nor any other Saint or Father of Holy Church was ever known to have performed in his living; for, there and then, before them all, he stripped himself to his doublet, and letting down his stockings to his knees, fastened them, with a wisp, at the same. Thus arrayed, he was the first to make his appearance before Madame. And when he had paid her his reverence, for her farther gratification, and that of the company, he next threw a great summersault, displaying his great big brawny arms and thighs, all hairy over like any bear. And after him came the Lord de Saintré, who, at a little distance, had undressed himself, his stockings all richly sown in pearl and gold. And he, too, came to pay his respects to Madame, smothering, as best he could, the mortification and humiliation of his soul. And presently they were facing one another; but before either of them had time to lay hold, Damp Abbot, all of a sudden wheeled about, and throwing himself imploringly on his knees before Madame, said to her, with uplifted hands, "Ah, Madame, entreat for me to the Lord de Saintré!"

Then Madame, who was well acquainted with Damp Abbot's powers, laughing, said to the Lord de Saintré, "Hey, my Lord de Saintré, we recommend to you our Abbot; do not, for our sake, be too hard with him."

To which the Lord de Saintré, who too well saw through all this raillery, only said, "Alas, Madame, it is he who will have to spare me."

And when he had said this, Damp Abbot and the Lord de Saintré closed, and made a feint or two. Then Damp Abbot put out his leg, and by a twitch of his foot sent the Lord de Saintré flying head over heels; the said Lord falling on the grass, on the flat of his back, with his legs in the air. Then Damp Abbot, striding across him, as he lay there, cried out, as in distress, to Madame—"Ah, Madame, recommend me to the Lord de Saintre!"

Then Madame, laughing as if she would burst, said to him, "Ah, Lord de Saintré, hear Damp Abbot's prayer!" but for the way she was tickled, she could not add another word.

Then Damp Abbot got up on his legs, and said aloud, so that all might hear, "Madame, what I have done, was out of love; the God of heaven, and the God of love have fought on my side, and avenged my quarrel. And if the

Lord de Saintré should now be disposed to assert that he loves his lady better than I do mine, here am I, all simple and naked as I am, ready and willing to attest the contrary."

"You are, are you?" said Madame.

"Aye, against him, or any other man," said Damp Abbot.

Then said Madame, smiling, to the Lord de Saintré, "What say you to this, my Lord de Saintré? surely as a gentleman and a man of honour, you are bound to take it up."

"Madame," replied he, "and as a gentleman, had it been toward a gentleman, I had taken it up, and in such a manner too as gentlemen alone are privileged to take such matters up."

"That is but an idle evasion," said Madame, "to get out of it. It should be taunt enough to raise the spirit of any gentleman, to be told that he dare not stand up in defence of his Lady; but faith, methinks whoever looks for spirit in you, will have to look hard before he finds it."

"Alas, Madame," said the Lord de Saintré, "and why should you say that?"

"I say it," said Madame, "because I cannot help saying it. Do not I see you this moment afraid?"

Then said the Lord de Saintré, "I see clearly, Madame, there is nothing for it but to commence again; and that there is no sort of excuse, however reasonable, to which you are disposed to lend an ear. So, since it is your determination, I bow to it."

Then Damp Abbot, as soon as he had caught his words, by way of farce, said, "Ha, Madame, pardon me this once; for if, by any chance, I have not justice on my side, he will certainly get the better of me, so sorely was I put to it in our last encounter. Madame, it is true all they say of him, nor does it at all surprise me. However, since I have brought it on myself, I suppose I must go through with it."

Then they each stepped back a few paces. Then Damp Abbot, who was by this, with excitement, half wild and out of his wits, began to cry, at the top of his voice, "Ha, Fidelity, guard now thy faithful slave!" And with this, he came a trick which had well nigh laid the Lord de Saintré sprawling. However, by a sort of miracle, he recovered his feet, but it was only to find himself, at the end of one or two closes, where, from the first, he too well knew he would have to come—the flat of his back.

Then said Damp Abbot to Madame, "Madame, you are our judge. It is for you to say, have I acquitted myself as became me? Which of us is the most loyal?"

"Which!" echoed Madame; "it is you that have gained."

Whilst the poor Lord de Saintré, broken-hearted to perceive not only that he had got the worst of it, but that his discomfiture was an occasion of triumph to Madame, could not so much as find a word to say. Then they both retired to dress.

All this while, the two Squires that Saintré had retained about him, had like to die with grief and spite, thus to see Madame and Damp Abbot twitting and laughing at the Lord de Saintré, than whom, in all the realm of France, there lived not, that day, a gallanter gentleman, or a nobler Knight. So, as he was coming away, they said to him, "Our Lord, it will be more than human in you if you forbear to revenge this day's brutality."

But he only said to them, "My friends, do not be distressing yourselves. Keep quiet; never fear, I'll put all this to rights."

Then the Lord de Saintré, who had now for ever extinguished in his breast all love or hope of Madame, indignant at such treatment from one whom he had so passionately loved and faithfully served, feigning to take it all in good part, carried himself as though he had not, in any way, taken his defeat to heart. So, good-humouredly, and as if half talking to himself, he said to Madame, "Alas, Madame, it is a thousand pities such a man as my Lord Abbot, of such a build and strength, should never have been brought up to the noble science of arms. Such a man should have been defending the marches of our Lord, the King. I much question if there are above one or two men in all this realm who would dare to meet him in an open field."

. Then Damp Abbot, on hearing so handsome a tribute to his prowess, scarcely now knowing whether he was on his head or his heels, turned another great summersault, to the no small entertainment of Madame and the remainder of the company. Then he sent for wine and cherries to refresh them all.

Of the Embassy from the Convent.

And while all these fine Olympics were going on, word was suddenly brought to the priors, and other more venerable ecclesiastics of the convent, all about the wrestling, and the taunting of Madame and of Damp Abbot. And as they had long been sufficiently scandalized with Damp Abbot's course of life, which they well knew to be not only such as it were unbecoming a churchman to lead, but such as it would but ill become any other man to lead, they came to the conclusion, there and then, that two of their body should be deputed to Damp Abbot on the part of the convent, and who were to expostulate with him as follows:—

The Embassy from the Convent.

"Right reverend father in God, and our very honoured Lord, the Priors and administrators of your convent, *unâ voce dicentes*, with their most humble and beseeming duties, accredit us to you, instructing us to apprise you how they have heard with pleasure that, on more than one occasion, you have entertained our ever-to-be-redoubted Lady, as well at dinners as at suppers, as on other occasions, for all which, seeing that she is at once our Lady and our Foundress, the convent cannot sufficiently express its obligation to you; and this the more, that it has been the means of procuring for our poor house the honour of the presence of such a Lord as the Lord de Saintré, of whom common rumour speaks so loudly, and whom we believe to stand most highly with our Lord the King. But seeing that, owing to some provocation on your part, this Lord was, as it were, compelled to wrestle with you; and not only that, but thrown several times, and after ridiculed by you; conduct but ill becoming any prelate or any churchman, under what reserve soever, but, least of all, openly, being a thing forbidden by our rules and statutes: for all this, our convent is exceedingly disturbed and distressed, and so we have to pray and beseech of you, that you will endeavour, in some way or other, to accommodate matters, and that, before he leaves, all causes of jealousy may be removed, as well from yourself as the convent in our persons. And we have to let you know that if any mischief, or misunderstanding whatsoever comes of it, to the damage either of us or of our house, we shall not hold you excused, but will, on the contrary, lay all the responsibility to your door. And for this you will be pleased to pardon us all."

The reply of Damp Abbot, and of the remedy he applied.

THE AUTHOR.

Damp Abbot, having heard all this sermon, and the remonstrance of his convent, replied to them, "Priors, return to your brethren, and tell them that all I did was out of pure frolic and gaiety of heart. Say, they are not to be uneasy, for, before he goes, I will have made it all right."

CHAPTER LXXXII.
How Damp Abbot appeased the Lord de Saintré.

AND after all this embassy from the convent had been received and dismissed, wine and cherries began walking round again, and every one was merry and jolly to their hearts' content. And when they all had drunk, Damp Abbot took the Lord de Saintré by the hand, and drawing him aside, said to him; "My Lord de Saintré, once, with God's permission, I had the honour of seeing you in my poor hotel, which, if you would deign to accept of it, shall be yours. And this, I had long wished for, so much had I heard of you. And now, as a favour, I have to ask you, if you would, again, with Madame, confer a like honour on me, and dine with me quietly to-morrow. You will not refuse me, I know: and, indeed, it is a gratification I shall not readily forget."

The answer of the Lord de Saintré, and the prayers of Damp Abbot.

SAINTRÉ.

"My Lord Abbot, for your first dinner, and the hearty cheer and reception I then met with, as sincerely as I can, I thank you. And for your second offer of a dinner to-morrow, I do no less cheerfully also thank you; and which nothing less than some affairs to be attended to in the good town, and which it would never do to neglect, could possibly prevent my accepting."

"Alas," said Damp Abbot, "I am sorry for this. Sir, if I did anything, out of mere thoughlessness and frolic to annoy you, I humbly entreat I may be forgiven. Sir, I have one of the best and handsomest mules in the kingdom, let who will have the second; I have as noble a falcon, whether for the water, or the wing, as any man alive; and I have three thousand écus. Sir, besides the King and the Pope, there is not the man in Christendom, save yourself, to whom I would part with one of them. As humbly as I can, I ask, entreat and implore, that, which you please, of my three offers, you will deign to accept at my hands; and that you will pardon me, and we may part good friends."

THE LORD DE SAINTRÉ.

"My Lord Abbot, as for the mule, it is not exactly the kind of thing which it is my manner to mount. Your three thousand écus, were I in any sort of want of them, believe me, I would not hesitate, one single half-second, to take them from you. As regards your beautiful falcon, it is otherwise. It shall be accepted, out of a respect to you. I will not, however, deprive you of it; use it for my sake, and should anybody, at any time, ever happen to ask it from you, you have only to tell them, that it is the Lord de Saintré's. One thing, however, in return, I have to hope, and that is, that you will not deny me the first request I ever make you."

"And what is it?" said Damp Abbot; "I am at your service: on my honour, if it is in my power, you shall most willingly be obeyed."

"Truth?" said the Lord de Saintré.

"Yes; on my salvation," said Damp Abbot.

Then the Lord de Saintré said to him, "All I would ask is the honour of entertaining you and Madame, the day after to-morrow at dinner."

"But that!" said Damp Abbot. "Then that I can answer for at once, for both of us. One thing, however, you must engage for: there is to be no sort of extravagance."

THE AUTHOR.

Then, the best friends in the world, and all made up and forgotten, the two of them come together to Madame, and the Lord de Saintré repeats his prayer. But the instant Madame heard it she as instantly demurred, nor would she listen, for a moment, to anything Saintré could say. Then Damp Abbot took her on one side, and said to her, "Indeed, Madame, but you must come. I have undertaken for both of us, and I have given him my word; and you will get me both into trouble and disgrace, if we fail to keep our word. Besides, Madame, think of how matters stand between you and me: our position is ticklish enough. It is the mischief to make enemies of these cocked-up, spiteful, sneaking rascals from the Court. One should have a heed of them, as they would of hot iron. And it was for this reason, Madame, I said we would go; and you must really come; for if we do, he will be conciliated, and all forgotten. Otherwise, he will never forgive me for having thrown him."

Then Madame, who could neither divert Damp Abbot, nor yet refuse him, at last said, "Well; be it, since you are so bent on it."

Then Damp Abbot, in great glee, called the Lord de Saintré to him, and said, "My Lord; my high and mighty Lady, whom you here see, merely refused you, fearing that it might have been your purpose to offer her something altogether too unconscionable, and out of all bounds. This she was wishing to spare you. However, I have assured her, that everything is to be as modest as she could wish."

Then the Lord de Saintré said, "Let us drop ceremony. To courtiers like ourselves, Damp Abbot, and Madame, a fine table can be but a poor treat. Now and then, to rough it, is a pleasant change. Something solid if we can;

and a glass of good wine, at any rate we will manage to provide. I am sure Madame will not be difficult for once, but will put up with it as if it were better."

And when he said this, the horses and the cobs were at the door. Then Madame and the Lord de Saintré thanked Damp Abbot, and took their leave of him till the following day but one. And when they got outside the gate, as hard as ever her horse could lay foot to the ground, Madame and her people made home. And as she was galloping, from time to time the Lord de Saintré would bring his horse along side of Madame's, and say to her, "Ha, Madame, what is it I have done to you? Is there the man, in this world, who dare assert that I have not loyally served you, or loved you with my whole heart."

"Truly, Sir," said the Lady, "you showed as much when you strove with Damp Abbot. You will oblige me by troubling me no more about such matters, and leaving me to myself."

The Lord de Saintrè, who saw, clearly enough, how matters now stood; and who neither wished to be restored to her good graces, nor would have deigned, even at her entreaty, to be again to her what he had been, in speaking to her, had only wanted to let her see that he was alive enough to the scurvy jest she had put upon him; though of her new amour, he might say nothing. And when they had got to Madame's hotel, and before he was able to alight, Madame said to him, "Now you may go, my Lord de Saintré, for I have affairs to attend to in doors; and you have after to-morrow's work before you."

So he got his leave to go, with an "Adieu, till after to-morrow."

Then the Lord de Saintré, whose head was full enough with all the matter of the past and coming day, put spurs to his horse, and made straight for the town, and the quarter where all his people were to be. And in a little time he was with them, finding them all waiting where he had ordered them to attend him.

Then he called to him his maître-d'hotel, and told him, that Madame and Damp Abbot were to dine with him the next day, and that he was to use all the diligence he could to get together provisions in plenty, and of the best sort; and good drink, as well for her as all her people. And he told him that he was to settle beforehand with the landlord for anything they might have spent, or would have to spend. And at the same time, he gave him ten écus for the use of the varlets and ostlers of the hotel. And he gave orders that, in the morning, his horses and his trunks, with the mass of his people, were to leave; some ten or twelve only remaining to follow with himself. And it was all done. And, after that, as soon as he was in his room, he sent for his host, and said to him, apart; "Good host, can you think of any Gentleman, or citizen of the place, something of the build of yonder great Squire?" pointing to one of his own people.

"Yes, my Lord," said the host, "more than one."

"But have they armour of the best, I mean the primest quality?" said Saintré.

Then he inquired, "Who it was had the best?" and when he was told, he then asked the host, "to be good enough to request the person named, to let the Lord de Saintré see him." And so he did.

And when the cit had come, and had made his scrape to the Lord de Saintré, who met him with all the civility imaginable, the Lord de Saintré said to him, "Jacques, who in this country has the best store of armour?"

"My Lord," said he, "many keep it; but, without vanity, I may say that I have four or five as complete suits as any gentleman or townsman of the place."

"Then, by the Lord Saint Jacques," said the Lord de Saintré, "it redounds to your credit. As you have a suit, no doubt that fits yourself; do you think you could manage to find another would answer to yon Knight?" indicating one of his party who was about the same size with himself, Saintré.

"My Lord," said he, "I can supply you; and they shall be such as you will in every way be satisfied with. But what sort of helmets will you have?"

"Jacques, my brother," said the Lord de Saintré, "I want them not too heavy; and two axes and daggers must be with them: and all alike; and make yourself easy about them; you shall be no loser by your bargain."

"Lose! what an idea," said Jacques, who could now scarce contain himself, so flattered was he to be in the presence of the Lord de Saintré. "There is nothing I have that is not at your service. But when must you have them?"

"Why, I should like them at once," said the Lord de Saintré, "but you must bring them in a bag or a trunk, for I would not wish any one to see them coming."

Then, as quickly as he could, Jacques went to his home, and brought, quietly, the two suits, all fine, and furbished up, and the two axes, and the daggers; and to see them, the Lord de Saintré was well satisfied. And when that night was passed, and the next day come, and the Lord de Saintré had heard mass, and sent away all his baggage and his people saving only twelve; and had seen the tables laid, and that all would be ready by his return, he got upon his horse, followed by all his company, and set out to meet and escort Madame. And when he had got about half way to her hotel, he met Madame and Damp Abbot in the fields.[16] And when they were about to interchange their mutual salutations, Damp Abbot commenced, and said, "Halt, there, my Lord de Saintré! Speak of the wolf, and you will see his tail, or his ears. My Lord de Saintré, but did you not hear our horns?"

"I hardly know, really," said he. "I rather thought you would have been coming by the road. But have you breakfasted, Madame, and you, my Lord Abbot?"

"We have," said Madame; "to keep out the fog, we took a snatch, with a little ypocras, and *à la poudre de duc.*"

"You certainly did right, Madame," said he, "and you too, my Lord Abbot."

And so chatting, they all continued together; Madame, however, always addressing herself to Damp Abbot. Then the Lord de Saintré, seeing that he might as well be talking to the winds, reining in his horse, fell alongside of Madame Jehanne, thinking to enter into conversation with her. But she only told him, "that, for the present, she could dispense with his civilities."

Then he went to Madame Katharine, then to Madame Isabelle; from each of whom he met with a like reception; for they had all been forbidden to show him any attention. Then he pricked on again to Madame, and to Damp Abbot; and in a few minutes after, they had all gotten to his lodgings.

Then the Lord de Saintré took Madame's arm, and conducted her into her chamber, her and her women; and then he led Damp Abbot into another. And when they were in their several chambers, readying themselves, he told his maître-d'hôtel, that as soon as he saw them all at table, he was, that instant, to have all the horses saddled, and all his people booted, and ready so to start at a moment's notice. And when the dishes were laid; and, to be brief, Madame and Damp Abbot had washed their hands, then he placed Damp Abbot, as Prelate, at the head of the table; and Madame, who could never be prevailed upon to be far from him, next. Then, the others he put at the end. But, for all they could say, or do, he would never consent to be seated; but, with his napkin on his

R

arm, kept going about, helping, first one, then another; now to this dish, now to that; with plenty of good wine between.

Why need I dwell on it any more? Damp Abbot was so taken with the condescension and forgivingness of the Lord de Saintré, that it would be impossible for any one to be more. And presently, when all their tubs began to be well filled, and their tripes well lined and larded; the Lord de Saintré, as if carelessly, asked Damp Abbot, "Had he ever had on armour?"

"Never in my life!" said Damp Abbot.

"Hey, God," said the Lord de Saintré, "but it would become you, too! what say you, Madame, would it not?"

"Damp Abbot would look well in anything;" said Madame; "and for that matter, though some people might think it a good joke, I confess I can see nothing so very ridiculous about it."

"Madame," said the Lord de Saintré, "who is there joking here? I repeat again what I said before: I have rarely seen the man who, in my opinion, armed, would appear to more advantage than would Damp Abbot."

And, with this, he called to Peronnet, of his bedchamber, desiring him "to do as he had told him." Then Peronnet brought in two boards, and laid them on tressels, at the foot of the room; and then he put on one of them the larger and more gaudy suit; without, however, either axe or dagger.

And when Damp Abbot saw this beautiful and polished harness, and heard it so admired, he began to be delighted in his heart; for, surely, thought he, the Lord de Saintré, out of his good-nature, is going to give it to me; and it was for no other purpose that he invited me. So he made up his mind, within himself, that if asked to put it on, he would do it at once, without making any sort of difficulty about it. And then to show him how much he was taken with it, and how deeply he felt his kindness, he began loudly to express his admiration.

Then said the Lord de Saintré to him, trivially, "Since it seems to take your fancy, if by any chance it fits you, I am sure you are very welcome to it."

"Earnest?" said Damp Abbot; "then, for the love of Madame, I will neither eat nor drink till I have let you see me in it!"

Then they all began to cry out, "Away with the tables; we have eat twice too much already!"

Then Damp Abbot, now in his glory, stripped himself to his doublet.

Then the Lord de Saintré, a mallet in his one hand, with the rivets in the other, coming to him, and helping him on with the various pieces; having put the helmet on his head, made Damp Abbot all sound and tight. Next he handed him a pair of gauntlets. And when Damp Abbot found himself thus all armed, he began to turn himself, first this way, then that; then he would stick his hands upon his hips, all the while inquiring of Madame and her women, "What think you now of your monk, in his new rôle of Knight? Is he not worth looking at, eh?"

"Monk," said Madame, "such men are rarely seen."

"Hey, God," said then Damp Abbot, "if I now had but an axe in my hand, and any one had a mind to settle an account, or pick a quarrel with me!" Then, as a good jest, he said to Madame, "Troth, Madame, this here surplice is a wee bit heavier than the one in which Damp Abbot usually officiates of a Sunday. However, since I have won it, I will keep it." But as he was saying this, the Lord de Saintré, interrupting him, said to him, "Stay, my friend, not so fast; you have not won it yet: in a minute or two, however, you shall." Then he had the other harness brought in, and instantly began putting it on. And when Madame had taken in more fully what the Lord de Saintré had just said, and saw him hurrying himself into the other armour, she began to be uneasy as to what was like to come of it; so she said to him, "My Lord de Saintré, what is it you are about?"

"Madame," said he, as soon as he was ready, "you will see presently."

"Will see!" cried Madame; "Sir Coward, and are you then going to attack a priest?"

Without so much as answering her, the Lord de Saintré, who was now fully armed, turning to his people, said, "Look well to the door, and see that neither man nor woman enters in or passes out." Then he ordered Madame, and the other Ladies, and the monks present to withdraw, all of them, to the foot of the room, telling them, "that the man or the woman of the lot of them that budged from thence, but the tenth part of an inch, he would cleave them from their jaws to their hips."

Then might you have heard them curse the hour they had ever set their foot in that hall. Then coming to Madame, he said to her, "Madame, of your own accord, and without any manner of difficulty, you condescended to be judge in the affair, the other day, between Damp Abbot and myself; so, in return, I have now to beg and entreat of you, as humbly as I can, that you will deign again to be as much of another sort of a tussel, and one in which I happen to be somewhat more of an adept. And I have to hope, Madame, that you will be on my side, and second my proposal to Damp Abbot."

"What proposal?" said Madame. "Any insult offered to him, I shall take as offered to myself. He is under my protection."

Then the Lord de Saintré turned to Damp Abbot, and said to him, "Damp Abbot, at Madame's request, and yours, I wrestled with you two times, and each time was thrown, as more than one aching bone this moment reminds me; nor, for anything I could entreat or urge, would one or other of you listen to reason. There was nothing for it, but I must go through with it. So now I beg and require of you, and for the sake of the Lady whom you have so faithfully loved, that you and I may try a fall at the sort of combat which I have been taught to wage."

"Ha, my Lord de Saintré," said Damp Abbot, "I never could do anything in armour."

"Possible," said the Lord de Saintré: "however, you can do at least as I did, you can try: you shall go through with it, or through that window, at your choice."

Then said Madame, now trembling before the fearful sternness of the Lord de Saintré, "Lord de Saintré, we will and command you, under the penalty of incurring our highest indignation, this moment to disarm; as also Damp Abbot. And if you do not, we will publish you everywhere for a coward and vindictive, and we will take very effective measures besides to see you requited for this day's liberties."

And when the Lord de Saintré saw himself thus vilified and menaced, and all out of her partiality and regard for Damp Abbot, turning and looking upon her, he cried aloud before them all, "O false and disloyal traitress, as you are; and this to me: I who have so long and faithfully loved and served you; ay, as never woman yet was loved or served of man! and now for this whoreson monk I am cast off; yourself debased, defiled, dishonoured and disgraced! And in order that you may carry in your recollection, and to your dying day, what it is to trifle with and to rouse the anger of the Lord de Saintré, I will make of you both examples, and you first, such as shall be well remembered, and to all time, of all such apostate dogs and bit—s." With that, raising one hand, he seized her by the hair of her head, and with the other was about to smite her on the face; but suddenly he curbed himself, recalling to his mind all the many kindnesses, on a time, he had received from her; and that, besides, it was not to be defended. Then releasing her from his grasp, he let her fall upon the form; now crying, and well nigh dead with agony, and shame, and fright. Then he called to his people to bring in the two axes and the two daggers which he had had prepared. And when they were brought, he ordered them to hand them to Damp Abbot to make his choice. Then coming towards him, he said to him, "Damp Abbot, Damp Abbot, bethink you now of all the injuries you that day heaped in my presence, on Knights and Squires; Knights and Squires whose days and nights are spent in arms, and all whose thoughts are virtue and are honour; or now the hour of vengeance is at hand!" With that he closed his vizor; fiercely bidding his people to do the like with Damp Abbot's. And then he went up to him; and when Damp Abbot saw that there was no possible escape for him; but that, will he, nill he, he was in for it; now furious and desperate, he raised his axe, and rushing on him, brought it down with such a force, that, had it lighted on Saintré, infallibly it had knocked him down, or killed him out of hand, for he was by much the stronger, as well as the heavier and bigger of the two. And this would have been what would have pleased Madame well. But, by the grace of God, and thanks to all the experience he had had in every kind of fray, he managed to evade it. And a moment after, thrusting his axe under a plait in Damp Abbot's armour, he carried him before him right up to the bench whereon Madame was lying. Then he tumbled him over it, Damp Abbot falling with such a crash, that sure they all thought the whole place was coming in about their ears. Then when Damp Abbot saw himself down, he began to cry, "Mercy, mercy, Madame! Ah, my Lord de Saintré, for God's sake, mercy!"

Now the Lord de Saintré, mad with all the provocation he had received; and all the infamies and insults you have heard were heaped upon him, had determined, in his own mind, to make an end, for good and all, of Damp Abbot. And to this purpose he had raised his arm, when suddenly remembering the ever-blessed words of our Lord JESUS CHRIST, where he says in Deuteronomy, in the Old Testament, and the sixth book of the Bible :—

Quicumque fuderit sanguinem humanum ; fundetur sanguis illius.

And, again, where it is said in the Passion :—

Non edificabis michi domum, quoniam vir sanguinum es.

As also, again, where he says by the mouth of David :—

Viri sanguinum et doli non dimidiabunt dies suos ;

As, again, by the lips of David :—

Virum sanguinum, et dolosum abhominabitur Dominus ;

As also, where, in the same place, he says :—

Si occideris Deus peccatores : Viri sanguinum declinate à me ;

and, with them, so many other touching entreaties, remonstrances, supplications, instances; and which, by his own example, he had illustrated, the Lord de Saintré relented, and resolved to spare him. However, as a just vengeance, and, as it were in obedience to the divine injunction, which, by reason of Damp Abbot's manifest and crying sins, had permitted him to have the better; throwing his axe from him, and taking his knife in his hand, and opening Damp Abbot's vizor, he said to him, "Damp Abbot, Damp Abbot, allow you now, be God a just judge, or be he not ; when, not all your arrogance, nor all your might, nor all your insolence, nor all your menaces, have been able to save you from this day's disgrace ; ay, and before the face of her, too, in whom was all your confidence ; and to curry whose smiles you have so basely lied, and reviled Knights and Squires and their order. And for this your lying tongue is now about to pay its forfeit." With that he split his tongue in two; and having driven first his dagger home through either cheek, he then left him, ere he went, inquiring of him, however, "Damp Abbot, have you not now well and honourably won your harness?" Then he had it taken off him; and when they both unarmed, and he saw Madame with her hair all about her, and her clothes all disordered, lying on the floor, he said to her, "Adieu, Madame, of women falsest!" And as he was saying this, he looked, and spied about her waist a belt of satin, blue, and edged round with gold. And when he saw it, he ripped it from her with his knife, saying to her, "How, Madame; and have you then the assurance to show yourself in such a colour? Blue is the emblem of faithfulness. Ill beseems it such as you; you shall no more of it." Then rolling it up, he put it in his pocket. This done, he advanced to the Ladies and Gentlewomen, with the monks and attendants, who were by this all huddled together in the farthest corner, shivering and shaking like a lot of sheep; piping, and half dead with fright; and said to them, "You have been witness to everything that has been said and done, in all this unhappy matter; and into which, to my infinite regret, I have been forced. And for all the annoyance and, I fear, fright I have caused you, I do entreat I may be pardoned. And now God be with you all." Then they opened the door for him, and he went down stairs, presently saying to the host, "Should Damp care to keep the larger harness, he is to have it. But the smaller, and the two axes and daggers, you will return to Jacques, and tell him to let me see him speedily. Good host, have you been satisfied?" And as he said this he got upon his horse, and setting spurs to him, called, as he vanished, to his host, "Adieu, mine own host!"

And now I will say no more of him, as he went straight to the Court; but will tell you of Madame and of Damp Abbot, and of all their people, who, you need hardly be told, were not a little disturbed when they came to understand more distinctly the nature of all that happened to Madame and to Damp Abbot.

CHAPTER LXXXIII.
Of the state in which Madame, Damp Abbot, and all their people were left.

THE AUTHOR.

AND when Madame had had her hair and things put to rights, and they had all cried themselves sick, and Damp Abbot had been disarmed, they then sent for a surgeon. Then they all began to cry afresh, and roar, and blubber, and curse the day they had ever set their foot in good host's house. Meanwhile Damp Abbot, who could not now speak, had his clothes taken off, and was put to bed; so that, needs was, Madame had to leave her friend. Then she broke out into such a paroxysm of lamentations, and tears and sighs, that, had all her family and friends been dead, it could not have been greater. But all the comfort she met with from her women, was, the one, "Ha, Madame, we thought as much would come of it as soon as we saw him arrive, and heard Damp Abbot speak of Knights and Gentlemen the way he did;" and the other, "Ay, and to see him treated, and kicked, and knocked about as he was!"

"Whatever was done," said Madame, "take my word for it, it will not be forgotten. As soon as Damp Abbot is up again, he will have his revenge; as, besides, that he should have dared to treat me the way he did: and to take away my belt, scoundrel and murderer that he is!"

And now I will forbare to speak of Madame, or of

Damp Abbot's recovery, or of how, for two months after, they managed to be good company to one another, and to enjoy themselves even more than ever they had done; the close of which, however, was somewhat bitter.

CHAPTER LXXXIV.
How Madame returned to the Court.

THE AUTHOR.

AND whilst Madame and Damp Abbot were thus enjoying themselves; the King and my Lords, his brothers, no less, could not help wondering what it was could be keeping Fair Cousin so long away ; so that at last they spoke to the Queen. The Queen, who had a secret presentiment that all was not right, to save Madame's honour, said, "She knew nothing about what it was could be detaining her." However, on their pressing her to write, desiring her at once to return, she told them, " that she had already written to her, and sent to her two parties ; and that she might come exactly when she had a mind ; for, for her part, she was not going to write again."

Then the King and my Lords, who clearly saw by the Queen's manner, that she was, in some way or other, annoyed, wrote letters themselves, and sent them by one of their own chaplains. Then, on seeing them, was Madame mortally wounded, to find she would have to leave her holy father. And so she appointed a day on which, without fail, she would be back in town. Then the good chaplain took his leave of her, and she of him ; he returning to the Court.

THE AUTHOR.

Ha, false traitor, Love ! cursed and insatiate as Hell, which never crieth, *Enough !* will you never be wearied of your triumphs, your slaughters; to vaunt you of your sick of head, your sore of heart! God and nature have heaped on you such a power, that you are for ever taking and harrying in your toils, hearts of Popes, hearts of Emperors; hearts of Kings, of Queens; of Dukes; of Bishops, of Archbishops; of Patriarchs; of Marquisses, of Marchionesses; of Princes, of Princesses; hearts of Abbots, of Abbesses; of Counts, of Countesses; wights of every mortal state, temporal as spiritual! Ah, many is the wretch, as many a tale attests, an history tells, whom first you have lured on, and then have spurned from you! Ha, how many of them have you driven to madness, despair, to vengeance, and to crime; aye, even to the perdition of their souls, had not God had mercy on them, and made them to be vindicated in the eyes of men! But to return to my story, which is as follows, I will say no more about you, you rascal!

THE AUTHOR.

And when Madame saw that there was nothing for it, but she must return, her distress and agony were greater than I can find any words to describe. However, as Damp Abbot faithfully undertook to pay her a visit quietly, from time to time, disguised; on the strength of this little comfort they were able, at last, to tear themselves asunder; and, had it not been for the parting, and the dinner, the rest of her visit would, on the whole, have been pleasant enough.

CHAPTER LXXXV.

How Madame came to the Court, and of the good reception she met with.

THE AUTHOR.

THEN Madame, all pensive and out of heart, came to the Court, accompanied by Lords, Counts, Barons, Knights, Squires, in numbers, who had gone before to meet her. And when she was come, she made her reverence to the King, who received her civilly enough. Then on going to the Queen, the Queen said to her, a little drily, "Your stay was somewhat long: it seems you liked your native air."

Then she went to my Lord Dukes, who received her as did the King; that is, civilly. Then they said to her, laughing, "It is us you must thank, fair Cousin, that we have the pleasure of seeing you back."

Then all the other Lords, Ladies, Gentlewomen, Knights, Squires, advanced to pay her their respects and congratulate her. And, from this time, a month slipped away. And at last it came, one lovely night, as the King and Queen were sauntering after supper, in a fair meadow, with all their Lords and Ladies round about them, that the Lord de Saintré said to the Queen and the Ladies, "Now sit you all down here, and I will rehearse to you a true story, and a most marvellous history, which, lately, and most curiously, came to my ears. In fact, it comes from beyond the seas."

"That we will," said the Queen; "'fore God, let us hear it. Madame, here!"

Then she called to her Madame, Fair Cousin. Then she said to the other Ladies, "Now, Ladies all, sit you round, and let us hear this wonderful tale, which the Lord de Saintré is going to give us."

Then the Queen sat down, and made Madame sit next to her; then the other Ladies and Gentlewomen, in a ring; the Knights and Squires among them. Then, laughing, she said, "My Lord de Saintré, grand master of the novellists, commence your tale."

CHAPTER LXXXVI.

How the Lord de Saintré, without, however, naming any one, gave them the history of Madame, Damp Abbot, and himself; and how he gave Madame back her belt: present the Queen, and many other Ladies and Gentlewomen.

The Author.

THEN the Lord de Saintré began his tale, with all the art and grace of which he was capable. And he said, "Madame, there lately came into my hands the account of a truly marvellous and authenticated history, and which, but a little ago, fell out in Germany. It is of a very noble and powerful dame, who, of her own good pleasure, having elected, as her choice, a very graceful little lad, so heaped upon him wealth, distinction, affection, love, honour, discipline; that, with time, she caused him to be accounted one of the most accomplished Knights of Christendom. And so faithfully and ardently did they love one another, that, as my story goes, never were loves more loyal, more secret, or more true. But, as says Boethius, of Fortune, the traitress—

> '*The pride of fickle Fortune spareth none;*
> *But, like the floods of swift Euripus borne,*
> *Oft casteth mighty princes from their throne,*
> *And oft the abject captive doth adorne.*
> *She cares not for the wretch's tears and moan;*
> *And the sad groans, which she hath caused, doth scorn.*
> *Thus doth she play, to make her power more known;*
> *Showing great wonders, when man's fickle state*
> *One hour hapless doth see, and fortunate.*'

"So was it, Madame, with this unhappy wight, now so established in the graces of his Lady, that sure never man was loved of woman more. And, as fortune would have it, to prove as well to her how much he loved her, as for the enhancement of his name, on a time he came to France in quest of glory and of arms; which arms he found, and from which he returned with honour. And now you must know, that while thus absent on this foreign field, it fortuned to this Lady to make the acquaintance of a certain lickerish, powerful, well-built monk, Damp Abbot, of a fair and rich abbey; and quickly came to such an understanding, the Lady and the monk, that he who so passionately loved her, and had loved her, was far away, had done and suffered so much for her, was as clean forgotten as though he had never been." "Then," said the Queen, interrupting him, "she showed a very villanous disposition to forsake, for the like of a monk, any such man."

"Madame," said the Lord de Saintré, "but, nevertheless, so it was. It is so written in my history, and so it must be true. However, listen, Madame, to the continuation, and how it all fell out."

"Go on, and let us have it all," said the Queen.

Then, taking up his tale, he went on and told them how this faithful servant found the Lady and the Abbot together in the fields, hawking; and how the Abbot had asked the Lady, "If she would wish the gentleman to be retained to dinner," and of the answer she made; and of how the lover staid to see the farce out, remaining without any sort of difficulty, and of how the Abbot and the Lady made themselves merry, at the expense of chivalry, of Knights and Squires; of how the lover was drawn into the wrestling-match, and of how the Lady sat as umpire; and of how they undressed and wrestled; and of the fine summersaults the Abbot threw; looking on the Lady; and of all the pleasantry, the mocks and the raillery that followed the match, the embassy from the convent; and, to be brief, how the Lady and the Abbot come to dine at the hotel in the town; how they both got to be armed, and of the fight; also of the way the Lady carried herself toward her former lover, reviling him and threatening him, and all for the sake of her new; how he put out his hand and caught her by the tuft of her hair, pretending as though he would strike her; what her former servant said to her; how he took the belt from off her, telling her "that it was not for the like of her to be tricking herself in such a colour, for blue was the emblem of faithfulness and of constancy;" short, the whole story. And when he had got to the end of it all, then was the Lady, whom they all thought to be in Germany, loudly blamed, and cried "shame on!" of all the company present, and the hero of the battles which had been so gallantly gone through with, as loudly praised. And the more they talked and chatted of this most famous story, the more it seemed to tickle their fancies, and the more it made them laugh, with the exception only of poor Madame, who sat, without a word to say, trembling and frightened half out of her wits.

Then the Lord de Saintré said to the Queen, and to all the other Ladies round, "Madame and my Ladies, our historiographer has bid me ask, what is to be thought of this Lady: did she well do, or did she not? Madame, of you, I first inquire."

Now, when Madame, the Queen, had heard tell of the loves of a Lady and an Abbot, she had had her own suspicions, that possibly it might be question of Fair Cousin: but inasmuch as she had never heard any inkling of those of her and of Saintré, she could not be exactly certain with herself. So to see how Madame was likely to bear it, she put it to her, to be the first to give them her mind. But to this she replied, "Indeed, Madame, you must pardon me, for the fact of it is, I was thinking of very different matters, and hardly heard the half he said. If you please, let the rest first offer their opinions, and by then I will know more about it, and be able to give you mine."

Then the Queen said, "Since, I suppose, as being the Queen, I must deliver myself first, my opinion is this:— that the Lady was of the wrong sort, false and disloyal; so we will say no more about it."

Then said the Lord de Saintré, "Madame de Retel, and what may be your opinion?"

"I think," said she, "as the Queen thinks; and I think, besides, that she should be turned out of all decent society, that is, supposing her still to be in it."

"And you, Madame de Vendosme," said Saintré, "and what may you say?"

"I say," said she, "that she should be tied upon an ass, with her face to the tail, and then led about the town, with the rabble at her heels."

"And you, Madame de la Perche," said Saintré, "and what is your verdict?"

"I think," said she, "pretty much as the Queen thinks, and the two Ladies do who have spoken before me. And I am further of opinion, that she should be stripped naked, from her head to her hips, her head shaved, and when fat and sugar had been well rubbed into her, turned up for the entertainment of the town and the benefit of the midges and the flies. It were not one whit too bad for her, or the like of her."

Then, as soon as they had all delivered themselves, he drew from his sleeve the belt of blue and gold; and falling on his knees before Madame, said, looking on the Queen and all the company,—"Madame, forgive me that I have so long deprived you of it." And thus saying, he laid it gently in her lap. And when the Queen and all her said company had fully taken in that it was Madame, and all this marvellous history; if they were astonished, and if they stared at Madame, I need hardly tell you; nor need I, if she looked overwhelmed or hung her head. And from that hour began her fall, and forfeited she for ever all her honour, joy, and peace of mind.

And now I am come to the end of my tale, praying and beseeching of all Ladies and Gentlewomen, of citizens' wives, or wives of whatsoever degree it may be, that they have, as a warning, before their eyes, the pattern of this so noble and so idle Lady, who, by her riotousness lost herself; and that they will heedfully remember and carry in their mind the old proverb, "*never was there fire so covered, but of it came smoke.*" That is to say, that never was there good deed, or ill deed done, however secret, wary, covered, or obscure, but at the length it was brought to light. For so has ordered it, the great Author and disposer of all things: the good and the just, to bring to honour; the wicked and the unjust to punish for their sins; whether in their souls in the world to come, or in their bodies and their honours in the world that is; as he did this Lady, and many another, of whom history tells, for their disordered courses. And the further meaning of which is, that there ever will be in this world little, lying and malicious tongues, which will take their delight to scatter smoke without flame; that is to say, to blow upon the reputations of honest and of worthy men and women, and without cause. But as to fire, that they cannot kindle, but where the spark appears; and by which, as was this Lady, they are cast, become lost to themselves and to society; spurned and tortured to their faces, ridiculed and reviled behind their backs.

THE AUTHOR.

And here I will make an end of the history of this most famous Knight, who, besides being engaged in all the passages you have heard, bore a part in many another

S

engagement, as well by sea as by land. And more particularly, he was one of sixteen Knights and Squires who sought at Cairo, in the presence of the Soldan, twenty-two Christian renegades, and discomfited them in defence of the faith of Jesus Christ; and he travelled far and into more lands than I would have time to tell. And when at last the day was come, that God was pleased to take him to himself—by the hand of that death which spareth none; I say, the day was come in which his eyes were closed in endless night, he was esteemed, of all, the most valiant Knight of all the realm of France. And it was in the town of the Saint Esperit, upon the banks of the Rhone, that he rendered up his mortal spirit, having first received in the profoundest devotion the holy sacraments; and performed every office and duty to be attended of a good Christian in that so solemn an hour. And as they were digging the sepulture in which he was to be laid, one turned up a little slab, on which was graved,—

In this spot will one day lie the nonpareil of France and Chivalry; of all that have been, are, or are to be!

But this many take to be saying a little too much, and that it can only mean, the most valiant, of his time, in Christendom. However this be, as a tribute to his memory, I myself have been on a pilgrimage to his resting-place; and there have looked, with no ordinary emotion, on all that time has spared to us of this once famous Lord and Knight. And there I saw his monument on which was graven as under, in the Latin tongue:—

(15) Hic jacet Johannes DE SAINTRÉ, milles senestalus Andegavensis, et Cenamanensis, Camerariusque domini Ducis Andegavensis, qui obiit anno Domini milessimo CCCC. LVIII.; Die XXV. Octobris. Cujus anima requiescat in pace. Amen.

NOTES.

(1) The expressions, *To ride upon the high horse; To carry it with a high hand,* owe their origin to the habit which the young pages had, of riding, or leading the war-horses of their masters, to save them till such time as they might want them.

(2) It appears, about this time, to have been a general practice (at least among the higher orders) to retire to bed for a few hours, after dinner; which was usually at from about ten to twelve of the clock.

(3) It is but fair the reader should be informed, that all this part, and, indeed, all that regards heraldry, costume, or armour, has been awfully scamped in this translation. They are matters of which I know literally nothing. The *stockings* of the time were, I fancy, nothing else than *close-fitting hosen breeches;* in make, like the *tights* still worn by our dancers, tumblers, &c.

(4) There is, apparently, something omitted, about this place. Saintré's object in visiting the old lady was, probably, to deposit the money in her hands till such time as he might want it.

(5) I am unaware of either how or when the *Peacock* came to be *canonized;* for so, I suppose, he was. A duke of Burgundy is somewhere to be found, vowing (the peacock, dressed, on the table before him) to God, the blessed Virgin, my Lord St. Michael, the Ladies, and the Peacock.

(6) *Montjoie, St. Denis!* was the war-cry of the French in times of feudal France. The origin of the word is disputed and uncertain. According to *Pasquier,* one tradition is—that the last pagan King of France, on some imaginary interposition, (as the Christians told him), *of the true God* in his favour, was heard to cry, *Jesu Christ, mon joie!* Jesus Christ, my joy! or, *Jesu Christ, mon Jove!* Jesus Christ, my Jove! from that moment, declaring himself a Christian. The former supposition is the more likely of the two; though the latter is not improbable.

(7) There is something uncommonly *Irish* in the lady's fancying that any access of devotion, on her part, after the event, could be of any service to poor Saintré.

(8) The Pole was under an obligation to wear two rings of gold; one round his left arm, above the elbow; and the other round his ankle; each attached to the other by a long chain of gold; for the space of five years; if, within that time, he did not meet with any Knight, or Squire, of name and renown, without reproach, to deliver him. Such vows, I may add, were by no means unusual in feudal times.

(9) I cannot exactly make out, whether it was Saintré, *himself,* that the Lady dedicated; or only a *figure* of him; or, again, the

worth of his war-horse, armour, &c.; nor does the sequel throw sufficient light on the matter to clear it up.

(10) I conclude that this prodigious host must comprise *all* the Christians from whatever country they assembled. It is not, however, clear that they were not simply the German contingent.

(11) The *pennon*, carried by Squires, was a long streamer, pointed at the end. It became a *banner* when the pique, or tail, was cut off; leaving it a square, or parallelogram. The Knights only bore banners.

(12) I cannot, for the life of me, make out what it was that Saintré and his companions were to wear on their shoulders; whether it was a mask, a vail, or vizor. However, it matters little.

(13) As it may, perhaps, occur to the reader, that it is a little curious to find a gentleman and a lady, both in bed, calling for their night clothes; it may be as well to state, that, in the middle ages, the night shirt and the shift were presumed to be as sacred and inviolable depositories of a gentleman's or a lady's chastity, modesty, or virtue, as doublet, breeches, stockings, or stomacher. In fact there is considerable reason to believe, that it was not so much the *cut* as the *time of day* that constituted, among our ancestors, the difference between a night shirt and a day one. Or, possibly, the misapprehension, on this head, may have arisen, simply from the difficulty of expressing or conveying an equivalent. For instance, when we would say, *that a man put on his night shirt*; they would rather have said, *he kept on the one he had*. The custom was, as well with the single as the married, to take the shirt on them into bed. Among the *married*, however, it was not etiquette for the lady to pass hers over the side, till such time as the gentleman had shown her the example.

A king of France, wishing to be divorced from his wife, and swearing, before a court of justice, "that the lady was as much, that day, a virgin, as on the one she came to be queen," urged, among other proofs of the same, *that they had never been, without their shirts*, (*nu à nue,*) *in bed together!*

(14) *Damp* is a corruption of *Dominus;* and is the same with the Spanish *Don.* It seems to be of a value between that of *Sir* and *Lord.*

(15) What an admirable subject for a painter this wrestling-match would make. It caps all over the *Tournament of Tottenham.*

(16) Some hunting pleasantry is here indulged in, which I am not enough of a sportsman to be able to interpret. It, however, seems to be equivalent to the proverb, "*Speak of the devil, and he will appear.*"

(17) The translation of this inscription is, "Here lies Sir Jehan de Saintré, Knight, Seneschal of Anjou, and of Maine; Chamberlain to the high and mighty Lord, the Duke of Anjou. He died in the year of our Lord, 1458; the 25th of October, and may his soul repose in peace. Amen."

THE END.

www.ingramcontent.com/pod-product-compliance
Lightning Source LLC
Chambersburg PA
CBHW022055230426
43672CB00008B/1178